# To Be Gifted & Learning Disabled

## Strategies for Helping Bright Students with Learning & Attention Difficulties

Susan M. Baum, Ph.D.

Steven V. Owen, Ph.D.

We would like to acknowledge John Dixon
for his work and contribution to the first edition of
*To Be Gifted and Learning Disabled.*

Editor:
Rachel A. Knox

Thank you to Ellen Starmer for her help
preparing this manuscript for press.

ISBN: 0-936386-97-5

Creative Learning Press, Inc., P.O. Box 320, Mansfield Center, CT 06250
888-518-8004 • www.creativelearningpress.com

# Table of Contents

# List of Figures

# List of Tables

# Introduction

In an ideal world, school would be a wonderful place full of exciting opportunities for learning and growth, a place that nurtures talents, cultivates interests, and helps students understand and manage their particular pattern of strengths and weaknesses. Unfortunately, many classrooms are of the one-size-fits-all variety. Lessons are apt to be taught to all children in the same way, with student evaluations primarily contingent upon written products. In schools across the nation, exciting curriculum is often reserved for those precious few moments when all students have mastered basic skills.

There are some students who suffer considerably from this type of classroom because they cannot conform to particular kinds of learning. Students who are gifted, but who struggle with a learning disability or attention deficit, are a strange paradox—they have special intellectual gifts, but are unsuccessful with certain basic learning tasks. These students' potential are at great risk of going untapped and undeveloped because the major focus of educational intervention is on what these students do not know and cannot do rather than on nurturing their talents. These students present wild patterns of accomplishment and failure that require special attention, and it is vital that schools pay attention to the gifts as well as the learning difficulties.

To help these students, their parents, and the educators and other school staff with whom these students interact, we present both theory and practical strategies. In Part I, we explore the unique characteristics of gifted, learning-disabled (GLD) children and provide background information essential for understanding the GLD youngster. We describe several pioneering studies of GLD students and use those results to forge a clearer approach to educational intervention. Finally, we examine the confusion in diagnoses between learning disabilities and ADHD, especially with gifted students.

In Part II, we discuss the contemporary psychological theory and research that steers educational applications for GLD students. Before we can suggest specific ideas or strategies to use with gifted students with learning or attention difficulties, it is essential to consider how they learn and why particular learning strategies are sometimes successful and sometimes not. We first discuss intellectual profiles using a traditional definition of intelligence as measured by the Wechsler Intelligence Scale for Children, the most common measure given to identify GLD students. An examination of two intellectual patterns—Dispersive and Integrative—provides insight into why GLD students tend to have inconsistent learning behaviors. Next we apply Gardner's theory of multiple intelligences to understand why students with extraordinary strengths in some of the eight intelligences but not in others (such as linguistic) struggle in school. Finally, we extend this discussion of intelligence by examining attention and memory function and where problems may occur.

In Part II, we also examine several theories of motivation to explain how GLD students can be motivated for some kinds of activities and not others. Further, we explore why GLD children have difficulty using efficient learning strategies, especially when the task requires memory of unrelated facts or the organization of ideas, projects, or time.

While the previous sections provided important research and theoretical information about GLD students' need for effective learning, Part III presents practical strategies for meeting these needs. We offer guidelines for developing a comprehensive individual education plan (IEP) that assures gifted students with disabilities a free appropriate public education (FAPE); effective strategies for identifying GLD students; ideas for programs that nurture gifts and talents in students with gifts and disabilities; curricular strategies, modifications, accommodations, and compensation strategies that will enhance the learning and self-efficacy of the students; and finally, strategies for meeting the social and emotional needs of students with gifts and disabilities.

## Notes on the New Edition: Who are the Alphabet Children?

When we began to update *To Be Gifted and Learning Disabled*, we realized that many things that were simple in 1991 have become much more complicated a decade later, especially in terms of diagnosis and intervention. Since the first edition appeared, many students who may have been classified as learning disabled are now being diagnosed as having attention deficits. As the frequency of school disabilities attributed to attention deficits grows, it is becoming increasing clear that many bright children claimed to suffer from ADHD and other problems of concentration and behavior may be misdiagnosed. Often these gifted youngsters have learning disabilities causing some of the behaviors associated with both syndromes (ADHD and LD), or their restlessness and inattentiveness is a result of their giftedness being left unattended. The effects of treating one circumstance as if it were another or of neglecting the gift in lieu of remediating the weakness is producing greater academic, social, and emotional issues than those present at the onset of the problem. To explain the deterioration in student performance and school adjustment, many professionals are looking for additional diagnoses. As a result, we may see gifted (GT) learning-disabled (LD) students diagnosed with a multitude of conditions such as attention deficits (ADHD), oppositional defiant disorder (ODD), pervasive developmental disorders (PDD), general anxiety disorder (GAD), and more. These youngsters wind up with more letters after their names than do professionals with advanced degrees. We call these youngsters Alphabet Children. All these disorders with contradictory and often overlapping symptoms create a serious dilemma for those seeking to provide an appropriate education.

Recognizing that gifted learning-disabled students may be burdened with a ball and chain of cumbersome diagnoses, we have renamed this edition of the book *To Be Gifted and Learning Disabled: Alphabet Children in Today's Schools* and will use the terms *Alphabet Children, gifted, learning-disabled students (GLD)*, and *gifted students with learning and attention deficits* interchangeably throughout the book. To provide a more in depth discussion of the alphabet issue we have included a chapter on gifted students with attention deficits (see Chapter 4) in which we explore appropriate diagnosis and classroom intervention approaches.

This edition also contains three other new chapters on self-regulation, developing comprehensive individual educational programs, and sources of support and as well as greatly expanded chapter on classroom practices. We hope you find this new expanded edition helpful as you wrestle with finding innovative and effective ways to meet the needs of these special Alphabet Children.

# Part 1

# Who Are Alphabet Children?

How can a person be bright and dim at the same time? Why do some students appear "lazy" and "distracted" in the classroom, applying little or no effort to school tasks, but successfully commit themselves to demanding and creative activities outside of school? These behaviors can describe *gifted, learning-disabled* (GLD) students, and discovering answers to these questions will unlock the unique mysteries of students who are talented, but learning-disabled.

We'd like to introduce four young people who have suffered the consequences of being bright and creative as well as academic disasters. Their stories underscore the striking inconsistencies in the behavior of GLD students. By examining common themes, we can begin to understand the frustration and confusion experienced not only by the students themselves, but by all who interact with them. We can begin to appreciate the need for more information about their characteristics and how we can help these special students succeed.

## Neil

"School is like a basketball game, totally irrelevant to life!" shouted Neil, a high school student who was experiencing daily failure in school. While his teachers simply thought he wasn't applying himself, his assessment was all too accurate: school, like basketball, was irrelevant to him

3

when it failed to connect with any of his needs.

Convinced that Neil could do much better if he applied himself, his teachers described him as lazy. "When I talk to Neil, he has so much to offer, but he just doesn't produce," one said. His classmates, applauding his cleverness, viewed Neil as the class clown. But Neil saw himself as a misfit. He was baffled and frustrated by inconsistencies in his own abilities, his interpretation of people's perceptions of him, and his own feeling of inadequacy.

Neil began to have academic difficulty in the fourth grade. As he drifted through the grades, he accomplished less and less. By high school, he was in such a depressed emotional state that weekly psychological counseling became necessary. The psychologist suggested an educational evaluation. The results of the evaluation concluded that Neil had learning disabilities that were displayed as difficulty in written organization and sequential tasks for math and algebra.

Accordingly, Neil's curriculum was adjusted. He received supplemental instruction, and teachers made special provisions for testing and assignments, procedures usually recommended for learning-disabled students. However, unlike most learning-disabled students who begin to experience success and start to feel better about themselves when given more time or modified assignments, Neil's depression worsened. Although his grades had improved, Neil attributed it to the school's "handicapping" him, and he did not view those achievements as successes. Furthermore, Neil wanted to stay out of typical school-related competition and had removed himself to a safer place, away from competition at school, by "being his own person." Neil viewed his achievement in school as making him more like his peers, which was unsettling to him.

It was a different picture at home. His cultural background placed a high priority on school accomplishment and a college degree. He was constantly competing with the achievements of a highly successful father and a gifted younger brother.

Although Neil seemed to resist traditional modes of achievement, he had acquired an enormous wealth of knowledge on his own and pursued extracurricular interests with enthusiasm and commitment. He ran his own business as an entrepreneur and photographer. His photography won awards in amateur contests, and he was asked to photograph weddings and social events. He taught himself to play the piano and guitar and spent hours playing for his own amusement. Little wonder that he was unable to accept the school's claim of impaired ability to learn when, to the contrary, he learned so much on his own.

Photography best unleashed Neil's creative and insightful self. The statements that he made with the camera were powerful and signaled his depth of feelings, as shown in the photographic essay, "How I Feel About School," pictured Figure 1.1. Wouldn't simply using photography as an substitute for written work in school ease Neil's conflict? Unfortunately, the solution to overcoming learning disabilities is not as simple as tailoring a curriculum to the interests of GLD students. When Neil's school allowed him to substitute photographic essays for papers, he stopped taking pictures altogether, declaring, "Why can't I be like the piano player in Salinger's *Catcher in the Rye*, who used the piano for his own pleasure?" Photography was Neil's escape, an activity over which he had complete control. He didn't want teachers to evaluate his photography by their standards. In essence, Neil asked for attention to his strengths in their own right, not as a means to work through weaknesses.

## Jimmy

Nine-year-old Jimmy flopped down next to his dad and declared, "I'm going to conduct research and start a campaign to get kids to wear bicycle helmets. I know it will be hard, and some days I won't feel like working, but it's such an important project." On that day Jimmy became a researcher, and his study became his primary focus. After a visit to a professor in measurement and evaluation at a local university, Jimmy concluded that he would follow the professor's suggestion and add some open-ended questions to his survey and include adults in his sample. "I just can't wait to collect my data!"

Fourth-grader Jimmy had been diagnosed as mentally retarded during his preschool years. His parents were told that his cognitive development was delayed, and his potential was, well, uncertain. When Jimmy started school, new testing showed that he had strong intellectual ability, but he had great difficulty learning to read. A thorough assessment by a team of educational specialists showed that Jimmy had an Attention Deficit Disorder and problems in reading and writing. His full-scale IQ on the Wechsler Intelligence Scale for Children, Revised (WISC-R)

School is an ugly geometric existence.

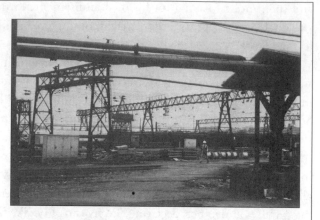

I feel that school has turned its back on me.

For me, school is a stepping-stone to nowhere.

**Figure 1.1.** Neil's photographic essay, "How I Feel About School."

Because it is irrelevant to life, it's but pieces of unconnected tracks, connecting nothing with nothing.

I know graduation is the light at the end of a very straight tunnel.

If I do make it out, what will I have gained? I feel like a barren tree, still reaching . . .

**Figure 1.1** *continued.*

(Wechsler, 1974) was 134 with a verbal IQ of 133 and performance IQ score of 129.

Jimmy hated school and often complained of headaches and stomachaches to avoid completing tasks or even going to school. In school his concentration was limited, distracted by everything and everyone. Could this immature, negative youngster be a young, motivated researcher? What explains these wild discrepancies? What could bring better balance to Jimmy's academic efforts and interests?

Jimmy's research interests were sparked in his special enrichment program, which focused attention on strengths and interests, not on deficits and remediation. Jimmy completed his research and presented his results to the police department. His poster summarizing the research showing the need for bicycle helmets was displayed in a local bicycle shop. Jimmy's parents and teachers reported positive changes in his attitude, motivation, and achievement that year. His fourth-grade teacher noted that "Jim finally feels that he has the ability to achieve and is putting forth greater effort in reading and writing." His parents could not believe the change in Jimmy's attitude about school, especially on Wednesdays, the day of the enrichment program. "We don't even need to set the alarm on his enrichment day. He's up early, prepared and eager to get to school."

## Debra

Feeling alone, rejected, and depressed, nine-year-old Debra had terrible difficulty making and keeping friends. She was knowledgeable and beyond her years in understanding the injustices of society. World hunger, child abuse, and death occupied her thoughts and conversations. Her dramatic flair in communicating her ideas only alienated her classmates who were already confused about Debra's inability to read and write. This sensitive, perceptive young actress could only reach out to adults. Unfortunately, her over-dependence on them often further alienated her from her peers. Debra's self-esteem was precariously low (at the third percentile on a widely used measure). Her teacher described her as defiant, distrustful, and easily hurt. She lacked confidence, concentration, and independence in approaching school tasks. Her short attention span and sharp deficits in reading and writing, despite a full-scale IQ score of

128 (Verbal IQ =119, Performance IQ = 132) on the WISC III, pointed to a learning disability. Debra had received remedial support in school since the first grade. Although her basic skills improved somewhat, her emotional well-being in school withered more each year.

Participation in a special enrichment program during fourth grade proved to be a turning point for Debra. "I never thought I'd be able to create my own slide and tape show. Is it really going to be shown at the museum?" Her eyes sparkled as she recounted her role as a director, writer, and actress in her historical research, "A Day in the Life of Jerusha Webster," a project she attacked steadily for ten weeks. Her excitement in researching, acting, and producing this project resulted in a sense of pride, confidence, and accomplishment. To complete the slide show, Debra had to coordinate audio and visual information. Because it was impossible to coordinate it all in school, Debra put it together at home, recruiting her six-year-old sister as a lieutenant.

Debra's classmates were astonished with the finished project. A new respect for her abilities permeated the room. Most importantly, Debra finally seemed to believe in herself!

### Bill

Bill, a high school senior, smiled with pride as he described his and his pal's award winning project: The Wounds that Glow. As Bill explained, "I'm a Civil War buff and my buddy loves science. We thought if we could team up, we would improve our chances of winning an award." These two young men impressed the judges enough to claim two first prize awards, one in the Siemens Westinghouse Competition and one in the Intel International Science Fair competition. Similar to the other students we've described, Bill's journey to these triumphs was obstructed by many roadblocks. School was not always an ideal environment for this youngster. Bill was diagnosed as learning disabled in 7$^{th}$ grade when the school system finally acknowledged that there was a two-year discrepancy between his ability and performance. But the problems with Bill had surfaced as early as preschool. Poor peer relations, inappropriate social behaviors, and a reluctance to complete written assignments punctuated his early childhood years. His parents requested a psycho-educational assessment of Bill when he was in fourth grade, but the psychologist declared that the discrepancy between his performance and ability was not large enough to merit special education services.

Fortunately for Bill, his fourth grade teacher was sensitive to his needs and skilled in working with youngsters who had learning differences. Her classroom, a learning laboratory, was often transformed into a museum-like setting, mirroring Ancient Egypt or China or some other venue related to the curriculum In this class, simulations, arts integration, and project-based instruction allowed children to learn in ways that best suited them, and knowledge was measured in many ways in addition to writing.

When Bill arrived in her class, the teacher recognized that he was troubled. He would hide under the desk and display other inappropriate behaviors, especially when confronted with writing assignments. She also saw his considerable talents as he engaged in creative projects. She arranged for the enrichment coordinator to work with Bill and several other boys with similar problems in small groups. They dug for dinosaurs on the school playground during recess and built models with Lego™ kits. Concerned about these boys' difficulties with writing, the teacher also arranged for them to have assistance in developing their fine motor skills. Bill was finding success in her classroom. When this teacher transferred to another school however, the support came to an abrupt halt, and Bill began a rapid decline.

The pupil personnel team thought Bill was just lazy and recommended remediation. His parents had him tested privately. His scores on the various WISC subtests ranged from the 4th to the 99th percentile. He was diagnosed as depressed and medication was recommended. His parents objected to medication and instead insisted that the source of the depression be the focus. Bill transferred to a school with a gifted program where he also received support in organization and learning strategies. Bill regained some success in this setting.

The family, including Bill, wanted Bill to be classified as learning disabled to ensure continued support at the secondary level. With an increasing discrepancy between Bill's ability and his performance, the team formally classified Bill as learning disabled. Throughout middle school and high school, Bill attended a resource class for academic support and was permitted to take AP courses. His high school offered a special counseling component for learning-disabled gifted students, which provided both academic and emotional support.

Even in this adaptive environment, Bill's work quality was sporadic. Listening to lectures and writing papers were not in line with his style of learning, and often he would become discouraged and withdrawn.

At those times, Bill and his family found outside activities to enrich and inspire him. He participated in a leadership program and attended college classes in the summer. These activities built his self-efficacy and attacked his depression. The award-winning science inquiry was extracurricular for both Bill and his buddy. It had been in his mom's laboratory that Bill and his friend conceived and conducted their research. Having the tools of the practicing professional at their fingertips and the opportunity to experiment on a topic of their choosing enabled these young men to pursue their passion with commitment and creativity. Bill observed the irony: " My teachers have no idea what I can do. I was afraid they would laugh at me if I told them I was entering these science competitions."

During his senior year, Bill began to make decisions about his education. He decided to take five years to complete high school. He used his fifth year to complete his English requirements by enrolling in an Internet English course, to earn elective credits as a teaching assistant in a chemistry class, and to continue his research and leadership activities.

## The Problem with These Students

Throughout time, anecdotal (and sometimes mythical) stories have described people with crazy-quilt patterns of strengths and weaknesses. Only recently have we learned more about people who have this curious mix of learning disabilities and gifts. It is increasingly clear that when the educational focus is on talent and providing learning environments that align with the student's natural ways of learning, dramatic changes occur in motivation, self-esteem, and behavior.

Traditionally, students who demonstrate a substantial discrepancy between performance and ability have been diagnosed as learning disabled. Once identified, learning-disabled students receive remediation in deficit areas, but little or no attention is given to strengths. Indeed, students diagnosed as learning disabled who also exhibit superior abilities are typically offered the same remedial menu as their average-ability, learning-disabled peers. Is the menu equally suitable for the two groups?

Or do GLD students have unique characteristics that suggest alternate educational practices?

As suggested by these case studies, spotlighting deficits can be self-defeating to a student who has special talents. Such youngsters appear to need both remediation and enrichment as well as special counseling to help them understand the paradox in which they must learn to succeed. With an ever-increasing emphasis on testing and writing, these students have little opportunity to shine. When all subject areas, including art and physical education, are additional opportunities to practice writing, many learning-disabled students with gifts and talents in specific domains are greatly handicapped, and the likelihood for emotional difficulties and behavior problems increases.

# A Matter of Definition

For many, the terms *learning disability* and *giftedness* are at opposite ends of a learning spectrum. Joining the terms results in an apparent contradiction stemming primarily from faulty ideas and incomplete understandings of each term. Before we describe the student who is both gifted and learning disabled, we need a clear understanding of the two individual parts and how the prevailing view steers services for bright students with learning disabilities. These understandings will form the foundation on which the rest of this book is built.

## Historical Perspective of Learning Disabilities

Learning disabilities as a syndrome began to appear in the literature as early as 1947 with the appearance of Strauss and Lehtinen's book, *Psycho-pathology and Education of the Brain-Injured Child*. In their view, learning deficits could be traced to some unspecified minimal brain injury that incurred before, during, or after birth, and that resulted in defects of the neuromotor system. Children diagnosed as brain-injured demonstrated problems in perception, preservation, or behavior. Many educators and psychologists objected to the use of the term "brain-injured," and a decade later, Stevens and Birch (1957) tried to shrink the emphasis on unobserved brain injury by terming such disorders "Strauss'

Syndrome." They also promoted a more observable protocol for defining these kinds of learning difficulties (these characteristics describe children who are today often diagnosed with attention deficit disorder or as having a nonverbal learning disability):

1. Erratic and inappropriate behavior on mild provocation
2. Increased motor activity disproportionate to the stimulus
3. Poor organization of behavior
4. Distractibility of more than ordinary degree under ordinary conditions
5. Persistent faulty perceptions
6. Persistent hyperactivity
7. Awkwardness and consistently poor motor performance

Thus, students with at least average intelligence—and sometimes superior intelligence—who were experiencing learning difficulties were thought to have some neurological dysfunction or central processing disorders whether or not specific brain damage could be verified (Clements, 1966; Cruickshank, 1966; Chalfant and Schefflin, 1969). Educational programs designed to help hyperactive, distractible students were based largely on the work of Cruickshank, Bentzen, Ratzeburg, and Tanhauser (1961). The approach was to structure the environment to minimize distractions, provide perceptual and motor training, and individualize learning for the students.

Within a few years, some researchers became increasingly dissatisfied with a perspective that seemed lifted from medicine. They objected to terms like *brain injury* and *central processing disorders* and argued that they had no meaning for practice or intervention. They promoted terms that directly described deficiencies in abilities. Roger Kirk (1963) first used the term *learning disabilities* to describe children who demonstrated developmental disorders in receptive language, speech, reading, and communication skills, and he ruled out children whose learning problems could be attributed to sensory, intellectual, or emotional deficits. Kirk and his colleagues argued that most learning disabilities resulted from underlying language learning problems, which in turn were based on some perceptual or cognitive processing difficulties. It was this use of *learning disabilities* that would eventually redefine the direction of the field.

With the focus now on aspects of learning, remediation for students relied on an evaluation of strengths and weaknesses in sensory processing systems. Practitioners aimed to help students use their strengths to compensate for weaker areas and provided training to strengthen areas of weakness. If a student's auditory memory was deficient, practitioners used visual programs to train memory and teach basic skills in addition to providing listening practice. Terms such as *reception, closure, sound-symbol associations*, and *memory* were popular among these theorists.

When the problem was defined in educational rather than neurological terms, the boundaries of *learning disabled* expanded broadly, encompassing many more students (Gallagher, 1983). For example, students who were underachieving but not hyperactive or distractible were now identified as learning disabled, regardless of ability level. Therefore, students with high cognitive abilities could now also be learning disabled. Theorists believed that students meeting the revised description needed only part-time special education placement, and the resource room emerged to serve the remedial needs of students with learning disabilities.

By the end of the '60s, bright students who were identified with learning disabilities were probably receiving remedial support in either a self-contained class (for students who were hyperactive or learning disabled) or in a resource room, depending upon the severity of their academic or behavioral problems. However, the high abilities of many of these students may have been obscured by their difficulties in learning and many of their talents might have gone unidentified and unserved. In all probability these students would neither have been identified as gifted nor enrolled in any academic program designed to nurture gifts and talents.

During the '70s, behaviorist ideas were gaining in popularity and practice. Behaviorists generally believed that theorizing about unobservable events—memory, attention, even learning—was unproductive and distracting. They argued that focusing on the causes of deficits and a student's intrinsic motivation toward learning diverted attention from the real problem: unacceptable behaviors. They replaced speculation about underlying causes and discussion of processing deficits with direct remediation of basic skills. Instead of theorizing why students were not learning, they encouraged teachers to break down behaviors into small tasks as a means of enabling students to master specific objectives in curricular areas. This new emphasis implied that deficits in academic skills could be eased by simply reteaching and reinforcing new learning.

The behaviorist position has caused major dissension among theorists. Those who favor neurological and underlying processes points of view suggest that a learning disability is relatively permanent in nature and may influence life-long learning and adjustment. Correcting a given skill does nothing for the larger problem, which is difficulty in learning. The behaviorist does not conjecture about future learning, but deals with observable behaviors as they present themselves and argues that present learning will assure future success (Bloom, cited in Chance, 1987). For proponents of the view that learning disabilities are a life-long problem, education should focus on compensation strategies, strengthening processing skills, and acquisition of basic skills. But non-behavioral professionals might question whether children assisted through a pure basic skills approach were truly learning disabled to begin with or were perhaps only improperly taught.

This widening rift among professionals continued to divide the field until the mid-seventies when considerable effort was expended to assure appropriate education for all handicapped children. Hope reigned high that a federal definition would silence the on-going debate in the field of learning disabilities. In 1975, after much debate and compromise, the federal government passed PL 94-142 (The Education for All Handicapped Children Act). This act defined categories of exceptionality and mandated appropriate identification and educational procedures. The learning disabled were now defined as

> Those children who have a disorder in one or more of the basic psychological processes involved in understanding or in using language, spoken or written, which disorder may manifest itself in imperfect ability to listen, think, speak, read, write, spell or do mathematical calculations. Disorders include such conditions as perceptual handicaps, brain injury, minimal brain dysfunction, dyslexia, and developmental aphasia. The term does not include children who have learning problems which are primarily the result of visual, hearing, or motor handicaps, of mental retardation, of emotional disturbance, or of environmental, cultural, or economic disadvantage.

> A team may determine that a child has a specific learning disability if (1) the child does not achieve commensurate with his or her age and ability levels in one or more areas [seven of

which are specified—oral or written expression, listening comprehension, basic reading skill or comprehension, mathematics calculation or reasoning] when provided with learning experiences appropriate for the child's age and ability levels; and (2) the team finds that a child has a severe discrepancy between achievement and intellectual ability in one or more of [these] areas. (US Office of Education, 1977, p.65)

Unfortunately, the official definition neither eliminated disagreement in the field of learning disabilities (Hammill, Leigh, McNutt, & Larson, 1981; Poplin, 1981), nor gave clear direction in identification issues (Harbar, 1981; Kavale & Nye, 1981; Olson & Mealor, 1981; Taylor, 1989). Instead it raised a host of new questions that contributed to further confusion. For example,

1. How great should the ability/performance discrepancy be before an individual is considered learning disabled?
2. Why are only children considered in the definition? What about adults?
3. Do all learning disabilities involve central nervous system dysfunctions or problems with psychological processes?
4. Cannot handicapped or disadvantaged children have learning disabilities?

Much disagreement continues to exist about how to define and identify this group of youngsters. (Mercer, Jordan, & Alsop, 1996). Many districts and schools use their own interpretation of federal and state definitions to select children who seem to be most in need of service, regardless of whether a specific learning disability can be identified.

To combat the conflict between the federal definition and local practice, professional organizations have offered their own definitions. The following definition, originally produced in 1981 and modified in 1988, was adopted by the National Joint Committee for Learning Disabilities (NJCLD):

Learning disabilities is a generic term that refers to a heterogeneous group of disorders manifested by significant difficulties in the acquisition and use of listening, speaking, reading, writing, reasoning or mathematical abilities. These disorders are intrinsic to the individual, presumed to be due to central nervous system dysfunction, and may occur across the life span. Problems in self-regulatory behaviors, social perception, and social interactions may exist with learning disabilities but do not by themselves constitute a learning disability. Although learning disabilities may occur concomitantly with other handicapping conditions (e.g., sensory impairment, mental retardation, social and emotional disturbance) or environmental influences (e.g., cultural differences, insufficient-inappropriate instruction, psychogenic factors), they are not the direct result of those conditions or influences. (NJCLD, 1988, p.1)

To avoid further confusion arising from their definition, the group offered the detailed rationale that you see in Table 2.1 explaining specific aspects of the definition.

The Association for Children and Adults with Learning Disabilities (ACLD) (1985) offered their own definition and rationale:

Specific Learning Disabilities is a chronic condition of presumed neurological origin which selectively interferes with the development, integration, and/or demonstration of verbal and/or nonverbal abilities. Specific Learning Disabilities exists as a distinct handicapping condition in the presence of average to superior intelligence, adequate sensory and motor systems, and adequate learning opportunities. The condition varies in its manifestations and in degree of severity. Throughout life, the condition can affect self-esteem, education, vocation, socialization and/or daily living activities.

In 1990, PL 94-142 was amended and renamed The Individuals with Disabilities Education Act (IDEA), Public Law 101-476. The latest version, created in 1997, defines *learning disability* as follows:

**General.** The term means a disorder in one or more of the basic psychological processes involved in understanding or in using language, spoken or written, that may manifest itself in an imperfect ability to listen, think, speak, read, write, spell, or to do mathematical calculations, including conditions such as perceptual disabilities, brain injury, minimal brain dysfunction, dyslexia, and developmental aphasia.

(i) **Disorders not included**. The term does not include learning problems that are primarily the result of visual, hearing, or motor disabilities, of mental retardation, of emotional

**Table 2.1. National Joint Committee for Learning Disabilities' 1981 Definition of Learning Disabilities (Hammill, Leigh, McNutt, & Larson, 1981, p. 336)**

| Definition | Rationale |
|---|---|
| *Learning disabilities* is a generic term | The Committee felt that *learning disabilities* was a global ("generic") term under which a variety of specific disorders could be reasonably grouped. |
| that refers to a heterogeneous group of disorders | The disorders grouped under the learning disability label are thought to be specific and different in kind, i.e., they are "heterogeneous in nature." This phrase implies that the specific causes of the disorders are also many and dissimilar. |
| manifested by significant difficulties | The effects of the disorders on an individual are detrimental to a consequential degree; that is, their presence handicaps and seriously limits the performance of some key ability. Because the NJCLD was concerned that "learning-disabled" is often used as a synonym for "mildly handicapped," the Committee wanted to emphasize that the presence of learning disabilities in an individual can be as debilitating as the presence of cerebral palsy, mental defect, blindness or any handicapping condition. |
| in the acquisition and use of listening, speaking, reading, writing, reasoning or mathematical abilities. | To be considered learning-disabled, an individual's disorder has to result in serious impairment of one or more of the listed abilities. |
| These disorders are intrinsic to the individual | This phrase means that the source of the disorder is to be found within the person who is affected. The disability is not imposed on the individual as a consequence of economic deprivation, poor child-rearing practices, faulty school instruction, societal pressures, cultural differences, etc. Where present, such factors may complicate treatment, but they are not considered to be the cause of the learning disability. |
| and presumed to be due to central nervous system dysfunction. | The cause of the learning disability is a known or presumed dysfunction in the central nervous system. Such dysfunctions may be by-products of traumatic damage to tissues, inherited factors, biochemical insufficiencies or imbalances, or other similar conditions that affect the central nervous system. The phrase is intended to spell out clearly the intent behind the statement that learning disabilities are intrinsic to the individual. |

      disturbance, or of environmental, cultural, or economic disadvantage.

  (ii) **In making a determination of eligibility . . .** a child shall not be determined to be a child with a disability if the determinant factor for such determination is lack of instruction in reading or math or limited English proficiency.

Current federal regulations (Final Regulations, 1999) elaborate on the basic definition and define the criteria for determining the presence of a specific learning disability. Regulations state that a team may determine that a child has a specific learning disability if:

- the child does not achieve commensurate with his or her age and ability levels in one or more of the areas of oral expression, listening comprehension, written expression, basic reading skill, reading comprehension, mathematics calculation, and mathematics reasoning, if provided with learning experiences appropriate for the child's age and ability levels; and
- the team finds that a child has a severe discrepancy between achievement and intellectual ability in one or more of the areas identified above.

The purpose of IDEA is to ensure appropriate practices with individuals with disabilities. Practices cover both appropriate diagnosis and educational accommodations. IDEA reiterates the need for a comprehensive assessment of the student conducted by a multidisciplinary team (including parents) that shares information essential for diagnosis, educational placement, and programming.

Although some elements mentioned in the earlier version of the definition of learning disabilities as well as the definitions offered by NJCLD and ACLD are glaringly absent in this most recent version, IDEA does specifically state that a learning disability can be present if "the child does not achieve commensurate with his or her age and ability levels in one or more of the areas." If a child is gifted and has the potential of performing above grade level but is struggling to stay at grade level, he or she can be diagnosed as having a specific learning disability. Unfortunately, many districts still use grade level performance to indicate the *absence* of a learning disability.

By now, you have sensed the problem: There is no one definition of learning disabilities. Some definitions defend the idea that students can be both gifted and learning disabled and others avoid the question. Thus, when we discuss learning-disabled students from a particular school district, we must take care not to assume that their characteristics and behaviors apply to students in every other district. Because of the wide disparity in the definitions, we have established our own philosophical position on the natures of learning disabilities and giftedness and use our definitions as a foundation in formulating goals, expectations, and teaching strategies to meet the needs of GLD students.

## Our Definition

For our purposes, we found the ACLD definition of learning disabilities (1985) particularly appropriate, especially their inclusion of the phrase "average and superior intelligence" and their contention that the disability can affect adjustment throughout life. It also allows for the possibility of a nonverbal learning disability where reading and writing are not major problems. Such youngsters may have difficulty planning and organizing, seeing the bigger picture, and understanding social contexts. Three assumptions about the nature of learning disabilities form the basis for our philosophical position and resulting educational strategies for students who are gifted and learning disabled:

1. These students are able to learn and accumulate knowledge in untraditional ways.
2. Because the disability is durable, compensation techniques are of primary importance.
3. The learning disability can cause the individual to face frustration and failure in specific areas where academic demands may be directly opposed to the individual's natural learning style. Accumulated unsuccessful learning experiences often result in poor self-esteem, social and behavioral problems, depression, poor self-efficacy, attention difficulties, and hyperactivity. These negative outcomes are thought to interfere with learning, but because they are often situation-specific, we view them more often as effects, not causes, of learning difficulties (Baum, Cooper, & Neu, 2001; Baum & Olenchak, 2002; Mooney & Cole, 2000).

## Historical Perspective on Gifts and Talents

As is the case with learning disabilities, there is no single conception of giftedness. On one end of the spectrum, beliefs are very conservative and restrictive, as reflected in state definitions in which giftedness means scoring in the 97th percentile or above on standardized intelligence tests. On the other, more liberal end are fully inclusive views that suggest that everyone has a special gift of worth to society (Taylor, 1986).

Until the advent of intelligence testing and the IQ score, giftedness was equated with productivity. Indeed, early civilizations recognized as gifted those citizens who exhibited strong talents or potential in specific domains valuable to the culture. Leaders, orators, scientists, artists, and great warriors were the gold of their societies. Those with influence and money made efforts to identify youngsters showing early signs of talent in such areas and provide them with special training to develop this talent. During the Renaissance, these practices continued. Because gifted individuals were highly valued, patrons provided encouragement and financial support to struggling young talent recognized by their work or creative product. It was Mozart's performances that brought him to the court's attention; the early works of Michelangelo likewise caught the eye of the de Medici family. In earlier times, school achievement and IQ scores had little to do with predicting giftedness. Rather, it was superior performance and dedication that forecast future greatness.

Today the stereotype of a gifted youngster conjures up the image of the straight-A student who boasts an IQ of at least 130. In some instances, test scores have taken precedence over talented behavior. In fact, we know that more than a few of civilization's most gifted individuals who did not do well in school— Picasso, Edison, Churchill—might very well be excluded from gifted programs by today's standards.

The shift from performance to test score began in the late nineteenth and early twentieth centuries when the movement toward testing and evaluating predictors of success slowly replaced the evaluation of products as indicators of giftedness. Sir Francis Galton started this transition.

Influenced by his cousin, Charles Darwin, Galton was convinced that genius was an inherited trait and that intelligence was tightly related to the keenness of one's senses. He argued that tests of sensory acuity could effectively measure intelligence or genius. At the same time, across the English Channel, the French Ministry of Education commissioned psychologists Alfred Binet and Theodore Simon to develop a test to identify children too dull to benefit from traditional schooling. After many unsuccessful attempts, they finally devised a scale based on specific skills that teachers felt students needed to achieve in school. They invented the concept of mental age to interpret test performance. The mental age concept eventually led to the first IQ (intelligence quotient). Binet warned against the overuse and sole reliance on a score to determine a child's capabilities, but the reign of the all-powerful IQ score had begun.

Before long the idea swept across the Atlantic, generating further excitement and support. Most important to the field of giftedness was the test's effect on Lewis Terman. Terman, a professor at Stanford University, translated and refined Binet and Simon's work and in 1916 published the first form of the Stanford-Binet test of intelligence. From then until the 1950s, giftedness was simply measured with an IQ test. Characteristics of gifted students were based on the landmark study undertaken by Terman and his associates (Terman & Oden, 1947). They identified 1400 students with an IQ score of at least 140 on the Stanford-Binet Intelligence Test and conducted a comprehensive, longitudinal study on the personality characteristics and later creative accomplishments of these young geniuses. Early findings created the "Terman Myth": "that gifted students are only those who excel in all areas of endeavor and score high on any achievement and aptitude test" (Whitmore, 1980, p. 13). There were doubters about this talented-in-everything depiction. Witty (1958, p. 62) asserted that "any child whose performance in a potentially valuable line of human activity is consistently remarkable" may be considered gifted. The movement continued with leaders voicing new ideas and opinions. Hildreth (1966, p. 147) argued that "Today the simple formula of 'giving a Binet' and deciding where to 'draw the line' no longer suffices. If giftedness is viewed as developed capacities and unusual performance in a wide range of skills and achievements, the identification of the gifted and talented requires a many-sided study of the individual's intellectual abilities."

This shift in emphasis away from using a high IQ score as the sole indicator of giftedness was further supported by other research. Wallach (1976) found that test scores do not necessarily reflect the potential for creative productive accomplishments (Renzulli, 1978, p.182). Getzels and Jackson (1962) and Guilford (1962) pointed to the importance of creativity as an ability separate from intelligence, and Guilford (1959) splintered intelligence into 120 separate skills. Pressure to broaden the view of human accomplishment eventually led to a revised definition by the federal government in 1978 (PL 95-561):

[The gifted are] children, and where applicable, youth, who are identified at the preschool, elementary, or secondary level as possessing demonstrated or potential abilities that give evidence of high performance capability in areas such as intellectual, creative, specific academic or leadership ability, or in the performing and visual arts, and who by reason thereof require services or activities not ordinarily provided by the school.

Although the federal definition allowed for a variety of superior abilities within specific fields, it failed to recognize non-intellective skills shown to enhance creative production (MacKinnon, 1965; Roe, 1953; Terman, 1959). In essence, according to Renzulli (1986), what seemed to be emerging were two different kinds of giftedness—schoolhouse giftedness and creative-productive giftedness.

This distinction between forms of intelligence is essential to understanding students who can be learning disabled and gifted at the same time. Schoolhouse giftedness refers to students who are exceptional test-takers and talented lesson-learners. Their superior performance in school not only indicates high cognitive ability, but also their ability to learn in traditional ways or work within the system. On the other hand, Renzulli explained that creative-productive giftedness occurs when students use their knowledge and problem-solving abilities to develop original products and ideas. These products often grow out of students' individual strengths and interests in areas of personal relevance.

Using research on creative production, Renzulli (1978) provided a definition of creative-productive giftedness that emphasizes specific behavioral traits, both intellective and non-intellective. In his definition, giftedness or gifted behavior is viewed as the interaction among three clusters of traits: above-average ability, creativity, and task commitment, that are brought to bear on a specific area of human endeavor (see Figure 2.1). For GLD students, we often find these traits in activities undertaken *outside* of the school setting where they are freer to pursue interests in ways they learn best. (We will discuss these traits of creative productive giftedness more fully in Chapter 10 when we focus on identification of gifted behaviors in learning-disabled students.)

In the late 1980s, Congress authorized a small federal program on the gifted and talented, The Jacob K. Javits Gifted and Talented Students Education Act of 1988 (PL 100-297), which greatly expanded the defini-

# Chapter 2

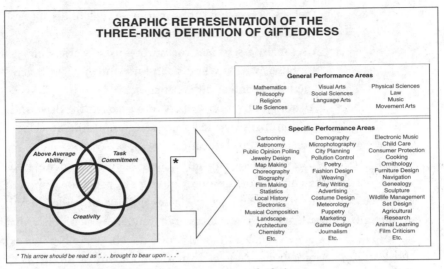

**Figure 2.1.** Renzulli's (1978) three-ring conception of giftedness.

tion of giftedness. A major goal of this act was to identify students who traditionally would not be considered for gifted or talented programs. The legislation specified that federally funded demonstration programs be developed that placed special emphasis on economically disadvantaged youngsters, students with limited English proficiency, and students with disabilities who are gifted and talented. The Act offered a broadened definition of gifted and talented with supporting guides for implementation:

> Children and youth with outstanding talent perform or show the potential for performing at remarkably high levels of accomplishment when compared with others of their age, experience, or environment.

> These children and youth exhibit high performance capability in intellectual, creative and or artistic areas, possess unusual leadership capacity, or excel in specific academic fields. They require services or activities not ordinarily provided by the schools.

> Outstanding talents are present in children and youth from all cultural groups across all economic strata, and in all areas of human endeavor.

To put these definitions into practice, schools must develop a system to identify gifted and talented students that

- Seeks variety—looks throughout a range of disciplines for students with diverse talents;
- Uses many assessment measures—uses a variety of appraisals so that schools can find students in different talent areas and at different ages; . . .
- Assesses motivation—takes into account the drive and passion that play a key role in accomplishment. (US Department of Education, 1993, p. 26)

As a result of the Jacob K. Javits Gifted and Talented Students Education Act and the enlarged definition of giftedness, programs appeared that focused on identifying and serving a wide range of students with unique gifts and talents in diverse areas. Finally there was a policy that not only acknowledged the existence of students who were both gifted and learning disabled but encouraged the development of programs to identify and serve these youngsters. (We describe several of these programs later in the book.)

Supporting the Javits initiative were changing views of intelligence (Gardner, 1983, 1999; Goleman, 1995; Sternberg, 1988, 1997) that steered away from using an IQ score to assess giftedness. This pluralistic view of intelligence encourages educators to view students in new ways and discover talents not measured by traditional IQ tests. Adopting the more expansive definitions of giftedness and intelligence opens the door for discovering all manner of gifts and talents in students with learning disabilities.

In short, the key points or assumptions we will use in discussing giftedness and gifted behavior within this book are as follows:

1. Giftedness may be creative-productive in nature.
2. Giftedness occurs in certain individuals in *specific* areas or domains at certain times.
3. Evidence for traits comprising creative productive giftedness can be found in any area of a student's life (in positive or negative situations).
4. Task commitment is not synonymous with attention span, high academic achievement, and homework done properly and on time. Rather, it represents "the capacity for high levels of interest, enthusiasm, fascination, and involvement in a particular problem area of study or form of human expression" (Renzulli

& Reis, 1985).

We see that early definitions of genius or giftedness involved talent or creative production that was culturally useful. However, as theorists became fixated on IQ, definitions drifted from actual performance to test scores. Today, we are returning to earlier views of giftedness. Beyond Renzulli's emphasis on creative production, others recommend looking at superior performances in specific areas. Gardner (1999) posited that there are multiple intelligences or areas of talents where individuals can excel. Tannenbaum (1983) argued that gifts are identified by teaching specific skills in specific domains and evaluating resulting performance. We make the larger case that gifts sometimes reveal themselves without formal instruction or assessment. Broadened conceptions of giftedness by theorists and policy makers help us puncture the myth that giftedness refers to extraordinary productivity in all areas. And perhaps more important, a wider vision suggests greater flexibility in identifying and promoting specific gifts and talents among LD students.

# Learning Disabled & Gifted: Who Are They & What Do They Need?

Who, then, is the student who is both gifted and learning disabled? Simply put, the gifted, learning-disabled student is a child who exhibits remarkable talents or strengths in some areas and problematic weaknesses in others. In recent years there has been a growing interest in and increased understanding about students who embody this paradox of behaviors. Research studies and scholars on traits and effective programs have revealed a body of knowledge about the learning characteristics of GLD students and what they need to fulfill their potential (Baum, Cooper, & Neu, 2001, Brody & Mills, 1997; Fox, Brody, & Tobin, 1983; Maker & Whitmore, 1986; Mooney & Cole, 2000; Reis & Neu, 1994; West, 1997). In this chapter, we introduce the three groups of students comprising the population of youngsters we refer to as GLD, highlight several of the research studies, and explore common themes concerning GLD students' unique learning traits and their educational implications.

## Three Varieties of GLD Students

### Identified Gifted Students Who Have Subtle Learning Disabilities

First consider the students whom everyone knows are gifted. These students are first noticed for their achievement and high IQ scores, and high grades often place these youngsters in programs for the gifted. However, over time discrepancies grow between expected and actual performance. These students may charm with oral talent while their spelling or handwriting contradicts this image. At times these all-knowing students may be forgetful, sloppy, and disorganized. When they reach middle school or junior high and face longer writing assignments and heavier emphasis on comprehensive, independent reading, these students find it increasingly difficult to maintain high levels of achievement. Well intended teachers, guidance counselors, and parents often lament, "If James or Tisha would only try harder. . . ." Such students may be able to put forth more effort, but it is unlikely to improve the situation because it dies not address the real issue: They simply do not know how to study or memorize. Like Neil, they may first blame the curriculum—it's boring—or they become class clowns to divert attention from their lack of success in the curriculum. Eventually they become depressed, confused, and discouraged about their difficulty in meeting curricular requirements and begin to doubt their own abilities. If the learning disability is not identified by high school, social and emotional problems can grow to accompany—or eclipse—the learning disability.

Because below-grade-level achievement is the usual signal for a psycho-educational screening for possible learning disabilities, these unfortunate bright students are often passed over. To many school personnel, a "C" average is no reason to refer a student for testing even though that same student demonstrates well-above-average learning potential. Unfortunately, few consider the resources it takes (effort, time, and support from family) for the students to maintain passing grades. Identifying a learning disability would help these students understand their situations. More importantly, professionals could offer learning strategies and compensation techniques to help these learning-disabled gifted students deal with the duality of learning behaviors.

However, just because a gifted student is not achieving to potential, he or she is not necessarily learning disabled. There are other reasons why bright students do not meet academic expectations. Perhaps teacher or parent expectations are unrealistic. Excelling in science, for example, is no assurance that high-level performance will also be found in other areas. Motivation, interest, efficacy beliefs, and specific aptitudes influence the amount of effort students apply to a task and the quality of performance. In other instances, the student's self-expectations are so high that a task is not—and cannot ever be—finished to perfection. As the student becomes dimly aware of the struggle between perfectionism and impossibility, procrastination may be an escape route, although that usually leads to other conflicts.

Underachievement can also result when a student perceives the curriculum to be unchallenging or irrelevant. Some bright students do not subscribe to the school's value system. Sometimes, for example, gifted students perceive grades as trivial, and these bright youngsters search out other rewards in other environments. If the curriculum had been so beneath student ability in the elementary grades, these students may have had little occasion or incentive to learn how to study or apply themselves when assignments require more memory, organization, and planning. It is essential to rule out alternative explanations before assuming a learning disability is present. In essence, one must ask whether the behavior is indicative of a learning disability or a signal of other curricular-related issues.

### Students Not Identified as Gifted or Learning Disabled

The second group of youngsters in which this combination of learning behaviors may be found are those who have not been identified as either gifted or learning disabled. These are students whose learning disabilities have been masked by their high intellectual ability. Their talent enables these bright youngsters to compensate sufficiently to perform at grade level. In an ongoing tug-of-war, their intellectual ability hides the disability and the disability disguises the gift. These students are difficult to spot because they are academically inconspicuous and do not grab attention with exceptional behaviors. The signs of their hidden gifts can emerge in specific content areas or with a teacher who uses more creative approaches in the classroom. Sometimes a talent emerges in particular learning environments in which written production is minimized in favor of projects, drama, debate, and discussion and in which less traditional teaching methods are favored.

Often the hidden disability is discovered in college or adulthood when the student happens to read about dyslexia or learning disabilities or hears peers discuss learning difficulties. By that time the student may have little confidence in his or her abilities and suffer from mild discouragement about school and learning. This scenario may be particularly relevant for students interested in the arts because their talents aren't valued in the classroom and they are seen as reluctant learners. Cowles (2000) interviewed 11 professional artists about their school experiences and discovered that 8 of them had experienced school difficulty. Of those 8, only 1 was formally identified as reading disabled and only 3 had received academic support. Although all were talented and some intellectually gifted as well, none received gifted services beyond participation in traditional arts classes offered to all students. As adults they felt that perhaps a subtle learning disability had impeded their learning. All agreed that it was their gifts that helped them get through a system that seemed blinded or indifferent about both their gifts and talents and learning difficulties. Table 3.1 summarizes the school experiences of these 11 students.

## Identified Learning-Disabled Students Who Are Also Gifted

The third profile group consists of students who are discovered within the identified learning-disabled population. Unlike the GLD students with a subtle learning disability, these bright children are often failing in two or more subjects. They are first noticed by school personnel for what they cannot do. This group of students is at serious academic risk because of the implicit message that accompanies the LD label: You are broken. When sensitive GLD students respond to the emphasis placed on their disability with genuine feelings of inadequacy, it can overshadow any positive feelings connected with their special gift or talent. And the school system all too often reinforces these negative, pessimistic attitudes. The usual approach is to work on the disability until a student is fixed and made normal again and then attend to the gift or talent. This practice values acquisition of basic skills over creative productive behavior. Reading, spelling, writing, and math take precedence over a student's talent in building bridges, gift of using art to explain conflict, or commitment to save whales by starting a city-wide campaign. Even if the gift is noticed, it may be misused or exploited, as seen in Neil's with his photography.

The prevalence of potential giftedness among this population is higher than you might expect and is often related to how school districts identify their learning-disabled populations. There may be as many as 180,000 learning-disabled students with above average IQs in American schools, and about 10% of high IQ children are reading two or more years, below grade level (Winner, 1996). In an earlier study examining the traits of high ability learning-disabled students, about a third of an identified LD population also had superior intellectual ability (Baum, 1985). Table 3.2 lists the

| Table 3.1. Artists and School Difficulties (Cowles, 2000) | |
|---|---|
| **Visual Artists (3)** | |
| School Experience | All received average to below-average grades in academics. None liked school. |
| Talent Identified | No formal identification. All excelled in art classes and were encouraged during middle school years at times. They were discouraged from pursuing art as a career. |
| Learning Disability Identified | One received remedial help in reading |
| Comments | "Wonderland." "I would sometimes fall out of my chair and have to stand in the corner. I hated school." "By middle/high school, I was not challenged for the type of person I was. I got A's in all subjects I was interested in, Ds in everything else. The subjects I was good in (drafting, mechanics, industrial arts, metal shop, pottery) were considered filler courses. If you weren't good in English and math then you were just no good." |
| **Storytellers (4)** | |
| School Experience | Two excelled in school; three enjoyed school. |
| Talent Identified | One identified as gifted, but received no intervention |
| Learning Disability Identified | Two had problems with math; one with spelling. No intervention. |
| Comments | "If I didn't like the way they were teaching, I just wouldn't do it. There was no reason to do it. Ability was never my problem. It was the situation, the times, who I happened to be and the family I grew up in. Those were my challenges." "My parents were disappointed in my career direction." |
| **Musicians (2)** | |
| School Experience | Both enjoyed the music aspect of school. |
| Talent Identified | Both involved in school music program and took private music lessons. |
| Learning Disability Identified | One had difficulty focusing and with reading comprehension. One received remedial help in fifth grade. |
| Comments | "I was identified as not a good test-taker, I didn't have focus as a young child . . . I had a verbal weakness I didn't enjoy sitting for long periods of time I remember only wanting to play the drums. It was my focus, my attention." |
| **Actors/Performers (2)** | |
| School Experience | Difficult journey, stressful |
| Talent Identified | One with IQ 135 was not recognized and received no gifted programming. One verbally identified as gifted but received no services. |
| Learning Disability Identified | One was identified as LD (reading and math). One was poor in math and terrified of making a mistake. |
| Comments | "My special ed teacher taught me to play to my own strengths to find my interests and challenge myself." |

percentage of identified LD students in grades 4-6 from 6 New England districts who attained an IQ score of at least 120 on the verbal or performance scales of the WISC. A score of 120 falls within the superior range of intelligence (Wechsler, 1974) and is claimed as a minimum threshold for high levels of creativity (Guilford, 1967).

| Table 3.2. Percentage of LD Students with Superior Abilities | |
|---|---|
| **District** | **% of LD Population with High IQ** |
| District A | 25 |
| District B | 6 |
| District C | 6 |
| District D | 20 |
| District E | 19 |
| District F | 33 |

An odd and unexpected finding was the extreme resistance of parents of bright LD students to allow their children to participate in the study. Parents of gifted students and parents of learning-disabled students with average ability had no such problem. The unwillingness of parents of GLD children implied that they were troubled and frustrated by current practices and procedures. Those parents fortunate to sample newer programs specifically designed for this population expressed relief and gratitude that the children's gifts were finally recognized and reinforced (Dixon & Baum, 1986).

To summarize, GLD children have well-above-average ability in specific areas, show a creative approach in specific situations, and are committed to some personal interest or real world problem. In addition, they are not performing well in certain academic areas because of identified deficits in learning processes. Table 3.3, which reviews the four students discussed in Chapter 1, presents such profiles.

## Characteristics of Gifted, Learning-Disabled Students

Viewed broadly, two sets of strategies exist in special education today. They are designed either to remediate weaknesses or to develop superior abilities. To understand how these strategies may be used with students who are both gifted and learning disabled, we will explore the cognitive and affective characteristics these students bring to the learning situation. The most relevant characteristics of GLD students are specific cognitive abilities, creative tendencies, self-concept, motivation, self-efficacy, and disruptive behaviors.

| | Above-Average Ability | | Creativity | Task Commitment | LD Problem |
|---|---|---|---|---|---|
| **Name** | **General** | **Specific** | | | |
| Neil | 120 IQ | Photo won first prize | Class clown, photographic essay, values | Taught self to play piano and guitar | Difficulty in remembering sequences in math and organizing throughout in written work |
| Jimmy | 134 IQ | Mechanical abilities, could take things apart and explain how they work | Excuses for avoiding tasks, compensation strategies developed on own to bypass weaknesses (used drawing to take notes) | Worked on survey even when tedious and boring because he felt it was important | Difficulty in reading and writing despite superior scores in verbal and performance areas of WISC-R |
| Debra | 128 IQ | Drama, interests in world | Great ideas in brainstorming activities, original ideas in architectural design with Legos™ | Wrote letter to President Reagan to protest nuclear war (even though she hated writing and could not spell); spent a lot of time on "A Day in the Life of Jerusha Webster" project | Poor self-concept, limited reading and writing ability, overdependence on adults |
| Bill | 133 IQ | History, science, building models | Developed an unique procedure for measuring growth of bacteria , first place winner of multiple science contests | Continuing research of identification of anti-body, on-going involvement with leadership training | Difficulty with putting ideas on paper poor handwriting and attention skills |

**Table 3.3. Sample Indicators of Giftedness and Learning Disabilities**

## Intellectual Skills

Most studies examining cognitive abilities of GLD students are based on patterns derived from the Wechsler Intelligence Scale for Children-Revised (WISC-R) (Wechsler, 1974). These studies have examined the possibility that certain intellectual patterns distinguish GLD students as a group. The results of three major research efforts give insight into the learning patterns of GLD students.

Fox and her colleagues at Johns Hopkins University (1983) studied the WISC-R profiles of 450 GLD students between the ages of six and fifteen with reading problems. Giftedness was defined by IQ scores of at least 125 on either the performance or verbal scale of the WISC-R. Documentation of a learning disability was provided by case history information, behavioral observations, reading achievement of at least two years below grade level, and evidence of a significant discrepancy between intellectual potential and academic performance. The researchers then organized subtest scores according Bannatyne's (1974) recategorization of the WISC subscales. The four categories—acquired knowledge, spatial, conceptual, and sequencing—are composed of three subtests, each shown in Table 3.4. Fox and her coworkers found that gifted LD students with reading problems perform best on conceptual and spatial tasks and worst on tasks requiring memorization of isolated facts and sequencing.

A second study (Schiff, Kaufman, & Kaufman, 1981) examining clusters of ability among GLD children found slightly different results. The researchers selected 30 students, ages 9 to 16, from a private clinic who were identified as gifted (as determined by an IQ score above 120 on either the performance or verbal scales of the WISC-R) and learning disabled (as determined by a significant difference between intelligence and achievement in some academic area, though the deficit area did not need to be below-grade level). These students displayed many behavioral traits associated with learning disabilities, such as hyperactivity and poor visual-motor or gross-motor skills. For most of these youngsters, their parents—not their schools—had requested special testing. In this study, verbal conceptualization and acquired knowledge subtests were strong areas, and spatial and sequencing abilities were weaker.

| Table 3.4. Bannatyne's (1974) Recategorization of WISC Subscales | |
|---|---|
| Category | Subtests |
| 1. Acquired Knowledge | Information, Arithmetic, Vocabulary |
| 2. Spatial | Picture Completion, Block Design, Object Assembly |
| 3. Conceptual | Comprehension, Similarities, Vocabulary |
| 4. Sequencing | Digit Span, Arithmetic, Coding |

There are two reasons for the differences between the Fox and Schiff studies. First, the populations of the two studies were different. Fox's study dealt with students whose reading abilities were two years below grade level; Schiff's study did not isolate reading problems or below-grade-level performance. Second, students in the Schiff study were performing at or above grade level, suggesting that they had found success in both verbal conceptualization and acquired knowledge areas. Both studies confirmed, however, that GLD students are able to conceptualize and think at abstract levels. It is their poor memory for isolated facts and deficient organizational abilities that interfere with school performance.

The third study is the work we have been conducting over the past several years investigating gifted students from identified learning-disabled populations (ages 9 to 13). We determined giftedness through observations of extraordinary performance in activities requiring problem solving and creative production in visual literacy, drama, or spatial design. After we determined whether a students was gifted or not, we analyzed WISC-R profiles for specific cognitive patterns. We identified strengths in Similarities, Block Design, Comprehension, Picture Arrangement, and Object Assembly, with Vocabulary and Information frequently appearing as secondary strengths. We found the typical weaknesses in Digit Span, Arithmetic, and Coding. These results have led us to theorize about the role Integrative Intelligence plays and its effect on learning and achievement with GLD children.

The familiar GLD cognitive pattern of nonverbal strengths is the focus of the West's book, *In The Mind's Eye* (West, 1997). West has written about the relationship between spatial ability and dyslexia. Dyslexia refers to neurological problems relating to language or words. This includes difficulty decoding written symbols into spoken sounds or verbal meanings, recalling names, remembering lines of text, finding the right word, or fluent speech. West provides examples of famous people from the past and the present, including artists, writers, scientists and others, who were able to achieve a great deal despite of having had some form of dyslexia or a learning disability. It is his belief that many of these individual may have achieved success or even greatness "not in spite of but because of their apparent disabilities. They may have been so much in touch with their visual-spatial nonverbal modes of thought that they have had difficulty in doing orderly sequential verbal mathematical tasks in a culture where such capabilities are so highly valued" (p. 19). (Chapter Five explores the topic of Integrative Intelligence and its educational implications.)

In summary, GLD students often demonstrate superior abilities in forming concepts and manipulating abstract ideas. For them, successful learning experiences depend on meaningful and complex interactions with subject matter. They do not assimilate isolated details that are not an important part of a "bigger picture." Although the minds of these students may be filled with broad abstractions and even grandiose ideas, they often cannot express them through organized written products because of difficulties in sequencing and lack of attention to detail. Education for these children must focus on abstract ideas and generalization. Teachers should provide organizational strategies to help these students achieve, assist the students in self-organization, and allow alternatives to writing as a means of communication. We will discuss these ideas more fully in the subsequent chapters.

## Nonintellectual Traits

Other studies concentrate on motivation, behavior, self-concept, and creative tendencies in bright learning-disabled students (Baum, 1985; Schiff, Kaufman, & Kaufman, 1981; Whitmore, 1981). The results of three studies provide a more complete picture of the typical GLD student. All these studies show that although GLD youngsters demonstrate superior abilities in certain areas and have often completed impressive creative feats (winning science fairs, breeding ants and tropical fish, producing a record, etc.), they tend to be unhappy and frustrated with themselves.

Schiff, Kaufman, & Kaufman (1981) conducted extensive interviews with the 30 GLD students in his study and their parents. He reported that these students were emotionally upset and generally unhappy because of their frustrations in activities requiring motor coordination and organizational abilities (for example, physical education, spelling, math computation). They felt powerless and vengeful. Schiff remarked that the emotions of these children were more unhealthy and troublesome than expected.

Whitmore (1981) confirmed these findings in her work with young gifted underachievers. Whitmore studied the emotional, behavioral, and creative characteristics of underachieving 6-8-year-olds, most of whom could be classified as hyperactive or learning disabled. As in the Schiff study, Whitmore found contradictions among achievement, motivation, and feelings of worth. While in school, the children were often aggressive, disruptive, and off-task. Their completed work tended to be sloppy and suggested weak effort. But in nonacademic settings these same students put forth sustained effort toward their own hobbies and interests. Whitmore found that these students were active problem solvers, analytic thinkers, and showed strong task commitment and effort when the topic was personally meaningful.

Schiff, Kaufman, and Kaufman (1981) and Whitmore (1981) based their conclusions on observation and interviews. Baum (1985) tested and extended these findings with more comprehensive measures. One hundred and twelve gifted or learning-disabled students in grades 4-6 participated in the study. Baum classified these students into three groups based on their intelligence: Superior, LD-Superior, and LD-Average. Students in the Superior group had an IQ score of at least 120 on the Performance or Verbal Scale of the WISC-R, and the local school district had identified them as gifted based on a discrepancy formula. LD-Superior students also had an IQ score of at least 120 on the Performance or Verbal Scales of the WISC-R and the local school district had classified them as learning disabled. The LD-Average students had a Full Scale IQ of at least 90 (but not exceeding a score of 119 on the Verbal or Performance Scale of the WISC-R) and the local school district had identified them as learning disabled.

Baum used a variety of instruments to assess and compare cognitive and motivational patterns in the three groups and found that the three groups were easily distinguishable. As might be expected, the "Superior" non-disabled students were plainly different from both learning-disabled groups. Teachers' perceptions of student creativity accounted for most of the difference. Teachers rated the superior students much higher on creative traits than they rated either group of learning-disabled youngsters. Predictably, the gifted students also felt more confident about their ability to do well on academic tasks (academic self-efficacy). Teachers viewed the LD-Superior students as more creative, and these students self-reported higher levels of interest in creative extracurricular activities than did their LD-Average peers, but they were more disruptive and frustrated in school. LD-Superior youngsters thought that school offered plenty of opportunities for failure, and they often ascribed their academic failures to shyness.

Overall, LD-Superior students showed high creative potential coupled with low levels of academic success and a tendency toward disruptive behavior. This profile runs directly in the face of conventional school expectations, and it invites misbehavior and frustration. The major factor distinguishing LD-Superiors from both other groups was a heightened sense of inadequacy in school. In contrast to Superior students, LD-Superiors experienced fewer school successes and considerably more failures. Even compared to less capable learning-disabled students, the LD-Superior group perceived themselves as failing more frequently in school. (In Part Two, we return to the problem of why bright LD students have such a poor sense of academic efficacy when they possess greater intellectual and creative potential, and we will make the point that poor self-efficacy fuels even more school failure and frustration for the GLD student.) Table 3.5 shows means and standard deviations for each of the three groups on the variables studied.

Gifted, learning-disabled students have learning, motivational, and perhaps emotional patterns different from those of their peers. The traits discussed above cause them to act variously gifted or learning disabled, depending on the educational or social context. At times they seem gifted and at other moments are disruptive and inept. We should wonder how many ordinary-seeming people, including adults, who show flashes of brilliance are actually GLD. A summary of these paradoxical behaviors appears in Table 3.6, and a discussion of each pair of traits follows.

### Knowledge of Concepts vs. Facts

GLD students' depth of knowledge can be simultaneously extensive and void. In areas of interest, GLD students may convey surprising and detailed knowledge of topics, especially if they are allowed to communicate in a mode that does not require written language. They can recite facts and information that they have gathered on their own within a meaningful context using strategies that are natural to them. GLD students generate many of their successes in learning on a personal need-to-know basis, acquiring facts within a meaningful context. Contrast that learning environment with one in which students must memorize a list of spelling words or math facts where ritual mastery rather than understanding is the objective.

## Table 3.5. Group Means and Standard Deviations for 24 Predictor Variables

| Variable | Group | | | | | |
|---|---|---|---|---|---|---|
| | LD-Average | | LD-Superior | | Superior | |
| | *M* | *SD* | *M* | *SD* | *M* | *SD* |
| **Self Efficacy for Academic Tasks** | | | | | | |
| Perceived success | 16.09 | 8.19 | 15.55 | 7.19 | 24.39 | 5.82 |
| Perceived failure | 4.47 | 4.04 | 5.73 | 4.56 | 1.00 | 1.44 |
| Perceived school skills | 11.63 | 11.24 | 9.89 | 10.28 | 23.38 | 6.72 |
| Overall academic self-efficacy | 78.81 | 11.12 | 78.00 | 10.10 | 91.19 | 6.77 |
| **Creative Potential** | | | | | | |
| Self-perception of creative traits | 20.74 | 4.15 | 22.64 | 3.71 | 23.50 | 4.06 |
| Teacher perception of creativity | 20.43 | 11.40 | 33.37 | 17.63 | 56.35 | 16.31 |
| Figural divergent thinking | 108.75 | 12.83 | 110.50 | 12.35 | 114.12 | 12.04 |
| Verbal originality | 94.90 | 15.11 | 100.17 | 15.03 | 108.91 | 14.62 |
| Figural originality | 112.18 | 23.98 | 111.04 | 24.29 | 116.27 | 20.57 |
| Creative interests | 22.58 | 14.36 | 26.62 | 6.20 | 22.20 | 9.11 |
| Spatial interests | .39 | .49 | .65 | .48 | .43 | .49 |
| **Disruptive Behavior** | | | | | | |
| Teacher perception of disruptive behavior | 12.43 | 8.00 | 14.33 | 11.93 | 5.15 | 6.28 |
| **Self-Concept** | | | | | | |
| Self-concept | 51.58 | 9.15 | 50.60 | 9.27 | 57.38 | 6.51 |
| **Locus of Control** | | | | | | |
| Internal control of success | 13.47 | 3.97 | 12.27 | 2.61 | 13.68 | 1.84 |
| Internal control for failure | 10.38 | 3.43 | 9.34 | 3.53 | 11.00 | 2.26 |
| **Attribution for Academic Success and Failure** | | | | | | |
| Success attributed to ability | 29.08 | 26.79 | 23.17 | 23.90 | 30.53 | 24.66 |
| Success attributed to effort | 32.38 | 21.25 | 41.34 | 29.08 | 31.44 | 17.02 |
| Success attributed to task difficulty | 28.42 | 24.54 | 37.09 | 29.26 | 36.66 | 23.90 |
| Success attributed to luck | 7.16 | 8.47 | 3.83 | 5.68 | 1.91 | 4.49 |
| Failure attributed to lack of ability | 4.62 | 10.53 | 1.70 | 4.99 | 4.93 | 16.31 |
| Failure attributed to lack of effort | 28.65 | 29.28 | 24.74 | 31.44 | 17.31 | 30.96 |
| Failure attributed to task difficulty | 21.12 | 32.99 | 32.99 | 39.42 | 15.00 | 29.95 |
| Failure attributed to bad luck | 6.36 | 9.82 | 10.71 | 24.64 | 4.95 | 16.85 |
| Failure attributed to shyness | 13.94 | 24.16 | 25.82 | 39.63 | 3.21 | 10.15 |

| Table 3.6. Paradoxical Behaviors | |
|---|---|
| Gifted | Learning Disabled |
| Knowledgeable about many things | Difficulty remembering simple facts |
| Creative | Generates many excuses; uses creative abilities as means to survive the system |
| Excellent sense of humor | Class clown |
| Task-committed when interested | Appears bored and aloof; boredom may be a call for help |
| Perseveres when in "flow" | Short attention span at times and a tendency to focus too long at other times |
| Excellent skills when using higher level thinking and problem solving | Fails to master basic skills; may be dyslexic, dysgraphic, or dyscalculic |
| High standards for success; perfectionistic | Sloppy, careless, puts forth minimal effort, doesn't turn in assignments |

### Creativity and Humor vs. Excuses and Clowning

Creativity and humor, like most human characteristics, can be productive or destructive. When a GLD student is in an appropriate learning environment, these traits usually manifest themselves in a productive fashion. When pursuing an interest, offering ideas during a class discussion, or designing an art project, the creative ability of GLD students is often superior. They can view a situation from unique perspectives and often their perceptions are off-center and humorous. However, in unsupportive environments, GLD students are likely to use their creativity to survive a system that is unfriendly and often hostile to them. They can invent many ways to avoid a task and get into trouble. It is as if GLD students had memorized the Nobel Laureate Juan Ramón Jiménez' words: "If they give you ruled paper, write the other way." These students could win awards for the most creative or funniest excuse for not completing homework. Indeed, some of these students become class clowns to divert attention from academic tasks they cannot perform and thus are able to preserve their positive but fragile self-concept as a gifted students.

### Task Committed and in "Flow" vs. Bored and Inattentive

Motivation, concentration, and persistence are usually strong when GLD students are involved in creative productive activities outside of school. These students often demonstrate their potential for giftedness by engaging in activities that align with their personal strengths and interests. At these times they persevere. They become "at one" with the activity, even giving up a meal in order to complete a model or finish an art project. Unfortunately, this absorption with an area of interest is sometimes misunderstood as *hyper*focusing or obsessing and thus not reinforced in the school setting. In traditional school lessons where listening, reading, and writing are required, many of these students appear restless, often do not complete tasks, and may behave as though they have attention deficits. Claims of deadly boredom should be assessed skeptically. When a GLD student asserts, "I would do the work if I were interested but it is too, too, too boring," the truth of the matter may be that they lack the skills or understanding to tackle the task.

### Mastery in Problem Solving vs. Failure with Basic Skills and Rote Learning

Performing tasks at different levels of thinking is another conundrum. GLD students are excellent at higher-level thinking and problem solving, but at the same time often show a deficit in lower level skills where automaticity is required, such as spelling, memorizing math facts, and handwriting. Unfortunately, schools subscribe to the belief of hierarchical learning—a fixed sequence of learning that assumes that mastery of basic facts must occur before the more creative, higher level applications can occur. "You can't do science if you can't read, and you can't follow math applications unless you have memorized the times tables."

### Towering Standards for Success vs. Sloppy and Incomplete Assignments

Quality of work is also an area of inconsistency for most GLD students. GLD students can be perfectionists, especially when pursuing and area of interest, but they are often apathetic about quality when completing mandatory school assignments. GLD students have high standards for success and are not be satisfied by accomplishments that they regard as watered down or simplistic, as was the case with both Neil and Bill. Even when they are pressed to complete assignments they think are as irrelevant, they may not perceive those as success experiences. If they find tasks too threatening and feel that even their best efforts may result in work beneath their personal standards they may opt to "lose" their completed work or simply not do it. They would prefer to fail from total lack of engagement rather than hand in a substandard effort and receive a poor evaluation.

Poor handwriting, spelling, and organizational skills often impede the GLD student's ability to hand in neat work. It is important to carefully evaluate an assignment's goal. If it is authoring a story, then using a word processing program with a spell and grammar check is advisable. Prohibiting these students from using the technology that will assist them in turning in work that meets their personal standards is counterproductive and educationally unsound.

### Educational Needs

GLD students have learning and motivational patterns different from those of their peers. Understanding and using these differences is critical to planning comprehensive programs for GLD students. An effective program creates educational contexts that suppress students' problematic behaviors, while simultaneously encouraging the emergence of more positive gifted traits. Results from studies and program evaluations (Baldwin, 1995; Baum, Cooper, & Neu 2001; Neilson, 2002; Reis, Neu, & McGuire, 1995; Weinfeld, Barnes-Robinson, Jeweler, & Schuetz, 2002) as well as anecdotal accounts from teachers, parents, and students (Abeel & Murphy, 2001; Mooney & Cole, 2000) about the plight of the GLD student provide strong suggestions about interventions that contribute positively to the education, health, and well-being of GLD students.

Chief among useful ideas is a GLD student's need to have attention focused on his or her strengths, talents, and interests. In addition, GLD students require a learning environment that supports their physical, intellectual, and emotional needs. Such an environment provides dually differentiated educational experiences that assure appropriate challenge, while offering instruction, accommodations, and compensation strategies that minimize the effects of the learning disability. Last, it is important to have counseling and advocacy support available both within and outside of the school setting. Chapter Nine extends the discussion of these factors essential to the healthy intellectual and emotional development of the GLD student.

# Alphabet Soup: ADHD and More*

*Blaine, a quiet but friendly and hard-working young man, is enrolled in a small, private academy. Depending on the subject, he worked at a variety of different grade levels. His teachers report that he is a willing participant in every facet of school and becomes fervent—even obsessive—about activities of particular interest. Showing superior grasp of academic concepts in his homework, class discussions, and projects, Blaine occasionally suggests alternatives to teacher-directed assignments so that he can demonstrate his comprehension and skill. While teachers are free to accept or reject his recommendations, they most often agree. As a result, Blaine's relationships with peers, older students with mutual interests, and adults continue to improve.*

This description, summarized from a middle school educational assessment, portrays a student whom most teachers would love having in class: intelligent, interested, engaged, and socially involved. But Blaine had a difficult time getting to this point. By the time he was eight years old, he was labeled with a confusing alphabet soup of disorders. The following excerpt from a neurologist describes a seemingly different child:

> . . . an eight-year-old boy being seen for neurological examination as part of a comprehensive child study team evaluation.

---

* This chapter reflects previous work by F. Richard Olenchak and this book's authors.

Information provided by mother and observations in the office setting indicate that difficulties displayed by Blaine have a multi-factorial basis, including: 1. Attention Deficit Hyperactivity Disorder; 2. mild Oppositional Defiant Disorder; 3. Generalized Anxiety Disorder; and 4. mild unevenness in skill development.

Recommendations

1. Ongoing individual counseling and family therapy
2. Ritalin and Clonadine
3. Social skills intervention to facilitate development of appropriate skills
4. Consistent behavior management at home and in school
5. No ot (occupational therapy) or pt (physical therapy)
6. Return to regular school in cooperation with special services

Notice that the summary makes no mention of Blaine's high intellectual ability (see Table 4.1) or his specific gifts and talents. The neurologist was keen to find problems, focusing on Blaine's anxiety and depression. This emphasis also punctuated the following report from the school

| Table 4.1. Blaine's WISC III Profile | | | | |
|---|---|---|---|---|
| Information | 19 | | Picture Completion | 14 |
| Similarities | 19 | | Coding | 8 |
| Arithmetic | 10 | | Picture Arrangement | 15 |
| Vocabulary | 19 | | Block Design | 18 |
| Comprehension | 19 | | Object Assembly | 9 |
| Digit span | 9 | | Symbol Search | 15 |
| | | | Mazes | 8 |
| | Verbal IQ | 142 | | |
| | Performance IQ | 119 | | |
| | Full Scale IQ | 134 | | |
| | Verbal Comprehension | 150 | | |
| | Perceptual Organization | 124 | | |
| | Freedom from Distraction | 98 | | |
| | Processing Speed | 109 | | |

psychologist. Though she acknowledged Blaine's superior intelligence in the body of her report, the school psychologist neglects to consider an interaction between the gift and his behavior:

> There is a side of Blaine that appears anxious and depressed, the origin of which may be directly related to his diagnosed ADHD disorder. Impulsivity is noted and in keeping with the situations in the past that have suggestions of endangerment to self, he needs to be monitored in school and at home. It is hypothesized that when Blaine's stressors have been reduced, he will improve in his outlook and his problematic and worrisome behaviors will diminish.

Blaine's situation is more common than you might suspect. Although the concurrence of learning and behavioral difficulties and giftedness is increasing (or at least being reported more frequently), professionals still appear to lack a general understanding about how it is possible for giftedness to coexist with learning difficulties. The usual intervention is designed with deficit in mind and ignores talents. But not recognizing and addressing talents can magnify behaviors and emotional outcomes, resulting in a search for additional diagnoses and creating even more labels for a child. Some of these youngsters have more letters trailing after their names than most degreed professionals who serve them.

The last decade has witnessed a dramatic increase in the recognition and diagnosis of a variety of syndromes to explain individual differences and resulting problematic behaviors, especially within the school setting. These new labels often have characteristics similar to other classification categories. In the case of gifted students experiencing problems, we have found that diagnosis has become increasingly muddied and confused. Not only are we finding gifted students with learning disabilities, but also gifted students with ADHD (attention deficit/hyperactivity), EBD (emotional and behavioral disorders), or AS (Asperger's Syndrome, a mild form of autism). (A gifted student with autism? Is that possible? Take a look at the web site "University Students with Autism and Asperger's Syndrome" (http://www.users.dircon.co.uk/~cns/).) While it is clear that multiple syndromes can exist simultaneously, confusion caused by overlapping characteristics and the cross-pollination of giftedness with a disability may result in underidentification, misidentification, or over-identification of multiple syndromes. The more labels, the more daunting it is to design suitable programs for these students, especially since many disorders have crossover characteristics (Baum & Olenchak, 2002; Crammond, 1994; Neihart, 2000).

In this chapter we try to sort the confusion out. We explore the many facets of ADHD and its interaction with giftedness. We also survey the landscape of gifted students whose presenting behaviors put them at risk of underidentification, misidentification, and ultimately receiving inappropriate services in schools. Our purpose is to reinforce why professionals and parents alike must be careful in pigeonholing children into convenient categories that may yield positive results in the short term, but thwart long-term development of the individual child's talents and gifts. Examining events leading to Blaine's pessimistic diagnosis will illustrate how lack of understanding about the characteristics and needs of gifted students obscured the professionals' vision and prevented them from suggesting appropriate diagnoses and treatment.

### Blaine

An alert little boy who seemed to need little sleep, Blaine loved being read to and playing with his Lego™ bricks. Though he began talking and walking later than expected, he quickly caught up, with his developmental levels in motor and verbal areas surpassing those of his age mates. Behavior problems first surfaced when Blaine entered nursery school. Impressed with his advanced vocabulary, wealth of knowledge, artwork, and ability to build structures, his teacher considered whether or not to differentiate his program to fit his unique learning needs. Ultimately, she chose to do nothing: "After all, he needs to learn to listen, follow directions, and accomplish tasks that are assigned." Because Blaine was becoming unhappy and school was increasingly aversive, his parents placed him in another nursery school where there was less emphasis on a predetermined structure and more opportunity for exploration.

When Blaine entered kindergarten at five, he performed quite well for the first few months. However, his teacher expressed concern about his tendency to blurt out answers, his difficulty learning his letters, and his motor skills that lagged sharply behind his extraordinary verbal ability. Described as impulsive, Blaine was becoming a discipline problem, especially when he was expected to tackle tasks he found difficult. As a result, the school asked Blaine's parents to complete the *Conners Parent*

*Rating Scales* (Conners, 1997), which includes items related to conduct disorders. Blaine was referred to a pediatric neurologist, who diagnosed him with ADHD. He began a regimen of Ritalin, the most commonly prescribed methylphenidate for addressing attention problems in children. That summer, Blaine attended summer school where he learned his letters in two short weeks.

When Blaine entered first grade, his behavior was under control, but he had difficulty learning to read and was placed in the lowest reading group. To encourage Blaine to read, Blaine's parents began to take him to the public library on a regular basis. In only a month, Blaine was reading fluently. Using books he chose—most of which were nonfiction—his literacy skills rapidly improved to the point that his teacher acknowledged that he now belonged in the top reading group. For unknown reasons, however, she never moved him. By midyear, Blaine once again had drifted into a pattern of inappropriate behavior and had become the classroom goat. Classmates teased him unmercifully, chanting "Blaine the Pain" and tossing things at him during recess or other semi-structured or unstructured activities. In the absence of any significant adult intervention, this sensitive six year old defended himself by lashing out physically. Adult fingers, though, pointed at Blaine. Explaining that physical aggression would not be tolerated and that Blaine needed to cope with teasing without resorting to violence, the principal placed Blaine on a behavioral contract. His behavior improved somewhat, but by spring, Blaine was suspended for provoking his teacher to such an extent that she threw a chair at him. (We know—the principal should have placed the *teacher* on a behavioral contract before she committed child abuse.)

During the summer between first and second grades, Blaine attended an enrichment program for gifted students and experienced no social or academic difficulties while working with intellectual and interest peer groups. At home, he read voraciously, plowing through four *Boxcar Children* novels by Gertrude Chandler Warner in three days. There was reason to expect that Blaine would have much improved school experiences ahead.

### Bad to Worse

But as second grade began, hopes were dashed for Blaine's sustained educational improvement. He complained constantly about writing assignments, and he refused to finish spelling and math assignments. The playground situation worsened, with incidents of cruel teasing escalating into fisticuffs. His parents requested the support of a playground assistant—their right under Section 504 of the Rehabilitation Act of 1973 provisions—but were denied. In desperation, Blaine's parents sought psychiatric support, which resulted in Blaine's medication regimen expanding to include Clonadine to enhance therapeutic control of hypertensive activity associated with anxiety that was diagnosed in addition to his attention problems. At school, the child study team chose not to classify Blaine for special education and instead initiated behavioral interventions, including 4.5 hours each day of individual instruction to address his cognitive abilities. Unfortunately, Blaine continued to display low tolerance for frustration, sometimes even ripping pages from his book after being asked to complete repetitious or dull work. And although he did not enjoy being separated from other children during class time, his peers continued to harass him on the playground. Consequently, Blaine contrived a pattern of stomachaches and other maladies so he could stay home from school. His parents struggled to keep him in school, but after several particularly aggressive episodes during recess and noncompliant behaviors during class, Blaine was removed from second grade and placed on homebound instruction. At this point, Blaine asked his mother, "Why did God give me ADHD? I wish I would die so other kids would feel sorry for me."

Continuing homebound programming into third grade, Blaine grew increasingly reticent. As a result, his psychiatrist diagnosed him as experiencing Major Depressive Disorder. To address the depression, homebound instruction was discontinued and Blaine was readmitted to school. Educators wanted Blaine diagnosed and classified for special education services associated with emotional disturbances, and Blaine's parents hired a professional special education advocate to help them make this classification. All the while, though, Blaine's teacher rebuffed any attempt to differentiate his instruction or curriculum, and his depression grew worse. During the process of classifying Blaine for special education, the family's advocate, along with an expert consultant, managed to convince the school district to fund Blaine's alternative enrollment at a nearby private school. The school, although not intended for students with special needs, admitted Blaine as a favor to his parents. It was thought that instructional and curricular adjustments would be more effective in the private setting given Blaine's cognitive talent coupled with his need for more individual attention..

In the private school setting, Blaine was accelerated in English and social studies to accommodate his strengths in those areas. An outstanding art program supported his spatial talents in the visual arts. Within their lessons, teachers offered projects as a learning outcome option, which was particularly appropriate for Blaine's profile of strengths and talents. Small class sizes, dependably less than 15, helped him focus his attention. His homeroom teacher worked with him to improve his social relationships, find acceptable responses to frustrating situations, and organize his work. Blaine's problems with written language and attention were substantially reduced by allowing him to use a computer for all written assignments.

Blaine graduated from eighth grade as valedictorian and is attending a public high school for gifted and talented students. In the summers, he is a teaching assistant in the same special enrichment program where his own gifts were first acknowledged.

Several important and complex issues come to our attention concerning Blaine: the lack of appropriate diagnosis, the role of the environment, and the addition of one diagnostic syndrome after another rather than changing the original diagnosis or the services offered. Of all the labels assigned to Blaine, which were justified? Did the original diagnosis of ADHD take into account the behaviors that might have been attributed to his giftedness? Did the problems cease when he was put on medication? Which of the behavioral manifestations were symptomatic of the stressful learning environment in which he was placed? Did his developmental lags and difficulty with spelling and handwriting indicate the presence of a subtle learning disability? Did the behavioral manifestations present clues to the rightful diagnosis? Was he ultimately a gifted student with an undiagnosed learning disability? Was he ADHD or was he gifted with both learning and attention difficulties?

To answer these important questions, we shall explore the usual approaches to diagnosing ADHD, including characteristic traits and typical interventions. We will then discuss how gifted behavioral manifestations may influence, confuse, and alter traditional diagnosis and interventions for students with ADHD-like behaviors. Last, we will suggest guidelines for appropriate diagnosis and intervention approaches for students who may be gifted with ADHD and learning disabled as well.

## ADHD Definitions and Characteristics

Despite the recent increases in diagnoses, ADHD is not a new disorder and there has been no sudden outbreak among children and adults. Noted in psychiatric literature as early as the mid-1800s, its emergence in this century began with the appearance of Alfred Strauss and Laura Lehtinen's 1947 text, *Psychopathology and Education of the Brain-Injured Child*. In the 1950s and 1960s, children who were of at least average ability and who exhibited the following symptoms (also mentioned in Chapter 2) were identified as having Strauss' Syndrome, hyperkinetic disorder, or minimal brain damage, representing researchers' assumption that the behaviors were created by some injury to the brain:

1. Erratic and inappropriate behavior on mild provocation
2. Increased motor activity
3. Poor organization of behavior
4. Distractibility of more than ordinary degree under ordinary conditions
5. Persistent faulty perceptions
6. Persistent hyperactivity
7. Awkwardness and consistently poor motor performance

(Stevens & Birch, 1957)

In the 1970s, professionals increasingly chose to disconnect these behaviors from brain injury because the connections were typically impossible to prove. So with the invented cause—brain injury—out of the way, researchers now focused on labeling a constellation of observable behaviors as the Hyperactive Child Syndrome. Early in the 1980s, psychologists reconsidered the role of hyperactivity as the central symptom of the disorder. They began to attach more importance to the inability among "hyperactive" children to sustain attention and control impulses. In fact, some of these students were not particularly jittery or jumpy but rather seemed to "drift off" during lectures, assigned reading, and written assignments. This observation led to the emergence of two terms to describe these children—attention deficit disorder (ADD) with hyperactivity or without hyperactivity (American Psychiatric Association, 1980).

Cited alongside other mental health classifications in the *Diagnostic and Statistical Manual-IV-TR* (2000) by the American Psychiatric Association, ADHD represents a renaming of the older diagnosis—ADD—that is now believed to be sloppy, given current research. Previously it was believed that the disorder was most characterized by attention problems and that, while hyperkinetic activity might accompany inattentiveness, professionals thought the substantive aspect of the disorder was not so much the exaggerated activity level as the inability to pay attention to a task. Recent studies have shown that many individuals with attention problems also occasionally exhibit at least some characteristics associated with hyperactivity (Barkley & Murphy, 1998). (While not denying that some children experience attention deficits *without* hyperactivity, some argue it may be an altogether different syndrome (Carlson, 1986).) But the great majority of children and adolescents with ADHD demonstrate significant characteristics of both inattention and hyperactivity-impulsivity. Consequently, the American Psychiatric Association formally changed the terminology to reflect the nature of the disorder as it manifests in persons of all ages. The current label reflects the position that the primary symptoms of the disorder are hyperactivity along with problems in sustained attention and controlling impulses.

### The American Psychiatric Association Criteria

Situated in the *Diagnostic and Statistical Manual* among disorders that are usually first diagnosed during childhood or adolescence, the core aspect of ADHD is that a pattern of inattentive or hyperactive, impulsive behaviors is exhibited with *more frequency* and *intensity* than in others at comparable developmental levels. Some of the inappropriate behaviors must have been observable before 7 years of age and must be problematic in at least two distinct environments where "there must be clear evidence of interference with developmentally appropriate social, academic, or occupational functioning (APA, 2000, p. 85). To fine-tune various combinations of behaviors and traits characterizing ADHD, three subtypes have been identified: ADHD, Combined Type; ADHD, Predominantly Inattentive Type; ADHD, Predominantly Hyperactive-Impulsive Type.

The Combined Type reflects six or more symptoms of inattention as well as six or more symptoms of hyperactivity-impulsivity that have persisted for at least six months. The Predominantly Inattentive Type encompasses six or more indicators of inattention but fewer than six symptoms of hyperactivity-impulsivity for at least six months, while the Predominantly Hyperactive-Impulsive Type involves six or more symptoms of hyperactivity-impulsivity but fewer than six characteristics of inattention for at least six months. Table 4.2 provides a synopsis of the characteristics used to diagnose ADHD as enumerated in *DSM-IV-TR* (APA, 2000, p. 92).

The behavioral criteria for identifying ADHD become especially important when one considers that there are no laboratory tests, neurological or attentional assessments, or other diagnostic instruments that have been convincingly validated in isolating ADHD (APA, 2000). As a result, the diagnosis of ADHD relies on behavioral observations where frequency, intensity, and recurrence of the behaviors are charted and where it can be determined that the behaviors negatively influence the individual in at least two settings.

| Table 4.2. Diagnostic Characteristics of ADHD | |
|---|---|
| **INATTENTION** | **HYPERACTIVITY-IMPULSIVITY** |
| Frequent failure to attend to critical details or frequently makes careless mistakes | Frequently exhibits physical restlessness – fidgeting, squirming, jiggling |
| Repeated difficulty sustaining attention in work or play | Often has difficulty remaining seated |
| Often does not seem to listen when addressed directly | Typically runs, climbs, or otherwise moves about where such activity is inappropriate |
| Recurring inability to follow-through on instructions producing incompletion of tasks | Tendency to be noisy during play or leisure activities and virtually unable to be quiet |
| Persistently weak at organizing tasks | Frequently animated and "on the go" |
| Frequently avoids, dislikes, or is reluctant to engage in tasks requiring sustained mental effort | Tendency to talk excessively |
| Habitually loses or misplaces tools needed to work on tasks | Often blurts our responses even before questions have been fully posed |
| Readily distractible by superfluous stimuli | Recurring inability to await turn |
| Usually is forgetful with activities | Often interrupts or intrudes on others |

**ADHD Characteristics and Interventions**

The American Psychiatric Association's most recent volume, *DSM-IV-TR*, expands discussion of ADHD to reflect the most current research conducted by the National Institutes of Health and private researchers. For example, people with ADHD-Predominantly Inattentive and Combined Types "tend to have academic deficits and school-related problems, whereas those with the Predominantly Hyperactive-Impulsive Type are likely to experience more peer rejection and accidental injuries" (APA, 2000, p. 830). ADHD behaviors are usually most conspicuous during the elementary school years, and with normal development, most identified kids appear to grow out of ADHD. But research results pertaining to adolescents who experience ADHD are ambiguous. Of particular interest is that the Combined Type is plainly the most common, and females are far less likely than males to experience the Hyperactive-Impulsive Type .

Studies on the identification of ADHD consistently reinforce concerns about confusion with other disorders or coexistence with other circumstances (APA, 2000; Barkley & Murphy, 1998). In fact, in a National Institutes of Health Consensus Statement (1998), a team of the leading psychiatric and psychological researchers admitted that so little compelling data had been collected about ADHD that the disorder presented a particular challenge to the mental health and educational professions. That same report noted that *no* significant data had been collected on ADHD–Inattentive Type, in which females appear to be over-represented, and that meaningful data regarding adolescents and adults with ADHD are virtually nonexistent.

Treatment of all types of ADHD continues to be concentrated in pharmaceutical intervention, though most research has focused on psychotropic drug therapy. Such studies tend to support the efficacy of stimulant medications like methylphenidate (MPH), dextroamphetemine, and pemoline over psychosocial treatments, but those conclusions are based only on short-term interventions (NIH, 1998). Further, while medications have been successful in controlling some inappropriate behaviors in schools, they are also suspected of inhibiting creativity and curiosity among bright children; anecdotal records and interviews suggest that spontaneity and sense of humor are reduced by medications in the methylphenidate family (Baum, Olenchak, & Owen, 1998). Although no conclusive research exists to explain the impact of such medication on other kinds of thought processes, especially those related to potentially creative, productive thought, Cramond (1994) observed, "perhaps we are lucky that medication was not available to stop the daydreams of Robert Frost and Frank Lloyd Wright" (p. 205). There is little doubt that in at least some cases, students of high ability are being "cured of their gifted-ness" as a tradeoff for docile and compliant classroom behavior. Corey, a bright 16 year old from a Houston suburb, elected to remove himself from his drug regimen of MPH because, as she puts it, "I do not feel like I am me—not the same person. I can't be myself with my girlfriend or my buds, and though I can sometimes seem to focus a little better on my class work, all and all, it isn't worth it to me. The little bit of increased focusing isn't enough to ruin my friendships. If I have to sacrifice my identity so that I can do school, I will find other ways to excel" (Olenchak, 2003).

Concerned that even with MPH or other pharmaceutical inter-ventions, children with ADHD continue experiencing at least some behavioral problems and show little enduring academic and social skills improvements, Barkley (1992) and Barkley & Murphy (1998) have ex-plored a variety of psychosocial interventions. These behavioral strategy interventions include:

1.  consistency management in school (e.g., point/token reward systems, timeout arrangements, and response cost agreements);
2.  parent training (e.g., child management and rearing techniques);
3.  clinical behavioral therapy (e.g., both teachers and parents use consistent management techniques both at school and home); and
4.  cognitive-behavioral treatments (e.g., self-regulation, verbal self-instruction, problem solving heuristics, and self-reinforcement).

To date, results of each of these types of behavioral strategies has been positive in producing improved school and social performance, though those of the cognitive-behavioral sort have not produced long-lasting im-provements in overall self-control unless medication has accompanied the therapy (Barkley & Murphy, 1998). However, results of some specific cog-nitive-behavioral techniques, including learning and using problem solving heuristics, when coupled with the clinical behavioral therapy approaches and with a program of family counseling, have produced marked improve-ments among older children with ADHD (Barkley, 1992).

Barkley's efforts are among only a few that seek alternatives to medication by targeting methods for addressing the behaviors themselves. Our position is that behaviors thought to result from the disorder are sometimes the result of a repressive environment where bright youngsters are required to conform to a slow-paced, unchallenging, and impersonal curriculum (Baum, Olenchak, & Owen, 1998; Zentall, 1997). Instead of providing an enriched, stimulating environment, schools are committed to force-fitting all students into a traditional "one-size-fits-all" structure. The explosion of high-stakes standardized testing has put great pressure on schools to create common curricula, common objectives, and common teaching methods. And within this scenario, the prevailing attitude is to focus on students' inappropriate behaviors rather than on their potential causes. Thus, although there are some professionals who believe ADHD identification and intervention can be quick and reasonably accurate, few of these professionals investigate alternative diagnoses, particularly identification related to giftedness (Baum, Olenchak, & Owen, 1998). Are these behaviors symptoms of a disorder or could they be responses to situations that provide inadequate accommodations for gifted students? This question is fundamental in understanding Blaine and finding a cause for his deteriorating situation. An analysis of the research literature related to attention problems, giftedness and creativity, intelligence, and learning disabilities will enhance our understanding of deficiencies in identification and service for students. In other words, there may be alternate hypotheses for the behavioral manifestations that are associated with ADHD. Each must be considered before a diagnosis is made.

### Other Perspectives

Several important views, flowing mostly from research on the gifted and talented, are rarely discussed when analyzing ADHD behaviors in gifted students. We address them here because awareness of this research base can enhance our understanding of the complexity of the situation. These topics comprise the emotional development of gifted students, creative behaviors, curricular and pacing issues, multiple intelligences theory, asynchronous development and adult reaction to the child's precocity. Each perspective presents unique factors that may contribute to the display of ADHD behaviors.

### Emotional Development of Gifted Students

The evolving theory of emotional development and the potential of gifted individuals (e.g., Dabrowski & Piechowski, 1977; Olenchak, 1994; Piechowski & Colenagelo, 1984; Piechowski, 1991; Silverman, 1993) offers a different lens through which we can examine the growing occurrence of hyperactivity and attention problems in gifted youngsters. Dabrowski's theory of positive disintegration aims to explain qualitative differences of human development. He proposed that gifted persons have "increased psychic excitabilities that predicted extraordinary achievement" (Nelson, 1989). Piechowski and Colangelo (1984) have described the concept of overexcitabilities as

> an expanded and intensified manner of experiencing in the psychomotor, sensual, intellectual, imaginational, and emotional areas. . . . As personal traits, overexcitabilities are often not valued socially. Being viewed instead as nervousness, hyperactivity, neurotic temperament, excessive emotionality and emotional intensity that most people find uncomfortable at close range. (p. 81)

Piechowski and Colangelo (1984) also described psychomotor overexcitability as an "organic excess of energy or excitability of the neuromuscular system. It may manifest itself as a love of movement for its own sake, rapid speech, pursuit of intense physical activities, impulsiveness, restlessness, pressure for action, driving the capacity for being active and energetic" (p. 81). Our interviews with adolescents talking about being jittery illustrate Piechowski and Colangelo's point: "'When I'm around my friends, I usually come up with so much energy that I don't know where it came from. . . . When I am bored, I get sudden urges and lots of energy . . . [in school]. I use this energy to goof off'" Another student we know described his need to get out and do something physical after completing a long assignment: "I suddenly get the urge to shoot baskets or ride my bike."

This energy seems stimulated as much from boredom as from the excitement of new ideas. Some students report great difficulty in sitting down and getting started writing. "I have to talk out the idea [aloud] or just put on the music and dance!" explained one young woman.

Cruikshank (1966, 1967, 1977), known for his classic work with hyperactive youngsters, came to consider hyperactivity and extreme sensitivity to the environment as a *positive* trait in bright students rather than an irritant. When gifted students act impulsively, blurt out or flail, they may simply be responding to the urge to explore their world (Piechowski, 1991). The curiosity these students display and their hunger for knowledge can take precedence over a prescribed curriculum fixed in time, sequence, and space. In this sense, the regular classroom can be too inhibiting—even disastrous for such youngsters. Jonathan Mooney (Mooney & Coles, 2000), a gifted hyperactive student, observed that if he is asked to be still and sit quietly he will *lose his ability to think*! For Crammond (1994), appraising whether hyperactivity enhances or distracts from learning and performance is essential to a diagnosis.

### Creative Traits

Many gifted students are also highly creative. Crammond (1994) compared "crossover traits" between creativity and ADHD (see Table 4.3). Definitions of creativity and ADHD are oddly similar, but possibly for different reasons. Declaring the trait positive if it drives creative production or negative because it inhibits the individual's productivity should help identify appropriate interventions. Crammond cautioned parents and teachers "to look carefully at behaviors exhibited by children for what may be potentialities instead of deficiencies" (1994, p.11). But no matter which diagnosis is decided, interventions should include nurturing students' creative traits so that they will be aimed toward achievement and success.

### Inappropriate Curriculum and Pacing

Another group of variables relevant to the emergence of ADHD-like behaviors involves aspects of curriculum and instruction. Inattentiveness, hyperactivity, and impulsivity are natural responses when the curriculum is perceived as repetitive, routine, and dull. Ironically, gifted students may be at risk for failure not because the lessons are too difficult but because they are too easy! Lack of a stimulating curriculum will invite them to find more interesting stimuli for their attention. If none are present, then the child may well invent her own stimulation. (See Chapter 7 for a discussion on arousal and stimulation.) We know that many bright students are being taught well below their instructional level and that they need less practice to master a skill (Gallagher, 1990; Reis et al., 1993). In a dramatic example of a curricular diet, Reis and her colleagues (1993) discovered that when up to 60% of the regular curriculum was elimi-

| Table 4.3. Creative or ADHD Indicative Traits | | |
|---|---|---|
| Trait | Creativity | ADHD |
| Inattention | Broad range of interest resulting in playing with ideas, visualizations, ease of making connections from what is said to other links; Capable of multi-tasking | Not paying attention, unfinished products |
| Hyperactivity | High energy for interesting tasks | Excessive movement, restlessness |
| Impulsivity | Risk taking and sensation seeking | Acting without thinking Thrill-seeking behavior |
| Difficult Temperament | Unconventional behavior Daring to challenge the system | Deficient social skills |
| Underachievement | Focusing on own projects Instead of those dictated by school. | Difficulty with achieving school goals |

nated, gifted students exceeded or equaled achievement levels of matched students who were required to digest the entire curriculum. Although these findings bode ill for all bright learners, those with attention deficits can be doubly affected, as their symptoms become worse when they are understimulated. These youngsters are automatically at odds with the school expectations that students be neat, obedient, and quiet for extended periods and remain interested in what the teacher is teaching . . . no matter how dreary the content or how banal the presentation.

Consider Blaine, who was once grouped with the slowest students to learn material he already knew. Blurting out answers—a characteristic on all checklists used to identify ADHD—seemed to have been triggered by his environment. How much patience should a gifted student show while waiting until everyone has a recitation turn in a lesson far too easy? In short, gifted children who are already active find it easy to butt heads with their school environment. They have an intrinsic need to discover, understand, and master new content, and they learn best by active engagement. However, when school tasks are mysteriously frustrating, lack perceived relevance, or are unchallenging, the student will find satisfying stimulation elsewhere. That elsewhere need not be another obvious activity; it is often in their mind's eye where daydreams are far more arousing than the school curriculum. The more obvious activities of clowning around, getting up repeatedly to sharpen pencils (whose points somehow keep breaking), and falling out of their seats are devices to gain attention and arousal. The point is that challenging gifted students with a meaningful and fast paced or in-depth curriculum can reduce or even completely head off many of the ADHD behaviors.

## Applications of Recent Theories of Intelligence

Recent conceptualizations of intelligence also cloud the understanding of identification and services conditioned on specific behaviors. Howard Gardner's most recent reflections about his Theory of Multiple Intelligences (MI) (1993, 1999) and Robert Sternberg's modifications to his Theory of Triarchic Intelligence (1995, 1997) continue to challenge the classic unitary perspective of intelligence. When schools operate in their traditionally narrow language and mathematical goals, their rigidity can obstruct high-ability students from competing successfully, because their domains of talent are neither recognized nor encouraged by schools. As a result, teachers frequently describe such youngsters as disruptive, off-task, and manipulative (Baum, Olenchak, & Owen, 1998). Yet, when involved in curricular and instructional activities that are at least partially in line with their talents, these same students show mental self-governance, direction toward excellence, productivity aimed at innovation, and striving toward demonstrable value (Sternberg, 1995).

Gardner's MI theory is very useful in understanding paradoxical behaviors of many ADHD students under certain circumstances. We have found that many youngsters with ADHD are particularly talented in visual and performing arts, engineering, and science (Baum, Cooper, & Neu, 2001). These disciplines rely on nonverbal intelligence, especially spatial talent. But because school transactions are primarily linguistic, these students seem inattentive and disruptive in traditional classrooms. When they are engaged in classes where teacher's reduce the amount of time they spend lecturing and emphasize active engagement in learning through experiences, projects, or the arts, these youngsters perform well. They can attend for long periods and complete complex projects. In one recent longitudinal study, Sternberg (1997) showed that 199 high school students achieved better than even their brightest peers when instruction and curricula were purposefully matched with their particular areas of ability and interests. Their school behaviors that had been viewed negatively were "magically" transformed to high levels of goal orientation and motivation.

Could it be that students with attention-related disorders are best served in an environment that values and incorporates alternate modes of thinking and communication? Perhaps attention deficits are connected to specific intelligences, an idea that has not yet been investigated.

Related to these ideas is the debate over the meaning of sustained attention. Children with ADHD have difficulty sustaining attention. They leapfrog from activity to activity, which interferes with their ability to finish their work. They seem almost driven by their own physical movements, stimulated by everything in the environment. These students seem to have little purposeful direction or focus, except to be distracted by novelty. They can attend for longer periods, and they seem to be absorbed and focused when they are engaged in activities "that are continuously reinforcing and automatic," such as video or computer games or reading for pleasure (Kaufman, Kalbfleisch, & Castellanos, 2000, p. 24). But absorption in such activities does not distinguish children who have ADHD from those who do not. What separates these two groups of children are tasks that require effort (Borchering, Thompson, Kruesi, Bartko, Rappaport, & Weingartner, 1988; Douglas & Parry, 1994). Kaufman, Kalbfleisch, and Castellanos (2001) have argued that because many of the tasks gifted youngsters face require little effort, their ADHD may be less apparent than in children with average abilities.

We make the opposite argument. As explained in Chapter 3, when gifted students are bored and are required to engage in tasks that are effortless, they experience problems in sustaining attention. Conversely, when tasks challenge an area of weaknesses (e.g., listening, reading, or writing), inattention increases (Baum, Cooper, & Neu, 2001; Berg, 2003). In this situation, attention problems can be attributed to a student's learning disability as opposed to ADHD.

The debate intensifies over the idea that students with ADHD tend to *hyperfocus*, which is defined as excessive engagement in tasks that are interesting and have intrinsic value. The engagement can be all consuming and cause students to have difficulty switching tasks. In other words, the problem is not so much sustaining attention but regulating attention during tasks that are intrinsically unrewarding or that require effort— tasks that gifted students most often encounter in school (Kaufman et al., 2001). People without attention deficits are able to modulate, switching at will from one task to the next, but students with ADHD cannot sustain attention unless arousal is intense. Lacking that extra-strong "stimulus fuel," their focus fades, but once it is found, they are also prone to over- engage (Berg, 2003).

Hyperfocus can be confused with the idea of "flow." In Csikszentmihalyi's (1990) bestseller, *Flow,* he laid out his theory of happiness. Greatest personal satisfaction stems from engaging in difficult or complex experiences that demand sustained physical or mental effort. The form of experience is unbounded; it might be mountain climbing, reading, solving a math problem, or playing a piano piece before a large audience. He argued that these kinds of activities create a state of total absorption—flow—that people feel when they are so completely involved in an activity that they lose track of time, are unaware of fatigue, hunger distractions, or anything but the activity itself. In a sense they are lost in the present. The joy they get from the experience is totally intrinsic, worries disappear, anxiety evaporates, and they are truly "in the moment." In many ways, Csikszentmihalyi observed, "the secret to a happy life is to learn to get flow from as many of the things we have to do as possible" (1996, p. 113).

The determining factor between hyperfocus and flow is to what degree students can engage in areas of interest but still be able to redirect as necessary to more mundane tasks. Gifted behavior, as described by Renzulli (1978, 1985, 1997), occurs when students are engaged in producing something that demands above average ability, creative strengths, and task commitment. From this perspective, being highly focused through intrinsic motivation is a desired state, not one to be cured. We think it is vitally important to view intense engagement as a positive trait, without which one is unlikely to accomplish extraordinary feats. In the school environment, students who have in-depth interests can focus and learn in ways that are aligned to their strengths. It behooves us to then create learning environments that aim to meet individual needs rather than on insisting that individuals stretch or shrink themselves to fit the mold of the school.

## Developmental Asynchrony

Silverman (1993, 1997) documented how different aspects of development (say, physical, emotional, intellectual, or social) can sometimes be far out of coordination. She observed this frequent *developmental asynchrony* in gifted individuals and offered insight into how giftedness can influence the social and emotional behaviors often associated with ADHD. As a result of differing rates of cognitive, emotional, and physical growth, students with high levels of ability not only think differently but also feel differently than their chronological age peers. This incongruity of development prompts greater inner tension, motivating behaviors that are at odds with the typical demands of school classrooms in which movements often are restricted, openness of exploration discouraged, and instruction and curricula usually predetermined by some imagined group need. A bright child who visualizes one type of outcome from her efforts but whose development will not permit bringing that idea to fruition figuratively howls with frustration (Silverman, 1993). Another high-ability student copes with sharp classroom time limits for personal interest-based investigation by exhibiting seemingly random behavioral changes ranging from hypoactive daydreaming to hyperactive fidgeting (Olenchak, 1999).

## Adult Responses to Child Precocity

Some extremely bright youngsters have minimal or erratic structure at home. In some conditions, their verbal precocity actually intimidates adults in their lives, and as a result, caretakers may fail to exercise authority over the child's behavior (Rimm, 1994). In other cases, the parents may believe that the disruptive behavior is part of the child's disability and thus underestimate their ability to control it. In these cases not only is the child excused for misbehavior, but their misbehavior is explained away by adult assertions that the child cannot control it. Setting limits can greatly improve behaviors that seem due to impulsivity and hyperactivity.

We see that identification of ADHD in gifted students is complicated. Sometimes observed behaviors are reactions to an unfriendly environment in which professionals have ignored or failed to meet the needs relating to the students' giftedness. At the same time,, the students' gifts may exacerbate the problem or obscure attention problem from view. Coupled with problems that being gifted might invite, confusion over the overlapping symptoms of ADHD and learning disabilities (disorganization, weak executive functioning, or inefficient use of strategies) can lead to inappropriate diagnosis. Other problems often seen with ADHD are substandard performance in writing and complex mental operations.

These behaviors are better explained and addressed in terms of a learning disability rather than ADHD. Alternate perspectives and overlapping characteristics reinforce the need for more in-depth analysis about the causal factors underlying ADHD behaviors. These overlapping characteristics press professionals to consider behaviors from a variety of perspectives to gain a fuller understanding of the problem, which was sadly lacking in the case of Blaine. In Table 4.4 we present a summary overview of alternate explanations for the same constellation of behaviors.

## Understanding the Issues

Although Blaine's story seems like an unhappy movie script, it is not. Well-intentioned school personnel, as well as medical professionals, believed they were acting in Blaine's best interests. Their perspectives, based

| Table 4.4. Synopsis of Behaviors from the Literature by Category of Human Condition (adapted from Baum & Olenchak, 2002) | | | | | |
|---|---|---|---|---|---|
| Trait | **ADHD** (*DSM-IV-TR*, 2000) | **LD** (Baum et al, 1991) | Creativity (Cramond, 1994; Renzulli et al., 1976) | Gifted (Piechowski, 1991; Renzulli et al., 1976; Silverman, 1998) | Contemporary Theories of Intelligence (Gardner, 1993, 1999; Sternberg, 1995, 1997) |
| Sustaining Attention | Difficulty with sustained attention; daydreaming | Often poor memory unless in interest areas | Heightened imagination may obscure attention | Poor attention often due to boredom; daydreaming | Weak attention in situations unmatched to intelligence pattern |
| Listening Skills | Diminished ability to listen attentively | Auditory skills can be weak | Hypomanic to the point of not listening | Preoccupation with own ideas and concepts; appears bored | Non-auditory intelligences restrict ability to listen |
| Task Completion | Problems with independent task completion | Erratic task completion based on interests | Broad range of interests often prohibits task completion | Completion of tasks directly related to personal interests | Tasks often remain uncompleted when unrelated to strengths |

| Table 4.4 *continued.* | | | | | |
|---|---|---|---|---|---|
| **Motivation** | Avoids and dislikes sustained mental activity unless interested | Motivation governed by areas of interest and strength | Concentration favors self-selected work | Lack of persistence on tasks that seem irrelevant | Tenacity linked to thinking preference patterns |
| **Organization** | Messy and may misplace items needed for work; disorganized | Poor, sometimes nonexistent organizational skills | Finds order amidst chaos | Organization may be seen as unnecessary depending on the task | Organization in the eye of the beholder |
| **Following Directions** | Difficulty following directions | Difficulty with oral or written directions or both | Willing to take risks to satisfy creative plans and pursuits | Questions rules and directions | Directions not accounting for intelligences may be overlooked |
| **Energy Level** | Heightened activity level; | Hyperactive | High energy; sometimes erratic energy | Frequent high activity level | High energy level on work in strengths |
| **Impulsivity** | Impulsive; poor judgment in interactions (not waiting turn, interrupting) | Poor self-concept triggering poor social judgment; may act impulsively | Impulsive in actions and often disinterested in relationships; risk taking | Highly sensitive but judgment lags well behind intellectual development | Impetuous when trying to cope with tasks in nonstrength ability patterns |
| **Verbal Manifesta-** | Excessive talking | Verbal vs. ability to put ideas in writing | Asks questions about anything and everything | Magnified curiosity and need to probe yields much talking | Verbalization increased when working in preferred intelligences |
| **Reactions to Authority** | Problems adhering to rules for behavior regulation | Poor self-regulation skills | Freedom of spirit that rejects external parameters; uninhibited | Intensity that leads to struggles with authority | Self-regulation reliant on nature of tasks and relation to strengths |

on their earlier training, blinded them from considering hypotheses built from contemporary research in other areas. With their discipline-based myopia, the various adults involved in Blaine's case trapped themselves in the deficit model of diagnosing and remediating problems, still dominant in both medicine and education. No other course of action came to mind, and there was no drive to consider using a wide-angle lens to view Blaine's circumstances.

The psychologist's report illustrates such outdated and narrow thinking. Her conclusion articulated her concerns about Blaine's social and emotional adjustment, especially about to his growing depression and anxiety. The behaviors she described in her report reinforced her opinion that ADHD was responsible for Blaine's problems. However, a closer look at her observations suggests an entirely different conclusion:

- Enthusiastic in library and art class and had no behavior problems there;
- When he did blurt out answers, they were always correct;
- Problems arose in physical education class, playground behavior, and classroom written work.

In truth, Blaine behaved well in the class where his strengths were exploited. He was an excellent artist and had superior verbal skills. Problems cropped up in situations that demanded proficient motor skills. His assessments showed his deficiencies in those areas. In fact, within his WISC subtest scatter, there were dramatic discrepancies between his strengths and weaknesses. Blaine's WISC profile suggested the presence of a learning disability and could explain his growing anxiety about the wide contrasts between what he could do well and the areas in which he was frustrated. The school psychologist was stymied because she focused strictly on his diagnosis of ADHD. Blaine was on medication and still showed impulsive behaviors and depression.

The school psychologist did not perceive—or at least did not report—that Blaine's learning environment had a negative effect, although she noted that he had to skip recess to finish work he missed while being tested. His teacher's mindless adherence to classroom rules pointed to a jarring lack of sensitivity. Even for the brief period in second grade during which attempts were made to serve Blaine with strategies aimed at his strengths, the spirit of gifted education was violated. Instead of creating opportunities for Blaine to be with his intellectual peers, he was separated from fellow students for most of the school day and was force-fed repetitious, drill work assignments. In contrast, the summer program in which Blaine excelled after first grade placed him with intellectual peers who had similar interests and abilities to work on challenging, real-world problems. In that program, Blaine had experienced *no* problems of *any* kind. Almost certainly, the professionals working on Blaine's case would have profited from a multidisciplinary perspective. Specialists skilled in creativity, giftedness, and contemporary theories of intelligence could have assisted the child study team in developing a deeper understanding of the complexity of Blaine's situation. A cursory examination of Table 4.4's matrix suggests numerous interpretations that could legitimately account for the behaviors Blaine displayed. For example, when Blaine lashed out against peers for teasing him and calling him names, it could be interpreted as impulsivity from an ADHD perspective, or it might be viewed as extreme sensitivity coupled with weak judgment, which is often seen in the developing gifted child.

There are probably multiple factors and combinations of factors contributing to the difficulties that some gifted students experience in trying to navigate the classroom. Barkley (1995) has theorized a delicate interaction between the characteristics of the students and the demands of the environment. He argues that ADHD is best understood in terms of inhibition, which he views as a trait. Each of us falls somewhere along a dimension of extreme inhibition to no inhibition (see Figure 4.1). Excessive inhibition can paralyze one from engaging in any of life's activities. And those of us who fall at the other end of the dimension will show a startling lack of impulse control and an inability to delay gratification. Barkley defined deficits of attention as a special case of the latter extreme. For Barkley, ADHD is a portion of the inhibition trait. We argue that although traits are defined as enduring dispositions, there are environmental conditions that will invite a trait to appear or vanish in human behavior. That is, although the trait lies beneath the skull, its manifest behaviors depend partly on the environment. Thus, a generally self-regulated student under pressure of a high stakes exam can quickly degrade into inhibition and anxiety and even lose concentration altogether.

Creative people who are fueled by the high octane mix of energy and ability are less inhibited and more likely to take risks. Because they are highly motivated to accomplish their own goals, they may invent their own rules and be unwilling to postpone their agenda. Curiosity and a sensation-seeking urge can prompt highly creative people to take more and greater risks and to forge ahead with little thought of consequences. Students with high abilities are also driven to engage in new learning and challenges. These qualities place gifted and creative people on the *low* inhibition side of the dimension. When the environment becomes too restrictive and out of alignment with students' talents, they may find themselves pushed even more toward the end of the dimension, resulting in ADHD behaviors. For example, at age six, Blaine could not contain his responses while less able students were still trying to understand what the teacher's question was all about. His energetic personality and superior knowledge put him in a difficult spot for obeying classroom rules. Blaine's psychomotor immaturity on the playground, coupled with the barrage of teasing also contributed to his inability to inhibit his stress responses.

In stressful times, behavior of gifted and creative students may re-semble that of a smaller number of people who truly suffer from ADHD

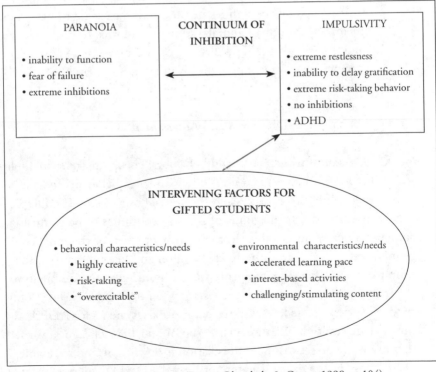

**Figure 4.1.** Continuum of inhibition (Baum, Olenchak, & Owen, 1998, p. 104).

due to neural or chemical imbalances. But regardless of the cause (environmental or neurological), a person at the low-inhibition end of the dimension has poor skill in regulating behavior without medical, cognitive, or psychological intervention. To make an accurate referral for ADHD behaviors, we must also consider the effects of the environment on the student's behavior. In other words, we must estimate to what extent traditional school environments and curricula prompt behaviors that look like they come from ADHD. If we can rule out important environmental influence, then we can be more confident that the ADHD behaviors primarily result from of neurological or chemical problems.

Remember that *under*identification of ADHD may be just as serious and possibly even more prevalent among gifted students. We must take care to consider when a student's over-reliance on strengths pushes the disability into the background.

> While emphasizing strengths may highlight a student's gifts and talents, it does not eliminate the reality of the condition and can, in fact, lead to a worse predicament in which the student distrusts his or her abilities because of the struggle to maintain them. On the other hand, if a student is allowed to acknowledge and experience the disability, he or she may learn appropriate compensatory or coping skills. (Kaufman, Kalbfleisch, & Castellanos, 2001)

## Diagnosis and Assessment

Using medical benchmarks and behavioral checklists (refer to Table 4.2 earlier in the chapter) and examining students' behaviors in at least two settings, a physician makes an official diagnosis of ADHD. Despite these standardized lists, diagnosis of ADHD continues to be confusing, sometimes nearly  impossible. In their study of seven of the most commonly used ADHD screening tools, Perugini and her colleagues (2000) found that even when instruments were administered in combination, the overall predictive power of the tests for identifying ADHD was only moderately acceptable level. Given that most assessments for ADHD do not include multiple instruments, Perugini and her colleagues warned that using any one instrument in isolation is downright undependable.

Because of the difficult nature of formal ADHD diagnosis, we will focus instead on informal assessment procedures that can be done in the classroom before a referral occurs. With the reauthorization of I.D.E.A. (scheduled for late 2003), the focus on classroom interventions *before* classification will become a reality. We support this idea and offer the following suggestions for evaluating student behaviors and determining when to seek more formal assessment:

1. Observe and document circumstances that seem to impair or enhance attention to tasks. Consider Gardner's notion of multiple intelligences. Are there adaptations of curricular presentations (e.g., visual or kinesthetic instead of verbal) that might grab and hold the student's attention?

2. Observe the student's behavior in different learning environments to estimate the optimal conditions for learning.

3. Observe parent-child and teacher-child interactions to see whether limits are set, if strategies for self-regulation are provided, and whether the student is able to self-regulate.

4. Observe the child on different occasions during the day to decide to what degree the student's creativity is appreciated, reinforced, allowed expression, or squelched.

5. Investigate whether there is any effort to develop the student's gifts or talents. If so, how does the student behave during talent development activities?

6. Pretest the student to assess prerequisite skills and evaluate appropriate curricular pacing.

7. Make environmental adjustments as needed, based on observations, and document the results. Make sure to consider the student's learning styles, intellectual strengths, talents and interests (see Chapters 8 and 12).

8. Decide whether you need to proceed with a formal diagnosis and, if so, make appropriate referrals.

The results of such observations may suggest specific strategies that can minimize learning barriers facing the student. The results may help eliminate the question, "Is this child gifted or ADHD?" and allow educators to focus on "How impaired is this student by ADHD?" and "How much can I help by adjusting elements within the classroom?" Some Alphabet Children are able to compensate for their ADHD (and neither they nor their parents or teachers may be aware of it), others are seriously handicapped. The best we can do is to identify the extent to which the child's adjustment is thwarted because of ADHD behaviors. We must try to figure out

1.  which students will profit simply from environmental intervention. Some students greatly improve when the physical environment is modified, curriculum and instruction differentiated to meet unique learning styles, challenging but relevant content and assignments are given, and self-regulation strategies are taught.

2.  which students will require medication? Some students are greatly helped by taking the appropriate medication and need little else. The medication helps them focus, sustain attention, and get along with their peers. When medication fails to improve achievement, consider testing the student for a learning disability.

3.  and finally, which students, like Blaine, will need both types of intervention?. While Blaine still needs a mild dose of Ritalin, he is performing exceptionally well in his challenging educational environment.

In the remaining chapters of this book we address how to create and manage curricular and instructional components meant to help all Alphabet Children fulfill their promise.

# Part II

# Measures of Intelligence & Recognizing Intellectual Strengths

In the first section of this book, we explored one central question ("How is it possible for a child to be both exceptionally talented and learning disabled at the same time?") by examining the seemingly contradictory behaviors a teacher and parent might see in a child. An analysis of students' patterns of intellectual strengths both on traditional measures of intelligence and from a multiple intelligences perspective (Gardner, 1983, 1999) will help further clarify our understanding of the GLD phenomenon.

## WISC Scores and GLD Students

Although school psychologists and learning disabilities specialists rely heavily on WISC patterns to diagnose learning disabilities and to plan appropriate educational programs, they usually do not consider the meanings that can be derived from the unique patterns suggested in Chapter 3. Professionals usually use intelligence subscores, along with other documented evidence, to confirm that there is a disability and to pinpoint the areas in which the student is having difficulty. Discrepancies between verbal and performance IQ usually dominate decisions made on the student's behalf, but subtest patterns are rarely used to identify giftedness or provide an environment that allows the gift to emerge and develop. In short, the traditional testing focus is on the problem, not the potential. However, these patterns of subtest scores can help to explain why a child demonstrates wild inconsistencies in learning behaviors.

## Integrative Versus Dispersive Intelligence

As mentioned in Chapter 3, researchers have found that GLD students are generally strong in abstract, holistic tasks and much weaker in tasks involving sequencing and memorizing isolated facts (Fox, Brody, & Tobin, 1983; Schiff, Kauffman, & Kauffman, 1981). Two of the studies described based their analysis on Bannatyne's (1974) recategorization model. This approach has given us insight into interpreting the learning behaviors of GLD students, but it falls short on implications for better serving this special population. John Dixon (1989) has suggested a more comprehensive and flexible model. He has theorized that these students have particular strengths in what he terms Integrative Intelligence. They also demonstrate severe weaknesses in Dispersive Intelligence. This discrepancy explains why GLD students can be brilliant in creative endeavors while simultaneously failing the weekly spelling test.

Integrative Intelligence is the capacity to understand and discover patterns and connections in broad expanses of information. This ability enables a learner to approach and solve problems in otherwise unanticipated ways. Its importance lies in the fact that remarkable creative accomplishments—whether of an artistic, scientific, or humanistic sort—require a deep level of integrated knowledge in the area of endeavor. Deep knowledge is so profound that pieces or elements of that knowledge can be changed, experimented with, manipulated, or viewed from an entirely different perspective without violating or losing a grasp of the essential principles, patterns, and connections in that area of knowledge.

Playing around within an integrated system of wisdom is almost a universal ingredient in creative accomplishment—in composing a symphony, writing a novel, creating a new mathematical formula, and discovering a new twist in the nature of matter. Integrative Intelligence is behind the "Aha!" experience in problem solving, what Konrad Lorenz meant when he talked about "gestalt" conception: "The scientist, confronted with a multitude of irregular and apparently irreconcilable facts, suddenly 'sees' the general regularity ruling them all" (Lorenz, 1951, cited in Dixon, 1983, p. 136).

It is not uncommon to find descriptions of this kind of thinking when great geniuses of history account for their own uniqueness. Einstein described his thought process thus:

> The psychological entities which seem to serve as elements in thought are certain signs and more or less clear images which can be voluntarily reproduced and combined. It is also clear that the desire to arrive finally at logically connected concepts is the emotional basis of this rather vague play. This combinatory play seems to be the essential feature in productive thought. (cited in Dixon, 1983, p. 93)

In a partly biographical accounting of intelligence, the mathematician Doug Hofstadter interpreted encounters with thinking similarly:

> As I have gotten older, I have come to see that there are inner mental patterns underlying our ability to conceive of mathematical ideas. Universal patterns in human minds that make them receptive not only to the patterns of mathematics but also to abstract regularities of all sorts in the world. Indeed, how could anyone hope to approach the concept of beauty without deeply studying the nature of formal patterns and their organizations and relationships to mind? (Hofstadter, 1985, p. 177)

Is this kind of thinking required or even expected during the school day? If so, which tasks require students to understand patterns and see the bigger picture? Creative writing, grasping the underlying idea of a story, drawing conclusions, seeing the patterns in numbers require integrative thinking. Other examples include designing and conducting a scientific experiment, building a model of the Titanic for a social studies project, or drawing a mural of Indian life. These activities all require a sense of the whole and how the pieces come together to form a meaningful pattern. Students must supply relevant details as they work to complete their envisioned plan. As we have noted, both gifted students and GLD students usually have little difficulty with tasks requiring this type of thinking.

Dispersive Intelligence, on the other hand, complements Integrative Intelligence. It allows us to remember and use isolated facts and associations that need not make sense in any big context, such as the name of a faded actress who slapped a policeman in Hollywood or your phone number. Not fitting in a big context does not mean that such information is trivial. Much factual information is required simply to move through the daily routines of life, and in that sense, Dispersive Intelligence is of equal importance with Integrative Intelligence. For example, unless you are writing lyrics for pop music, it is very important to be able to associate the spoken word "enough" with the letter sequence e-n-o-u-g-h rather than with the sequence e-n-u-f. From the point of view of the phonetic pattern consistency (that is, Integrative Intelligence), the second letter sequence seems more reasonable than the first. The strength of Dispersive Intelligence is that it allows limited association between a certain vocalized sound pattern, "enough," and a certain letter sequence to be accepted for what it is. This acceptance is done without interference from broader attempts at patterned understanding (phonetic consistency) which might suggest it should be otherwise.

Arithmetic offers another example. It is handy for a person to remember that "9 x 7 = 63" without having to discover or figure out that fact through some sort of reference to number patterning. Memorizing math facts is a little different from spelling in that one could arrive at a math fact by some process of pattern reconstruction such as "3 x 7 = 21" and "3 x 3 = 9"; therefore, "9 x 7 = 3 x 21 = 63." There are some children who use Integrative Thinking of this sort to reconstruct math facts, but it is a pretty clumsy and inefficient way to deal with math facts.

The extent to which a student possesses strong Dispersive Intelligence and uses it influences school success. For this child, it is perfectly acceptable to recall that *enough* is spelled e-n-o-u-g-h. It will not help much to construct a theory of spelling, a model of spelling, or a gestalt of spelling that would lead one to conclude that *enough* be spelled the way it is. This is the power of Dispersive Intelligence. It lightens the intellectual load when it is employed properly. On the other hand, a student with strong Integrative Intelligence may want to go far beyond memorizing and accepting the conventional spelling of "enough" and wonder how it came to be that "ough" would stand in for "uf," and why the "ough" in *enough* is pronounced "uff," but the same part of *cough* is pronounced "off, and in *through* it is "ooo." And how come *ugh* is pronounced "ug?"

The distinction between Integrative and Dispersive Intelligence helps explain why some children can be simultaneously capable and disabled. Dispersive Intelligence is the thing most extensively rewarded in most schools. No matter what other amazing things a child might accomplish, if she does not master the dispersive detail of reading, writing, and arithmetic, all else is likely to appear insignificant. The learner might create an intricately interesting sculpture or produce a TV program, but if he or she is unable to remember from day to day (or even minute to minute) the spelling of *enough* or that "9 x 7 = 63," the student is likely to be considered an academic failure. Incapable of remembering what was assigned for homework or where a math book was left, how can such a student be considered bright, responsible, or even gifted?

To stretch this idea further, consider the differences between the following written and visual expressions: A fifth grade teacher asked a GLD student to write an opinion of the 1991 war in the Middle East. He wrote four short sentences: "Hussein is a bad ruler. He is forsing Kuwayts out of there home. The U.S. and the Allies will try to stop him. Who will win." Knowing he had more to say, the student's resource teacher asked him to draw a political cartoon (see Figure 5.1). The differences between the two products represent the dilemma GLD students face. With poor

**Figure 5.1.** A fifth grade GLD student's opinion of the 1991 Gulf War.

verbal mechanics, they often cannot express their creative ideas in writing. Written work may call more attention to their disabilities than their abilities.

We have described students who appear to have strong abilities in Integrative Intelligence and much weaker abilities in Dispersive Intelligence. Are they gifted or disabled? The answer is both. The emphasis one places on the giftedness or the disability depends on the values brought to the judgment. If you are interested in creative production that rests on integrative thinking, you will set aside the disability to consider the potential the student demonstrates for gifted behavior. On the other hand, if you are judging children primarily in terms of high academic achievement, creativity might seem like an amusing but irrelevant sideshow. We know an artistic high school student who sketches characters he encounters in literature class as a means to grasp the essence of the plot, but his teacher asked him to put his sketch pad away during class. Unfortunately, the teacher did not understand that this creative sketching behavior allowed the student to focus his attention during the classroom discussion on the play, plot, and character. In the school classroom, when such differences between Integrative Intelligence and Dispersive Intelligence occur, Dispersive Intelligence usually rules.

### Assessing Integrative Intelligence

When professionals carry out diagnostic procedures to identify whether a child is learning disabled, they can use a number of tests. The number and variety of these tests invite confusion, but there is one point of common ground that runs through much of the testing: the WISC-III. The WISC-III is administered to more learning- disabled students than any other instrument, and rightly so: The WISC-III subtests catch many of the subtle patterns that distinguish most learning-disabled children.

However, the interpretive value of the WISC-III scores is, unfortunately, often overlooked. Professionals usually emphasize either a full-scale IQ score or the Verbal and Performance IQs and ignore the more meaningful subtest patterns. Oddly, researchers conducting studies on the WISC (all revisions) have never found that it divides neatly into a verbal section and a performance section. Although patterns underlying WISC subscores vary from study to study, they found consistently point to the difference between Integrative and Dispersive Intelligence. Such patterns are always more informative than the conventional verbal-performance split.

One way to organize the WISC scores is on the basis of subtests in which learning-disabled students do well and those in which they do poorly. The Australian psychologist Colin MacLeod (1965) brought together information from eight different research studies that made this kind of comparison. The findings, summarized in Table 5.1, are surprisingly regular. LD children dependably show certain weaknesses and certain strengths.

In a similar study of our own (Baum, Owen and Dixon, 1991), we examined the WISC patterns of 50 fourth-, fifth- and sixth-grade students diagnosed as learning disabled in language arts (reading, writing, or spelling) who spent their mornings in a resource room for language instruction. We were looking for learning-disabled children who had subtest scores high enough to suggest potential giftedness. The criterion for selection was a subtest score at the 97th percentile or higher. Table 5.2 displays the results.

The pattern that emerges from such studies reveals that LD students can be quite talented in spatial tasks such as Block Design. They also can do very well on tasks that require recognition of patterned sequences. Students may also display strength in abstract conceptualization, as

| Table 5.1. MacLeod (1965) Studies of WISC Patterns | | |
|---|---|---|
| Subtest | Number of studies in which subtest was a strength for LD student | Number of studies in which subtest was a weakness for LD student |
| Block Design | 5 | 0 |
| Picture Arrangement | 4 | 0 |
| Comprehension | 4 | 0 |
| Picture Comprehension | 3 | 0 |
| Similarities | 3 | 0 |
| Object Assembly | 2 | 0 |
| Vocabulary | 2 | 3 |
| Digit Span | 0 | 3 |
| Information | 0 | 6 |
| Arithmetic | 0 | 7 |
| Coding | 0 | 7 |

| Table 5.2. Extreme Cognitive Strengths of LD Students | |
|---|---|
| Subtest | Percentage of LD students scoring in the 97th %tile or above |
| Object Assembly | 12% |
| Picture Arrangement | 12% |
| Block Design | 10% |
| Picture Comprehension | 6% |
| Similarities | 6% |
| Comprehension | 6% |
| Information | 6% |
| Vocabulary | 4% |
| Digit Span | 0% |
| Arithmetic | 0% |
| Coding | 0% |

shown on the Similarities subtest. On the other hand, they usually have problems on tests of detailed memory, as evidenced by the Arithmetic subtest where the student's ability to apply math concepts depends on fast recall of math facts. These students may also have trouble with random sequencing, as is required on the Digit Span subtest, and can be quite slow in processing details as measured by the Coding subtest.

Researchers sometimes use a sophisticated statistical tool called factor analysis to study the dimensions running through the WISC. Although the results depend somewhat on the kinds of children studied, the usual pattern appears in Table 5.2. The WISC subtests are arranged in the typical sequence of strongest to weakest performance for learning-disabled students. The top three areas often indicate distinct talent. The bottom three areas often suggest the presence of a specific learning disability. This factor analysis arrangement is consistent with the comparison of Integrative and Dispersive Intelligence. The top three groupings have their foundation in the capacity to discern broad patterns and connections in visual or verbal information—exactly what we mean by Integrative Intelligence. The bottom three areas are about accepting and remembering simple associations and arbitrary sequences. Such descriptions are part of Dispersive Intelligence.

The contrast between Integrative Intelligence and Dispersive Intelligence makes much more sense than the traditional definitions of learning disabilities. In legal terms, a learning disability is often defined as a gross discrepancy between intelligence and academic performance. When the child's school performance lags behind the level predicted by the IQ score, it is assumed that there must be some kind of specific dis-

**Table 5.3. Strength to Weakness Pattern for LD Students**

| | Integrative | Dispersive |
|---|---|---|
| Subtest Categories | Spatial Manipulation | Conventional Knowledge |
| | Block Design | Vocabulary |
| | Object Assembly | Information |
| | Pattern Sequencing | Detailed Memory |
| | Picture Arrangement | Arithmetic |
| | Mazes | Picture Completion |
| | Abstract Conceptualization | Quick Detailed Processing |
| | Similarities | Coding |
| | Comprehension | Symbol Search |
| | | Meaningless Sequencing |
| | | Digit Span |

ability. But this traditional definition offers virtually no implication for understanding the student's cognitive behavior.

Another popular definition is based on a discrepancy between the Verbal IQ and Performance IQ. Psychologists who use this definition look for the imbalance to go in either direction (e.g., Verbal = high and Performance = low, or the opposite pattern). This distinction is so general that it offers little of interest to the practitioner. It is like trying to get a sharp view of a specimen through a smudged lens. Professionals often interpret low scores on the Verbal Scale as a student's general ineptness with verbal information. However, a low Verbal IQ can come about even with high scores on verbal comprehension tasks and other language-based activities that are part of a meaningful context. Sub par Digit Span and Arithmetic subtest scores can also result in a low Verbal IQ (in which case it is fruitful to ask what Digit Span and Arithmetic have to do with Verbal aptitude).

Lumping Performance subtests together creates a similar difficulty. A child following a fairly typical GLD pattern will attain an average or higher score on Spatial subtests and a somewhat lower score on Coding. Averaging scores on the two types of tasks muddles specific information about the student. Unfortunately, this situation is typical for GLD students, and professionals often overlook documentation of specific abilities in complex cognitive activities.

From the very beginning of the learning disabilities movement, it was natural that looking at discrepancies should provide a way of thinking about these youngsters. Discrepancy is a metaphor for their lives. However, it is important for psychologists to continue refining the way discrepancies are defined. The discrepancy between IQ and school performance was a good start, and the discrepancy between Performance IQ and Verbal IQ was a small step forward. Our position is that the discrepancy between Integrative Intelligence and Dispersive Intelligence moves us closer to a sensible diagnostic scheme.

Fortunately, the WISC III (Wechsler, 1991) improved previous versions of this test by offering a means to separate problematic weaknesses from areas of strength. Instead of focusing solely on Verbal, Performance, and Full Scale IQ scores, the new version provides four additional factor analysis-based index scores. Two of these index scores are likely to be strength areas (Verbal Comprehension and Perceptual Organization) for students with learning disabilities. Some GLD students may exhibit strengths in both while others may tip more toward verbal or performance areas. The other two subscales (Freedom from Distraction and Perceptual Speed) are areas highly problematic for students with learning and attention problems. Table 5.4 lists the subtests that make up each factor-based index.

As seen in the table, the subtests comprising the Freedom from Distractibility and the Processing Speed Scales involve working memory, processing, and noncontextual learning or Dispersive Intelligence. Low scores on these indices will lower overall IQ scores, hiding the obvious intellectual gifts the GLD student may demonstrate in Integrative Intelligence.

In short, gifted learning-disabled students seem to have intellectual strengths in Integrative Intelligence that enable them to see underlying patterns and connections in broad concepts and abstract ideas. In contrast, they often show weakness in tasks involving Dispersive Intelligence,

### Table 5.4. Index Scales

| Factor I Verbal Comprehension | Factor II Perceptual Organization | Factor III Freedom from Distractibility | Factor IV Processing Speed |
|---|---|---|---|
| Information | Picture Completion | Arithmetic | Coding |
| Similarities | Picture Arrangement | Digit Span | Symbol Search |
| Vocabulary | Block Design | | |
| Comprehension | Object Assembly | | |

such as remembering isolated facts and associations for which they see no wider connection. As mentioned earlier in the chapter, this discrepancy helps explain why GLD students can have so much difficulty with seemingly simple tasks, while cruising through more creative and complex assignments.

In Table 5.3, we organized groupings of WISC subtests into particular cognitive skills and then divided them into Integrative Intelligence and Dispersive Intelligence. These patterns can help us recognize a GLD student's strengths and create more opportunities for school success. First, WISC subtest patterns can assist us in evaluating whether particular LD students demonstrate the potential for gifted behavior as documented by superior abilities in Integrative Intelligence. High scores on subtests included in Integrative Intelligence provide evidence that a student can think abstractly, see patterns, and make connections among ideas—all pieces of creative productivity.

We can also use pattern analysis to understand how a student learns best. This awareness coupled with knowledge of the student's interest are essential ingredients for providing students with optimum environments for success. In such an environment, not only can the GLD student achieve something of personal pride and importance, but he or she can also begin to identify strategies used to accomplish his or her goals. (We will elaborate more on developing such a learning environment using this approach later in the chapter.)

## Multiple Intelligences and the GLD Student

Howard Gardner (1983) and others (Sternberg, 1995, 1997; Goleman, 1995) posited that the traditional view of intelligence limits our explanation and understanding of human potential and talent. Gardner introduced his theory of multiple intelligences (MI) against the backdrop of a widely-held belief that intelligence is a unitary trait that can be adequately measured by an IQ test (Gardner, 1993). In at least two significant ways, MI theory challenges the idea of a single intelligence based on an overall IQ score. First, MI theory claims that we have several intelligences at work, not just one. And second, MI theory defines an intelligence as the ability to solve a problem or fashion a product valued in one or more community or cultural settings, not how well an individual performs on a narrow set of pre-ordained, short-answer questions (Gardner, 1993). MI theory argues that there are many ways to be smart and that those abilities are expressed in our performances, products, and ideas.

Using evidence from brain research, human development, evolution, and cross-cultural comparisons, Gardner initially arrived at a set of seven intelligences: linguistic, logical-mathematical, musical, spatial, bodily-kinesthetic, interpersonal, and intrapersonal intelligence (Gardner, 1993). He has added an eighth intelligence, naturalist, and is considering a ninth, existential intelligence (Gardner, 1999). Table 5.5 briefly defines the eight primary intelligences.

The idea of multiple intelligences is not the same as the notion of learning styles. Learning styles focus on which senses we use best (or prefer) for gathering information, whereas multiple intelligences represent particular content that the brain is processing—i.e., verbal, spatial, emotional, or musical. We know that some GLD students have difficulties with linguistic information, but when the information is spatial, they can perform at high levels. Consider the student whose spatial representation of the 1991 war with Iraq was a far superior expression of his understanding (as opposed to his essay). This youngster has much talent in spatial intelligence, but is at risk in linguistic areas. Gardner (2000) explained this dichotomy as *fruitful asynchrony*: "a deficit in one cognitive or affective area (intelligence) may go hand in hand with the capacity to develop strengths in another" (p. 196).

Gardner also postulates that certain intelligences naturally encode information in symbol systems such as number systems, pictures, musical notation, and scientific formulas. Thus, those who may be strong in a particular intelligence may be able to use the symbol system of that intelligence and still experience difficulty with other symbol systems. For example, a student who lacks skill at decoding written language may easily be able to decipher the spatial symbol system used in music.

In contrast to traditional conceptions of intelligence, MI theory argues that intelligence is not the same in all situations. Rather, thinking, learning, and problem solving demand fluid situational and task-specific approaches, and each individual taps different intelligences in different combinations to work though problems. MI theory also suggests that intelligences do not work in isolation. Any adult role requires a collaboration among intelligences. For example, playing the violin in an orchestra certainly requires musical intelligence, but also demands bodily-kinesthetic ability to master the physical demands of bowing and fingering, enough interpersonal intelligence to work with an audience or conductor, and perhaps intrapersonal intelligence to translate the emotion of a

**Table 5.5 The Intelligences in Gardner's Words (Checkley, 1997, p. 12)**

Linguistic intelligence is the capacity to use language, your native language, and perhaps other language to express what's on your mind and to understand other people. Poets really specialize in linguistic intelligence, but any kind of writer, orator, speaker, lawyer, or a person for whom language is an important stock in trade highlights linguistic intelligence.

People with a highly developed logical-mathematical intelligence understand the underlying principles of some kind of causal system, the way a scientist or logician does; or can manipulate numbers, quantities, and operation the way a mathematician does.

Spatial intelligence refers to the ability to represent the spatial world internally in your mind—the way a sailor or airplane pilot navigates the large spatial world, or the way a chess player or sculptor represents a more circumscribed spatial world. Spatial intelligence can be used in the arts or in the sciences. . . .

Bodily kinesthetic intelligence is the capacity to use your whole body or parts of your body—your hand, your fingers, your arms—to solve a problem, make something, or put on some kind of production. The most evident examples are people in athletics or the performing arts, particularly dance or acting.

Musical intelligence is the capacity to think in music, to be able to hear patterns, recognize them, remember them, and perhaps manipulate them. People who have strong musical intelligence don't just remember music easily—they can't get it out of their minds, it's so omnipresent. Now some people will say, "Yes music is important, but it's a talent, not an intelligence." And I say, "Fine, let's call it a talent." But then we have to leave the word *intelligent* out of *all* discussions of human abilities. . . .

Interpersonal intelligence is understanding other people. It's an ability we all need, but is at a premium if you are a teacher, clinician, salesperson, or politician. Anybody who deals with other people has to be skilled in the interpersonal sphere.

Intrapersonal intelligence refers to having an understanding of yourself, of knowing who you are, what you can do, what you want to do, how you react to things, which things to avoid, and which things to gravitate toward. . . .

Naturalist intelligence designates the human ability to discriminate among living things (plants, animals) as well as sensitivity to other features of the natural world (clouds, rocks configurations). This ability was clearly of value in our evolutionary past as hunters, gatherers, and farmers; it continue to be central in such roles as botanist or chef. I also speculate that much of our consumer society exploits the naturalist intelligences, which can be mobilized in the discrimination among cars, sneakers, kinds of makeup and the like. The kind of pattern recognition valued in certain of the sciences may also draw upon naturalist intelligence.

piece into sound patterns. Therefore, how intelligences operate is best considered in the context of a specific domain—that is, in the world of real problems and real behavior.

Intelligences also include sub-abilities. One is not merely "musically" or "linguistically" intelligent. One's musical intelligence may manifest itself in the ability to compose clever tunes (musical composition), hear and distinguishing patterns of harmony in a song (musical perception), or improvise while keeping time with other musicians (musical collaboration). In the case of linguistic intelligence, one's ability may emerge through creative expression (as in a story), the descriptive language of a presentation, or in subtle and deep understandings of narrative passages.

This view of intelligences fits well with what we already know about GLD students who often excel at solving problems and fashioning products in particular domains that tap their strengths and interests, especially in contexts outside of school. These domains often involve intelligences and symbol systems outside of linguistic and logical/mathematical intelligences. For example, Project HIGH HOPES (see Chapter 11], purposely looked for talents in visual and performing arts, science, and engineering among the learning-disabled population because those are the domains in which many gifted learning-disabled adults find remarkable success.

In short, MI theory seems to offer an authentic description of intelligence as it operates in the real world and offers much advice to school practitioners and parents (Baum, Viens, & Slatin, with Gardner, in press). MI theory can help educators understand the circumstances in which GLD youngsters perform at their personal best, identify where their gifts and talents lie, and isolate those areas where GLD students needs support. This information is essential in designing appropriate instructional experiences for GLD students. Using an MI-informed approach usually involves an iterative process between curriculum, instruction, and assessment. MI theory helps teachers frame activities that make many "entry points" into subject matter available to students. Teachers use their knowledge about students' intelligences and preferences (from observing their students engaged in classroom activities) to inform subsequent instruction. Teachers who offer varied pedagogical approaches and allow students to explore differing perspectives are far more likely to reach more students more effectively.

## Why We Need Both Views of Intelligence

Working effectively with GLD populations requires knowledge offered by both approaches to intelligence. Legally, identifying students as learning disabled requires isolating a variety of discrepancies. These quantitative discrepancies include the difference between potential and performance as well as differences among subtests and IQ indices. Analysis of WISC profiles generates information that explains difficulties in cognitive functioning, including memory, attention, and comprehension, which helps confirm the existence of a specific learning disability. Subtest analysis can also highlight students' cognitive strengths in spatial or verbal areas, which can be useful in identifying students as intellectually gifted.

No matter how good they are, standardized intelligence tests cannot assess all human abilities. Wechsler (1974) himself cautioned about overreliance on these test scores. Using MI theory as a lens through which we can view the student offers more practical information about programming and educational approaches to curriculum and instruction as well as for counseling and parenting. Observing students and noting when they are at their personal best versus times when they are struggling alerts us to how these youngsters process information. For example, if a student is on task, communicating knowledge, and demonstrating higher level thinking when engaged in an improvisational activity, we might guess that she is strong in both bodily kinesthetic intelligence and the personal intelligences, especially in the domain of acting. Researchers have found that such students write better if they are allowed to become the character in order to describe its personality and motivation (Baum, Owen, & Oreck, 1997; Baum, cooper, Neu, & Owen, 1997). Writing ability has not improved; rather, changing the context to fit the student's strengths and interest has improved performance. In addition, using authentic assessment within specific domains, as Gardner (1983) recommended, will allow us to identify many LD students as gifted within particular areas. Instead of simply determining whether the child has a high IQ score, an MI approach enables us to design talent development programs that align with the abilities of the students.

Table 5.6 delineates how MI and the WISC complement each other in understanding GLD students.

| Purpose | WISC Scores | MI Perspective |
|---|---|---|
| **Table 5.6. Complementary Uses of Two Perspectives on Intelligence** | | |
| Identification of learning disability | To substantiate discrepancies between potential and performance or among subtests | Not applicable |
| Identification of gift | To identify abilities in abstract thinking and conceptualization; to identify academically talented students | To identify gifts or talents in specific domains |
| Understanding how student learns | To distinguish between strengths in Integrative vs. Dispersive intelligence | To identify when student is at his personal best (e.g., "student as engineer or performing artist") |
| Curriculum differentiation | Not applicable | To align the scope and sequence of content and activities to reflect the student's strengths |
| Instructional approach | Not applicable | To identify appropriate entry and exit points for learning (e.g., using improvisation as an entry point or as a learning assessment) |
| Accommodations | To determine accommodations such as more time on tests, memory strategies | To create instructional sequence (e.g., doing an experiment to begin a unit on magnets before reading the chapter) |
| Counseling | To assess level of cognitive functioning | To facilitate personally appropriate strategies for intervention |
| Parenting | To understand the child's academic functioning and potential | To recognize and nurture strengths, interests, and talents |

## Using Information About Intelligence

So far we have described two approaches for understanding the intellectual strengths of students who are both gifted and learning disabled and discussed how particular WISC-III subtest patterns could provide evidence of Integrative and Dispersive Intelligence. In addition, we explored MI theory as a way to assess how youngsters learn. To understand how to use a student's WISC pattern and MI profile to design appropriate educational experiences for GLD students, we consider two case studies, Louis and Mike.

Both Louis and Mike had been identified as learning disabled and had been nominated by their parents or teachers to participate in a state-funded program for GLD students. Our first task was to determine whether these students had strengths in Integrative Intelligence. If Mike and/or Louis did, we then had to decide what particular abilities the youngster demonstrated and how he applied these talents to real life endeavors.

## Louis*

Louis, a sixth grader, had been identified as learning disabled because of his extreme difficulty in learning to read and write. His teachers also reported that he was easily distracted and a real "itch" in the classroom. Over the past two years his parents and teachers had noticed a decline in his enjoyment of school and an increase in inappropriate behavior in the classroom. Table 5.7 shows Louis' WISC-R scores categorized into Integrative and Dispersive Intelligences.

| Table 5.7. Louis' WISC-R Profile | |
|---|---|
| **Integrative Pattern** | **Dispersive Pattern** |
| Block Design  12 | Arithmetic  10 |
| Object Assembly  11 | Digit Span  9 |
| Picture Arrangement  11 | |
| Mazes  — | |
| Similarities  13 | |
| Comprehension  18 | |
| Vocabulary  18 | |
| Information  13 | |

**WISC Patterns.** Louis' performance on subtests involving Integrative Intelligence is high. He does extraordinarily well on tasks that required understanding of social expectations (Comprehension), using and comprehending the spoken word (Vocabulary) and noticing details especially in a visual context (Picture Completion). These abilities are essential in writing, acting, and social interactions of all sorts.

**Multiple Intelligences Perspective.** When we interviewed Louis, he described how much he enjoyed writing stories, poems, and songs for his own enjoyment. To gain more information on the kinds of activities Louis preferred, we administered two inventories: Ways of Learning Scale (Dixon, 1986b) and Myself and Others (Dixon, 1986). His re-

---

* Case study written by Gail Herman.

sponses indicated that he preferred self-initiated, creative activities that involved verbal, social interaction. For example, his favorite school activities required speaking in front of the class and doing group assignments.

We have found that students such as Louis often think, learn, and communicate much like actors. Such students use the larger context, visual and social, to comprehend and remember the details of a situation. They communicate best what they know through dramatic expression. In fact, they often create their own drama whenever possible. It should be no surprise that many GLD students find a home on the stage in their adult lives.

According to Gardner (1983), acting involves strong skills in (at least) bodily kinesthetic and personal intelligences. People with these skills have a talent for accurately reading people and situations. They are particularly sensitive to social and emotional dynamics in their environment such as moods, subtle meanings, and interpersonal relationships happening around them. In fact, these nonverbal messages often take priority over other verbal information simultaneously conveyed. These individuals respond to both motion and emotion to make sense of their world and to communicate what they know. Like actors, storytellers, and mimes, they are often able to incorporate other people's temperaments, motivations, and intentions into a spoken or dramatic presentation. These abilities are crucial in a variety of real world endeavors. For example, successful counselors, politicians, lawyers, social workers, health care workers, and teachers all must have the ability to decode and encode verbal and nonverbal messages in a variety of social contexts.

When we find this pattern of strength in GLD students, we must first help them sharpen their abilities in oral or dramatic expression. Next we need to assist these students in understanding the strategies they use in mastering tasks involved in the expressive area. Third, we must teach these students to use these strategies in other tasks. Special enrichment programs purposefully designed to accentuate a particular talent can help accomplish these three goals. In Louis' case, we created a ten-week program in dramatic expression in which students such as Louis had the opportunity to use and sharpen their dramatic ability for a real world purpose.

**Louis' Program.** At the first meeting of the program in dramatic expression, the mentor (a professional storyteller) explained to the students that they were chosen because they had a particular talent in drama.

Louis became noticeably excited about the possibility of performing in the State Storytelling Festival to be held later that spring. The mentor encouraged Louis to choose one of his own stories and helped him master the techniques of the professional storyteller so that he could perform with pride at the State Storytelling Festival.

First, Louis needed to find a way to remember his story so that he could tell his story within a six-minute limit and appear fresh each time he told it. Two methods that helped him were visual mapping and the incorporation of mimetic movements, facial expressions, and gestures with his characterizations. The visual map, a graphic depiction of the story's settings and important events, served as a picture in his mind's eye. The movements and gestures were kinesthetic cues that linked one emotional event to the next in the story.

To find the most comfortable delivery, Louis practiced the beginning of his story while standing, sitting, and moving around freely. He worked on using eye contact and looking at the top of people's heads to keep from being distracted. Because there would be a microphone at the festival, he practiced with one. During feedback sessions, Louis sought constructive criticism. He tried some of the ideas, discarding a few and keeping others. The results showed great variety of movement and voice. Louis had become, in fact, a professional storyteller, focusing his attention on the effects his verbal and nonverbal behaviors would have on his audience.

Louis attended the State Storytelling Festival and shared his story with students from many other schools. The amount of time and concentration he gave to his story showed his devotion to the art form, and his stellar performance underscored his talent. This achievement greatly enhanced Louis' motivation and self-efficacy for storytelling and contributed to his positive perception of his academic abilities as well. In the context of his talent development program, Louis and his teachers began to understand the ways in which he learned best.

## Mike

Because of poor skills in writing, spelling, and articulation, Mike, a twelve-year-old LD student, had been placed in a self-contained classroom for LD students. Teachers described his reading as slow and labored, but just this year his reading comprehension scores had reached grade level. Mike was, according to teachers, "struggling with school work, worrying constantly, and . . . [had] little self-confidence." Table 5.8 summarizes Mike's WISC scores.

**WISC Patterns.** From the scores in Table 5.8, we can see that Mike is highly able in tasks requiring Integrative Intelligence. Unlike Louis, however, Mike's strongest areas are spatial. His ability to see connections among things is probably responsible for his high Similarities score.

**Multiple Intelligences Perspective.** Mike's profile suggests that he is a spatial thinker, and information about his learning style preferences and interests corroborates finding. His responses to items on the Ways of Learning Scale (Dixon, 1986) confirmed his strong interest in spatial

| Table 5.8. Mike's WISC-R Profile | |
|---|---|
| Integrative Pattern | Dispersive Pattern |
| Block Design 14 | Arithmetic 13 |
| Object Assembly 18 | Coding 9 |
| Picture Arrangement 10 | Digit Span 10 |
| Mazes 13 | Picture Completion 14 |
| Similarities 15 | |
| Comprehension 14 | |
| Vocabulary 15 | |
| Information 14 | |

mechanical ability. He consistently chose answers that showed a strong desire for choices and a preference for visual information over verbal activities.. His hobbies included building models and sketching out ideas before solving a problem.

This pattern of exceptional abilities in spatial areas is prevalent in many GLD students (Dixon, 1983; Silverman, 1989; West, 1997). These students typically score well on spatial manipulation and pattern sequencing subtests on the WISC-R. They spend time at home with such things as blocks, building models, clay sculptures, paper folding, and creating other three-dimensional constructions. Puzzles and games that require actual manipulation such as Pick-Up Sticks, Tip It, and Rubik's Cube can provide hours of amusement for these youngsters. Some prefer two-dimensional activities involving painting, drawing, and other artistic activities. Architecture, engineering, and careers in the visual arts are some real word applications of spatial abilities.

Although these students may have differing interests and specific talents based on other areas of strengths, they share similarities in the way they think, organize information, and communicate what they know. Dixon (1983) described such individuals as having "the capacity to put the world together inside one's head such that all things relate to all others in precisely understood ways. The distance and directional positioning between a whole host of objects is so well understood that all become part of an interconnected system" (p. 9). For example, it is this kind of ability that allows a person to walk through a complex building without becoming confused. It is as if people particularly strong in these abilities carry a mental three-dimensional map. These students usually prefer to use visual rather than verbal methods to solve problems, generate ideas, organize information, and communicate what they know. Many show an exceptional ability in mathematical reasoning and in appreciating the scope and significance of history. Because they think in images and can see a variety of patterns and interconnections among things, they tend to have rich imaginations. However, because solutions often pop suddenly into view, they may have little idea about how they arrived at their conclusions.

Spatial intelligence can be manifested in activities that are mechanical or visual. Mike showed a definite preference for the former. He thoroughly enjoyed designing and building models. For example, in an activity created to spot engineering talent, Mike's class was asked to construct balloon-driven model cars, with a prize going to the students whose car went the farthest. Mike's attention to details—reducing friction on the wheels, getting more traction, increasing thrust— showed that he had more technical knowledge and problem-solving skills than his peers did. His model won him a place in a specially designed program for young engineers.

**Mike's Program.** At the onset of the program, the instructor of the class told students that they would be required to build an original model of something that interested them. Soon after the program began, Mike brought in an article he had read about the efforts of engineers to build a rover vehicle for exploring Mars. The article described the problems such a project entailed, especially the challenge Mars' craggy landscape presented. Mike was so excited about this challenge that he decided to create his own prototype. It would have to include such features as remote control and a special arm for manipulating objects. The instructor was somewhat concerned about the complexity of the problem, but Mike would not be dissuaded. He argued that he had been studying the article and already had a picture in his mind of what the vehicle would look like. He now had to work out the details.

Mike devoted himself so thoroughly to his goal that it took precedence over all other activities. He first listed all the things he would need to complete the project. He then drew a multicolored diagram of the complex inner wiring that his plan would require. Luckily, his father was an electrician, and Mike was able to discuss his ideas with his dad as he planned the project. He also asked his dad to help him obtain the necessary materials.

The class was awestruck when Mike displayed his model vehicle. No longer was he the shy and insecure student his teachers and classmates usually saw. Rather he exuded confidence about his ability and pride in his achievement. Like Louis, he was a practicing professional whose performance was of an excellent quality. Also like Louis, Mike was able to understand how to be successful.

—

The possibilities for helping students believe in their promise rather than focus on their flaws are endless. However, as we have pointed out in this chapter, success depends upon understanding the natural learning strengths of these students and helping them feel efficacious about their own learning abilities. The WISC III patterns and an analysis of the students' MI profiles are a very useful foundation for identifying potential gifts and talents, offering talent development opportunities, and providing appropriate instruction and compensation strategies that accomplish these goals.

# Cognition & Problem Solving

In psychology, cognition encompasses all the mental processes of thinking, memory, and learning: that is, how we acquire, store, and use information. Even external behaviors—movements—are tied to cognitive activity since many of them are planned, observed, and evaluated inside the head. At the highest level, often called *metacognition*, mental activities involve awareness and personal control of various strategies to learn and to perform. We will consider several theoretical and well-researched points about memory, thinking, and forms of problem solving and then apply these points to gifted and learning-disabled students.

Although the philosophy of behaviorism dominated psychology for much of the 20th century, it falls short in explaining thought and memory. As a result, interest in cognitive psychology has surged over the past 20 years. Since thinking and knowing continue to be unobservable and difficult to measure, cognitive research must make inferences about mental processes by proposing models of mental behavior and then judging how well external evidence fits the models. A typical cognitive model is termed *information processing* and computer programming has shaped this offshoot of cognitive psychology. Just as the computer manipulates sets of data, the brain transforms information to solve problems. The brain, of course, does more. It is already active and does not need an operator to turn it on or to instruct it. It can fashion new, original ways of processing information, and its plans are not so rigid as computer programs. It is flexible and insightful. And it makes errors.

In the information processing view, human beings seek information, interpret it, organize, transform, and file it in memory. They also merge the information with other data already stored in their heads and act on the basis of it. The centerpiece of all this processing is memory.

Without memory, we could not learn. We could not even qualify as intelligent animals. Each time we reached into a tree to pluck a banana, we would have to discover anew that we had to peel the fruit before we could eat it. Each time we roved the shore in search of dinner, we would find out that oysters are edible and rocks are not. So, in effect, we are what we remember.

The brain's tangled interconnections of some 100 billion neurons offer quite a bit of storage space. But the capacity of the memory is even more awesome. Ordinary folk, in a lifetime, store billions of items of information in their memories, including some 50,000 words and a greater number of images. Extraordinary folk may perform even more impressive feats of memory, at least in special ways. Leonardo da Vinci needed to see someone only once to draw a perfect likeness. The conductor Arturo Toscanini could set down accurately the score of a symphony he had not heard in forty years. A one-time Russian newspaper reporter known to psychologists only as "S" indicated that the potential of memory might be virtually boundless. Given a list of seventy unrelated objects, S could repeat it flawlessly, top to bottom or bottom to top, years later. S quit journalism for the stage, where in three shows a night he invited audiences to pepper him with nonsense syllables. After the audience ran out of nonsense, S would write every syllable on a chalkboard. The chalkboard was soon scrubbed, but S's memory was not. Many performances later, he could still come up with the lists of syllables of any earlier night. S ascribed much of his curious ability to the phenomenon that he "tasted" and "saw" oral sounds and musical tones. Every voice, for him, had its distinctive color. A musical tone of a certain pitch and loudness felt, he said, like borsch on his tongue and appeared like a brown strip edged with red tongues in his mind (Luria, 1968).

Memory—even with someone as unusual as S—seems to have three distinctive storage systems: sensory, short-term, and long-term. Although it is convenient to think of these systems as separate, it is more likely that they are related levels of a single, coherent memory structure.

## Sensory Storage

Great quantities of information in the form of environmental stimuli bombards us in great quantity and enter the sensory storage system. Evidence suggests that sensory storage holds accurate images of incoming stimuli while the brain searches for recognizable features or patterns. When familiarity is established (within a couple of seconds), information is passed to short-term storage. The irrelevant information decays immediately, and the sensory storage busily attends to new stimuli.

Can sensory storage attend to all incoming stimuli? Probably not. Researchers believe there must be a filtering mechanism that sifts through the information and have advanced several hypotheses about this filter. Although there is little agreement, a popular theory promotes something called an attenuated filter (Triesman, 1964). This filter includes a threshold that may be set at high or low, depending on the intensity of the stimulus bombardment. In the ordinary setting, the filter lets only some of the stimuli through for examination. Certain important stimuli, such as your name, will leap over the threshold and demand immediate and conscious attention. Other stimuli are let in the perceptual door, but are not awarded such high status. This stimuli may sneak through consciousness and into behavior without your being aware of it, unless you happen to think about what you are thinking or doing! Awareness, though, and intentional control of memory's behavior is the foundation of self-regulated learning, and therefore an important skill for gifted students with learning disabilities.

### Short-Term Storage

Awareness of thinking or behavior seems to takes place in short-term memory storage. Consequently, some psychologists call short-term storage *working memory*. Ironically, though short-term storage performs extremely important functions, its capacity is pretty puny.

First, short term memory holds information just long enough to sort it out and determine whether or not it merits keeping. If you remembered everything that happened to you, every inane conversation along with all the significant ones, your head would soon be cluttered with trivia. In short-term storage, we dismiss the trivia and pass on the worthwhile data to long-term storage. Sorting the trivial from the significant is an important function of short-term storage, and it does this by encoding, or interpreting, the images of stimuli sent from the sensory register. If you were asked what you have just read, you probably could not reproduce each word. The image has already decayed. But you could relate the general meaning of the words, thanks to the encoding process. In general, short-term storage has only a maximum of twenty or thirty seconds to sort and encode. When a lot of information is competing for attention, it may last only four or five seconds in short-term memory. After that time, information is either passed to long-term storage or lost from the system. Of course you can extend the short interval by re-entering the information: by reading, looking at, saying, or hearing the information again. You can even re-hear it silently by thinking of it.

However, you can't stretch the usual thirty-second time limit into ten minutes. There will be other information bumping the thoughts out because of a second limitation to short term storage: it simply can't hold much. In a classic article entitled "The Magical Number Seven, Plus or Minus Two," George Miller (1956) argued that we have space for five to nine bits of unrelated information at a time or, on average, seven. Many demonstrations have borne out Miller's contention. Today we know that the capacity of short-term storage develops with age. At age two, it can handle two bits of information, increasing gradually to its tiny maximum of about seven bits by age fifteen.

Just as we can extend the thirty-second focus of short-term memory by re-entering information, we can also pack in more information by grouping or chunking it. Thus you should be able to dial a ten-digit phone number without looking back and forth in the phone book if the digits are chunked in a handy way. For example, the brain probably treats the toll-free number 800-333-5555 as three bits of data, leaving enough short-term capacity to recall who you are calling and why. The apparent limitations of space and time in short-term storage also require that when you are introduced to someone you process the name into long-term storage right off. Short-term storage will not have the room or staying power to keep it for you because incoming stimuli will boot the name out of the way very quickly in order to process more incoming stimuli.

## Long-Term Storage

On the other hand, the capacity of long-term memory, as we remarked earlier, is awesome. However, most of us tend to think of it as rather limited and believe that if we do not use what we have learned fairly often, we will forget it and lose it forever. Many studies have shown this belief to be faulty. Some evidence for the durability of long-term memory comes from hypnosis, under which people recall events that elude them under normal conditions. Early evidence comes from electrical stimulation of the brain. In the 1940s Canadian neurosurgeon Wilder Penfield tried to locate the sites of epileptic seizures in the brain. Prodding with an electrode in a memory area, he found that patients, still awake, seemed to remember long-faded occurrences. Moving the electrode released memories of different occasions. Despite this discovery and more recent magnetic resonance imaging of the brain at work, finding specific locations that house memory is proving to be a challenge. It seems that memories may be scattered in several locations, and there may even be "backup" areas for safekeeping knowledge.

The psychological structure—what activates long-term memory, how images are coded and stored, and how information is retrieved—is also unknown. Various researchers have proposed many coding systems. One of the simplest and most widely used is the two-part system suggested by John Anderson (1995). In Anderson's view, information may be coded as declarative knowledge (knowing what) or procedural knowledge (knowing how). Obviously these systems communicate with each other. A procedural skill typically requires knowledge of height, weight, location, name, purpose, or other declarative information. For example, the student who knows how to store data on a computer's hard disk can probably also name the various parts of the keyboard (and will be most pleased to tell you).

No storage theory can explain how information or images are converted to biochemical matter and then reformed into thought or behavior. But, if the molecular route is too bewildering, then what can we learn from the larger picture of routine behavior? One of the most important big-picture discoveries is that long-term memory is not a passive storage device. It is active—although beneath our awareness—as it merges, creates, and modifies information. This constructive view of memory presents something of a paradox. On one hand, it is an astonishing strength. It allows the formation of useful knowledge from the inside and the creation of new ideas by merging others. It also permits, somehow, the comprehension of novel arrangements of information, such as a sentence that you have never read before.

On the other hand, the activity of long-term storage can blend data into faulty or downright stupid information. As an example of long-term memory's constructive activity, Loftus and Palmer (1974) showed adults a film of an auto accident then gave each participant one of two questionnaires. One questionnaire asked, "About how fast were the cars going when they *smashed* into each other?" The second asked, "About how fast were the cars going when they *hit* each other?" [Italics added.] The subjects who had been given the smashed question estimated the cars' speed at 30% greater than did those who had the hit question. A week later, all subjects were asked, "Did you see any broken glass?" Of the subjects who had responded to the questionnaire using the word "smashed," 32% said they had seen shattered glass. Only 14% of the other group claimed to have seen broken glass. In reality, NO glass had been broken in the mishap. This sort of creative but unintended restructuring has led some researchers to question the accuracy of eyewitness testimony in criminal trials (Loftus, 1996).

In short, evidence indicates that we pull together information from several sources to construct a "memory" of an event and may employ, in retrieving from memory, information beyond our actual experiences. Long-term memory is a process that is highly active. We reorganize ideas and facts as we gain information, even if the information is incompatible with our experience.

### Memory and Exceptional Students

Presumably, a student with a specific learning disability can have trouble in any of the three sequences of memory, from the sensory register to long-term storage. Difficulty in sensory storage, for example, might result from an inadequate filter, causing the youngster to attend to irrelevant information while ignoring the important. In short-term storage, the child may have trouble retaining or coding short sequences of information long enough to stash them into a more permanent location. When a faulty filter shovels meaningless data into short-term memory, the child may become bewildered trying to coax the information into long-term memory. Two external conditions increase the child's frustration. First, teachers and parents usually convey an unmistakable expectation that a student must learn lesson content. Second, when observing other students who appear to be catching on, social comparisons speak loudly to the child struggling to merge material with memory.

Problems with long-term memory might involve overactive combining of information into incorrect beliefs, weak connections among related bits of information, difficulty retrieving information, or lack of self-regulation and awareness of learning behaviors. (Chapter 8 elaborates on self-regulation problems and how to mitigate them.) As we have said, the portions of memory are not isolated. Trouble with one memory process can impair other processes.

By contrast, the gifted child may have sharper attentional and filtering capacity in sensory storage, strong coding skills in short-term memory, and much more efficient access routes to information stored in long-term memory. Most notably, gifted individuals have large storehouses of personally meaningful information squirreled away in long-term memory. The material seems to be placed along well-constructed scaffolding, so that there are clear routes from certain information to other information. The gifted person with creative talent also seems capable of rapidly erecting new scaffolding, especially along unpredictable routes.

What about the youngster who is both gifted and learning disabled? As usual, they are complex and little is known about whether their memory processes might be different. We can speculate, though, from personal observation and self-reports from such students. On the surface, they appear to have trouble with the stimulus filter in sensory storage and with the contents—the flow of consciousness—of short-term memory. They frequently seem inattentive to important points in a lesson. When the teacher is discussing proteins in the DNA molecule, Laurie is fantasizing about building an origami molecule. When Laurie actually starts fiddling around with a page torn from her notebook, her inattention becomes obvious. To the teacher, Laurie is locked in a cycle: the less she pays attention, the poorer the learning, and the poorer the learning, the less she pays attention. However, one might ask whether Laurie is doing anything useful with her memory when she appears inattentive. The answer is that she probably is, but the material being coded and rehearsed diverges from the lesson plans. The challenge for the teacher is to motivate Laurie to approach rather than to avoid classroom fare.

Alphabet Students are frequently quite interested in classroom topics, but their mental drumbeats get them marching out of step with the lesson. The child may be following a jazzy improvisational line, skimming here and dwelling there. Meanwhile, the teacher bangs out a methodical, even beat. A discussion about the Wright brothers' first manned flight in Kitty Hawk may set off imagery about strapping a jet propulsion engine onto the original rickety craft. Or it may stimulate a mental spin into a different area of long-term memory, resulting in private analogies. For example, the child might wonder why flying animals do not use propellers or jet engines, or why planes must. If the student makes the analogy public, an unprepared teacher will probably have difficulty fitting the analogy to the lesson plan.

As for the GLD student's long-term memory, the variety of information stored is about as jagged as Pinocchio's profile. In content or skill areas of interest to the child, there is a sustained commitment—almost devotion—to the topic. During the period of commitment, a remarkable assortment of study behaviors steps forward. The child will seek more information about the topic, from both people and written work. He or she will set about organizing the content in a way that is personally meaningful. And frequently the student will initiate some way of transforming the learning into a performance or product. This collection of behaviors is exactly the sort of outcome we expect of schooling: self-regulated learning (Zimmerman, 2002). The end result of all this effort is a substantial bank of information in long-term memory. Unfortunately, the accumulation may occur at the expense of other school topics, which means that long-term memory for those topics may be shallow and perhaps disconnected to other information on the mental scaffolding.

All humans, as we explain in the next chapter, seek arousing stimulation from their environment. Unless they have been taught to be helpless, they are curious and hungry to learn. To the extent that academic fare is made attractive, students will gobble it up. But like foods, careful selection and balance of choices is essential. The student with deficiencies in specific knowledge or behavior needs academic supplements; the youngsters obsessed with a topic need encouragement to consider a more well-rounded academic diet. In one sense, both types of imbalance are characterized by underperformance. By definition, academic deficit involves poor learning or performance. Academic excesses create deficits indirectly because they limit opportunity for other types of learning. Remember that the GLD student is usually quite successful in areas or skills that are personally important. That simple observation implies that the GLD student has a repertoire of learning strategies that have been used effectively. However, the GLD student may need reminders, and possibly demonstrations, that learning strategies can be useful in other situations. After enough practice, the student should become proficient enough at strategy generalization that no external reminders are needed. The student's learning is now self-regulated. In Chapter 8, we detail three case studies that show how strategies may be generalized to make new learning more interesting and efficient for the GLD student.

# Motivation & Self-Efficacy

In the first part of this book we discussed the motivational patterns of the GLD child. At home and almost anywhere outside of school, these students can be highly motivated to tackle innovative and complex tasks. At school it is often a different and perplexing story. When these students complete assignments—and frequently they don't—their work lacks effort and precision. In addition, many learning-disabled students seem to have difficulty paying attention to particular tasks and appear unmotivated. We suspect that this difficulty stems not so much from an inability to attend, but from an environment insensitive to the youngster's strengths and needs. Lastly, GLD pupils may set unreasonably high standards for themselves; when they cannot reach the mark, they view themselves as failures. Eventually, the cycle of high expectations followed by perceived failures settles into task avoidance and feelings of helplessness. But what exactly is motivation and how can we help GLD students tap into it in a constructive instead destructive way?

## What Is Motivation?

Twenty minutes into your lesson, you become aware of two boys in the back of the room who are obviously not paying attention to your carefully prepared lecture. One is staring out the window; the other is scribbling and squirming. Have you bored them already? Do they not want to learn? What do you do now? These questions and their answers address motivation in the classroom, a topic that has prompted much research and generated a lot of theory, but little agreement. So before we discuss what to do about inattentive pupils like these two boys, let us consider some theoretical points about motivation.

In approaching the topic of motivation, the first step is to determine what motivation is. Almost any teacher will assert that a motivated student is one who enthusiastically tries to master whatever the teacher wants the student to learn. Thus an *unmotivated* student is one who does not enthusiastically engage in learning, who may, in fact, actively and enthusiastically avoid learning.

Such a definition seems simple enough for the layperson, but psychologists will want to add their two dollars worth. Although their definitions vary, most theorists think that motivation embodies two components: energy and direction. Theories of motivation try to explain what energizes behavior in the direction of some goal. Why do people, including students, behave in certain ways, persist in those ways, and change their ways?

The teachers' consensus, then, that eager students are motivated and unreceptive students are unmotivated is far off base. Both kinds of students are motivated, one kind to achieve a goal that requires study and the other kind to avoid study. The second kind may manifest motivation in a number of ways: by remaining passive, by actively resisting, by distracting the attention of the class, or by being disruptive, to cite only a few.

Because motivation spans all human behavior, most theorists have found it useful to discuss more specific parts of motivation. In fact, there are now so many theories about motivation's sub-parts that it would take a couple of books to survey them. We will consider only a few of the more credible, better-researched aspects.

## Arousal and Sensory Stimulation

There is considerable evidence that all organisms require stimulation to survive. Stimulation of the sensory apparatus—hearing, sight, touch, taste—serves to arouse the organism. Arousal, while part of motivation, is not all there is. We must blend in some sense of direction. Arousal is the essential beginning; it sets the stage for goal-directed behavior.

The scientific status of this idea was strengthened back in the mid-1950s when McGill University students volunteered to enter an environment in which they would do nothing but lie on a cot. They had short breaks to eat and use the bathroom. They received translucent goggles to dim vision, cuffs on the hands and arms to impede the sense of touch, and earphones that delivered constant "white noise." They earned twenty dollars a day, a hefty allowance at the time, but few students could take more than a couple of days of the experiment. They reported unmanageable stress, extreme boredom, hallucinations, and mental dullness, among other unpleasant effects. (The researchers found that the outcomes were short-lived and disappeared after students returned to their routines.) These findings suggested that sensory deprivation is unhealthy, or, conversely, that humans have an inborn need for arousal,

Combined with other research, the McGill experiments help to confirm an important principle of arousal summarized by the well-known inverted U curve shown in Figure 7.1. Too little stimulation, as happened in the deprivation studies (and which also occurs when people are isolated or bedridden), impairs learning and performance. Too much stimulation works the same way. Studies of people whose jobs are chronically overstimulating, such as overworked airport controllers, show unhappy outcomes: easy distraction, errors and degraded performance, ulcers, insomnia, nightmares, headaches, colitis, asthma, and hypertension (Baldwin & Baldwin, 2001). The moral sounds simple: Moderate stimulation produces optimum attention and performance.

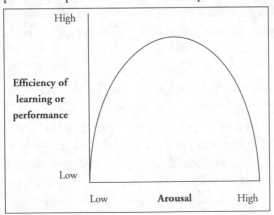

**Figure 7.1.** The inverted U-curve of arousal.

Unfortunately, it is not easy to translate that moral into classroom practice. Different students have different optimum arousal points. Some students, for example, have low arousability and require considerable stimulation. Others are aroused by low levels of stimulation (Farley, 1986). Such wide individual differences offer a stiff challenge for teachers trying to assure optimum attention and alertness in twenty youngsters. Plans for classroom activities that are optimally stimulating for one students may be monotonous for another. The solution is to aim for a Golden Mean: Arrange activities that will be arousing for the majority and offer enough variety so that each student will be optimally aroused at least some of the time. Listed are a few classroom variables that teachers can alter without too much difficulty:

- Type of activity
- Amount of student participation
- Tempo or pace
- Amount of structure
- Domain stressed (cognitive, affective, psychomotor)
- Formality versus informality
- Stimulus complexity
- Style of feedback
- Cooperative or competitive activities
- Form of reinforcer

Because arousal is essential, people are motivated to behave in ways that gain optimum arousal. If the classroom environment provides too little stimulation, students will invent their own means of arousal. When that happens, students are motivated toward goals that probably differ from classroom objectives and their resulting actions are usually called misbehavior. Although misbehavior has many sources, effective teachers can reduce optional routes to arousal by focusing on student strengths and interests, thus heightening interest in lessons. When students are optimally aroused, learning, enjoyment, and a sense of efficacy come naturally.

In our studies, we have observed dramatic changes in attitudes, enthusiasm, behavior, and quality of work when students are encouraged to explain what they have learned in their preferred mode. For example, a group of fifth graders had been studying colonial American history. One learning objective required students to compare and contrast growing up in colonial times and today. We first asked the students to write a brief essay on the topic. Predictably, the best essays came from the best writers. Next, we repeated the assignment with a twist: The students could choose how they wanted to communicate their learning. They could use drama, drawing, building, or, if they wished, even writing. This time, 90% of the projects were of superior quality. The finished products were neat, organized, and sophisticated. Effort, arousal, and time on task had improved. The students were also enthusiastic and pleased with their accomplishments. More importantly, though, the products of the learning-disabled youngsters were indistinguishable from those of the other students.

## Arousal and Hyperactivity

One of the chief complaints about misbehaving youngsters is that they fidget constantly, act impatient, pay little attention to what is being taught, and have difficulty following instructions and organizing tasks. This profile, of course, dictates that they will have trouble finishing school assignments. Many of these students—more often boys—are tagged with the important-sounding label, "attention-deficit/hyperactivity disorder (ADHD)" (American Psychiatric Association, 2000). It is hard to calculate how many students are ADHD because of local and regional variations in how to interpret the characteristics of ADHD. Although learning disabilities are thought to be different from hyperactivity, Lyon and Cutting (1998) estimated that up to 80% of certain learning disabilities (e.g., reading disorder) are accompanied by hyperactivity.

Despite public outcry over the past decade, the preferred method of managing hyperactive youth is medication, usually stimulant drugs such as Ritalin. A recent summary of psychiatric medications prescribed for youths (Zito et al., 2003) shows a dramatic upward trend over the last decade. It is possible that the surge reflects increased awareness of hyperactivity, but Jellinek (2003) argues that the upsurge is *not* founded on careful research and that perhaps we should exercise more caution in prescribing psychotropic drugs to children and youth.

Stimulant drugs seem to have a paradoxical effect. When they work, children are calmer and more attentive. Clarizio and McCoy (1984) offered a different explanation: Hyperactive people seem to have an "underpowered" portion of their brain that regulates arousal. They thus are much more active in seeking sensations from their environment. According to this theory, stimulant medication does not have a paradoxical effect. It simply provides internal stimulation so that the child does not need to squeeze every drop of stimulation he or she needs from the environment.

What causes hyperactivity? Certainly there is a genetic component (Ross & Ross, 1982; Hendley, 1998), but there is also evidence that aspects of the environment will heighten or reduce it. For example, some people react very poorly to stress. It is now well established that overreaction to stress contributes to anxiety disorders and cardiovascular disease. In addition, there may be lesser reactions, such as hyperactivity. Thus, when students with learning difficulties find certain classroom demands exceedingly stressful, they may become jittery, inattentive, disorganized—in other words, excessively aroused.

As discussed in Chapter 4, the school environment is very clear about its demands: students should be docile, neat, quiet for extended periods, and interested in what the teacher is interested in. Students who need more stimulation are automatically at odds with these expectations, and the GLD student with hyperactivity stands in double jeopardy. On the gifted side, the child has an intrinsic urge to discover, understand, and master, and prefers active engagement in learning. On the LD side, when a school subject is mysteriously frustrating or not meaningful, the student may dodge that stressful arousal by searching for optimal arousal elsewhere. When the classroom is highly structured and students are expected to be passive for much of the school day, the GLD child is almost certain to show higher levels of activity than is acceptable. In her study of upper elementary GLD children, Baum (1985) found that these children struggled with feelings of inefficacy in academic behaviors. Their sense of scholarly ineptness probably increased motivation to avoid the usual school tasks, and a predictable result was disruptive classroom behavior.

## Self-Efficacy

Self-efficacy, one's belief that he or she can successfully organize and carry out some behavior, is an important subset of Albert Bandura's (1986) social cognitive theory. In the social cognitive view, it is a sense of *agency* that allows people to have some control over their behaviors, the environment, and their futures. The most discussed sense of agency is personal self-efficacy, which refers to the idea that an individual can accomplish some specific task. Bandura (1997, 2002) has also considered two other forms of agency:

1. *Proxy self-efficacy* means that individuals try to enlist others

to effect change. For example, feeling unable to quiet your neighbor's dog howling through the night, you might call the animal warden for assistance. Or in school, a 7th grade whipping boy might ask the guidance counselor for help to get the bullies off his back.

2. *Collective efficacy* occurs when groups combine individual efforts to create a desired outcome. For example, a neighborhood group begins a block watch program to observe, report, and thwart crime. What goes on in this situation is not just the sum of the individuals working independently. Neighbors share information, discuss what works and what does not, create plans, and reinforce each other for making useful contributions. They have, in addition to their own sense of personal agency, a belief that *the group* is important and capable. Consider the idea of *collective teacher self-efficacy*, where teachers working together believe that the group can effect some desired outcome. Two items from a questionnaire about collective teacher self-efficacy provide examples of collective efficacy:

   • "I believe in the potential of our school's faculty to establish innovative approaches to education even when faced with setbacks."
   • "I am confident that we as teachers can develop and carry out educational projects in a cooperative manner even when difficulties arise." (Schwartzer, Schmitz, & Daytner, 1999)

Perceptions of collective efficacy are extremely important when students work on collaborative projects. It won't do to have four group members who each have strong personal self-efficacy, but weak collective efficacy. Such a group will have scattered and feeble outcomes because it cannot function smoothly as a team. Sports coaches are keenly aware of the importance of collective efficacy and are quick to bench a talented player who cannot, or will not, collaborate. The implication for teachers who assign collaborative projects is to monitor carefully the group dynamics. The best grouping arrangement combines students of differing talents where all of the talents are needed for the project's completion.

Self-efficacy is now claimed to have a central role in motivating human behavior. Compared to those with weak self-efficacy, people with a robust sense of efficacy are more likely to

- freely engage in the task,
- spend more energy on the task,
- concentrate and plan more carefully for the demands of the task,
- persist longer on the task,
- set more challenging goals for themselves,
- continue in the face of barriers and occasional failure,
- enjoy performing the task, and
- succeed.

Efficacy expectations seem to span all three domains of human behavior (psychomotor, cognitive, and affective). The psychomotor domain is the most obvious. Efficacy beliefs, after all, use some form of behavioral performance as their frame of reference. On the cognitive side of self-efficacy, a person must consider a goal, imagine working toward that goal, and make a prediction about success. The affective side is a poorly understood dimension ranging from reluctance, shyness, and anxiety about performance to exuberance, enthusiasm, and confidence. Self-efficacy is thus a reciprocal mix of cognitions about performances plus a motivating torque of confidence. Confidence spurs a person to try behaviors and improves the odds for success. As a person succeeds, self-efficacy is reinforced, and the heightened self-efficacy increases motivation to pursue similar tasks. In other words, when I succeed at something, it boosts my self-efficacy, making it more likely that I will succeed again. The opposite also holds. It is easy to predict that a student accustomed to failure will have low academic self-efficacy and his perception will motivate him to avoid classroom goals.

## How Does Efficacy Information Get Into the Head?

As we have implied, successful actions are the strongest contributors to self-efficacy. A second influence is imitation learning. Respected models demonstrating skilled performances convey important information about how to carry out a task. They also instill efficacy information: "When I address a problem this way, I can succeed. If you pay attention and do similar behaviors, you can succeed to." This influence does not suggest that models can or should always demonstrate effortless performance in front of observers. Models who often succeed and occasionally struggle send an important message: "Sometimes failures happen, but I can still have robust self-efficacy." Effective models may also be symbolic, such as plausible heroes in novels. Implausible models, as from commercial television, are imitated mainly when their behaviors are within reach of observers. These behaviors are ordinarily modest—trademark phrases, dress, and gestures.

Incredible behaviors—winning fist fights every ten minutes, arguing fluidly and persuasively no matter how silly the cause—have little imitative importance no matter how much the model is reinforced. That a few folks do try to copy astonishing behaviors testifies to their innocence. After a few ineffectual trials, they come to understand that their environment is not as supportive as the ones shown on TV.

Verbal persuasion is a third influence on self-efficacy. Teachers, preachers, parents, and peers spend much of their professional lives trying to persuade listeners to exhibit certain behaviors. Pleading, exhortation, and rational arguments become powerful only when they are coupled with successful performances. When a failing student is advised to follow a strict regimen of homework and study, but finds immediately that it is hard work and slacks off (fails), he chalks up one more example of free but useless advice. Therefore, verbal persuasion is most effective when the talker can arrange the environment so that success is highly probable.

Finally, interpretation of signs of arousal alters self-efficacy. When, for example, a student experiences severe test anxiety and performance falters, the student quickly comes to expect that anxiety will accompany the next test. If that prediction comes true, anxiety becomes more tightly tied to test-taking behaviors and may well spread to associated activities such as studying and attending class. As anxiety increases, effective effort wanes, failure becomes more likely, and self-efficacy about academic performance dwindles.

There are abundant practical applications of self-efficacy theory. Teachers should consider, for example, how to assure success experiences, especially in classes of mixed-ability students. Teachers may want to rethink their role as model, even when student imitation seems unlikely (as with adolescents), and they will want to know how to assess students' self-efficacy quickly and easily. Students with bloated confidence will make poor estimates of task demands and effort needed, and they are likely to engender failure. Those whose confidence is beneath their competence will lack endurance in school tasks and may even avoid them.

### Enhancing Self-Efficacy

It is important to remember that GLD students have high standards for success. Acceptable performance in a watered-down curriculum will likely not be considered success. We repeatedly hear these students appeal for material at their grade level and for help so that they can achieve the same quality of work as their gifted peers. And interestingly, students with high standards and high self-efficacy, *but who are dissatisfied with their recent accomplishment*, will generally be far more motivated on their next attempt (Bandura & Cervone, 1986). With these principles in mind, we offer several specific suggestions that will help boost self-efficacy by increasing perceived success:

1.  Carve big tasks into smaller pieces to increase the likelihood of success. Smaller steps lead to more frequent and nearby goals, which by itself improves self-efficacy (Stock & Cervone, 1990). Use more frequent evaluations of progress, rather than a few massive ones.

2.  For genuine progress, hand out reinforcers liberally. Consider public reinforcers as well as private ones. Praise—public and private—is an inexpensive, natural reinforcer, and it can be extremely powerful. Ken Blanchard (co-author of *The One Minute Manager* (1983)) remarks that praise needs to be dished out about four times as frequently as criticism. Why? Studies with adults show that even when praise is twice as frequent as criticism, morale is weak. If adults need the four-to-one rule, why be stingy with kids?

3.  Nonetheless, be careful using praise as a reinforcer. New teachers probably heard about the importance of praise in every teacher training course they took, but they often use it so carelessly that it loses effectiveness. Keep in mind the following guidelines about effective praise (adapted from Brophy, 1981):

    *   It is not delivered randomly or unsystematically.
    *   It shows spontaneity, variety, and other signs of credibility.
    *   It rewards attainment of specific performances (including effort).
    *   It gives information about competence and the value of performance.
    *   It uses past performance as the context for describing present

performance.

- It recognizes noteworthy effort or success at difficult tasks.
- It attributes success to effort and ability, implying that similar successes can be expected in the future.

4. Remember that occasional failure may be challenging to the student with strong self-efficacy, but discouraging to the learner with feeble self-efficacy. You may have to invent ways of minimizing failure for students with low expectations. As you raise their expectations, they become more resilient and can bounce back from obstacles and barriers.

5. Try to make tasks meaningful. Use events, illustrations, and applications that are important to the learner. Build new learning on what has already been learned. This task can be extremely difficult when it is time to begin a new lesson and some students are nowhere close to mastering the previous one. But if your lessons are hierarchical—that is, if new content builds on previous work—and the student is not ready to move forward, failure will loom no matter how cleverly you present the material. When the youngster believes that new and valued content is within grasp, she will perceive learning as a reasonable and worthwhile challenge.

   Learning-disabled youngsters often perceive irrelevant lessons as intense demands on their limited skills. Efficacy beliefs can buffer the demands (Bandura, 2002). When a student has strong self-efficacy, then the demands create only modest stress. But when self-efficacy is in short supply, feelings of stress become overwhelming, and hyperactivity may be the most obvious result.

6. Use peer tutoring, cooperative groups, and team projects. Peers usually act like coping models (who succeed, but with effort), and coping models are frequently more influential than mastery models (who show effortless performance).

7. Communicate expectations clearly. Tell learners exactly what you want accomplished (using instructional objectives), and accompany it with positive expectations.

8. Beware of accidentally communicating negative expectations. Good and Brophy (2003) summarized seventeen unintentional

teacher behaviors that offer hidden lessons (e.g., less eye contact with low achievers, giving high achievers (but not lows) the benefit of the doubt in grading written work, calling on low achievers less often to answer questions).

9. Reduce possible aversion to time on task. Listed are some typical aversive events for students. Each of them, with practice, can be altered.

   - Receiving too few praises and too many criticisms
   - Being pressured to move too quickly with difficult material
   - Being offered too much material at once
   - Being required to concentrate on reading or writing for an activity when you are disabled in reading or writing
   - Asking permission for an alternate way to communicate learning, but being told that writing is the only acceptable method
   - Being ignored or dodged after requesting help
   - Taking poorly written tests
   - Being told to stop an attractive (and worthwhile) activity
   - Not being able to distinguish important material from trivial
   - Listening to an unenthusiastic, poorly organized, monotone, or uncaring teacher

10. Use criterion-referenced measurement and evaluation. Grades are based on what students can or cannot do, rather than where they rank in the class. Ranking students is norm-referenced evaluation; older students often call it "grading on the curve." It is more honestly called "grading on ability," and it typically results in a few persistent winners and a group of students with an academic life sentence of losing. In short, less capable students are forced into unfair competition because no matter how much improvement they show, they still fall toward the bottom ranks. If a school system cherishes norm-referenced evaluation, teachers can at least try to mix in some criterion-referenced grading.

Robert Slavin (2003) offers a practical example of stirring criterion-referenced measurement into a traditional classroom recipe (see Figure 7.2). In Slavin's example, students receive extra points for personal progress, and the teacher adds these extra points to the actual quiz score. Every couple of weeks, the teacher recalculates a new base line. Slavin also suggests incorporating other elements (e.g., written praise) according to the number of improvement points and communicating with parents about what you are doing and why.

There is ample evidence that students' academic self-efficacy improves when classroom tasks are collaborative and focused on producing an acceptable product. This orientation is more akin to criterion-referenced evaluation. On the other hand, when teachers insist on norm-referenced evaluation, demanding individual work and emphasizing competition and the highest marks, self-efficacy shrinks (Andermann, Eccles, Yoon, Roeser, Wigfield, & Blumenfeld, 2001).

### Let's Be Honest!

Self-efficacy is an important energizer of behavior, and it makes sound educational sense to try to instill a sense of confidence in your students. But it is important for students to have realistic appraisals of what they can and cannot do. It will not help Tina to create hokey success experiences, deliver insincere praise, or inflate her grades. She may see through the ruse, and you will lose credibility. It is also possible that your bluffing will work, and Tina's efficacy beliefs will be raised far beyond her capabilities. Kruger and Dunning (1999) studied the issue of inflated self-efficacy. In their article "Unskilled and Unaware of It," they demonstrated that the college students who were the *least* capable were the ones with the most exaggerated efficacy beliefs, which caused a host of problems: "Not only do these people reach erroneous conclusions and make unfortunate choices, but their incompetence robs them of the . . . ability to realize it" (p. 1121). When skills improve, Kruger and Dunning pointed out, self-efficacy may

---

**Calculating Points for Personal Progress**

Calculate baseline scores for each student by finding the average percent correct from past quizzes and tests (or at the beginning of the year, use the previous year's average). For each quiz, compare the student's score with his baseline and award improvement points as follows:

| | |
|---|---|
| 5 or more points below baseline | = 0 improvement points |
| -4 to +4 points above baseline | = 1 improvement point |
| +5 to +9 points above baseline | = 2 improvement points |
| +10 above baseline to a perfect score | = 3 improvement points |

**Figure 7.2.** An example of criterion-referenced measurement (Slavin, 2003).

actually lessen as learners discover that their skills are limited. We can draw two lessons from this study: First, we should not sacrifice honesty simply to raise student self-efficacy. And second, we should help students make realistic assessments of their talents and deficits.

Self-efficacy is related to arousal theory. Teachers who feel efficacious believe in their ability to produce optimum arousal, and they probably are more effective in doing so. Students who feel efficacious are automatically more alert and attentive because they expect success, are motivated to work toward it, and tend to enjoy the tasks that bring success. In summary, it is a good thing to have self-efficacy and to encourage its development in learners. Because self-efficacy is not an enduring personality trait, it can respond to changes in the classroom environment, and that makes teachers more important than ever!

## Attributions for Success and Failure

There are other self-beliefs that influence motivation and accomplishment in the classroom. Bernard Weiner (1992) and his colleagues have developed a theory that considers how people explain outcomes of their behavior. In the classroom, this theory relates to why students believe they succeed or fail on achievement tasks. Weiner's ideas reflect what social psychologists call attribution theory*, for reasons the following examples should make clear:

- Danny got a C- on a test. He attributes his mediocre grade to the test's being too tough.
- James also got a C-, but he had not studied much before the test and figures he was lucky to get what he did.
- Esteban received an A. He feels his ability earned it.
- Brian also got an A. He credits extra study for several days before the test.

Weiner devised a scheme for classifying attributions that uses each of the four boys' explanations. The classification focuses, as Figure 7.3 shows, on two dimensions: locus of control and stability.

Stable characteristics such as ability are enduring and difficult to change; unstable characteristics such as effort can be readily increased or

---

* Attribution theory also extends to the explanations teachers give for their own successes and failures, as well as explanations they have for their students' performances.

decreased. The difficulty of a task—test, recitation, homework—is relatively stable but impersonal; someone else determines it. And luck, of course, is perceived to be unpredictable.

"Interesting," you may be saying to yourself, "but what will I do with that in the classroom?" Adding the dimension of stability provides important clues to what turns students on and off in school and what

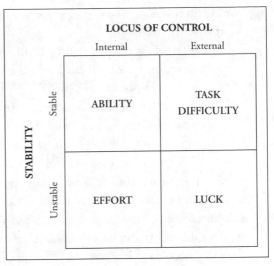

**Figure 7.3.** The attribution framework.

teachers can do to help turn them on and off, and that is what motivation is about.

## Attribution in the Classroom

All these aspects of attribution—ability, effort, task difficulty, and luck—are perceived, but not necessarily objectively real. Danny perceived the test as too hard, but James perceived it as fair enough. The subjectivity of perception helps explain why students behave so differently under the same conditions—that is, why their motivation and performance vary when their environment does not. For example, students have bigger gains in self-efficacy and show more persistence at a task when they ascribe success to their own efforts. And their attributions also influence their preferences among tasks: Students seek tasks that agree with their usual attributions. If students judge that ability is the explanation for their past successes, they will favor tasks that require competence rather than luck or special effort.

The attribution process occurs with our perceptions of others' behavior as well as our own, and teachers' perceptions of students probably influence much of what goes on in the classroom. In a series of studies summarized by Weiner (1972), teachers received data about some imaginary pupils—how the students ranked in ability, how hard each tried on a test, what each achieved on the test. Teachers then had to respond to the question *"How much reward or punishment did the students merit?"* Weiner found that

1. Regardless of their exam performance, students who were believed to have tried harder were better rewarded than those who appeared not to have tried.
2. Regardless of effort, students of little intellectual ability were rewarded more generously than those of high ability.

Add up the two outcomes and you will find that students with little ability who put forth a lot of effort get the best deal. Teachers seem to value effort above ability, especially if the student has surmounted the obstacle of low ability by strong effort. On the other hand, when failing students seem not to try, teachers dish out abundant criticism. We should wonder if anything invites as much teacher scorn as the capable-but-refuses-to-work-hard student. As it happens, this pattern is exactly what some GLD students display, students whose gifts may be apparent, but whose disability is misinterpreted by the teacher as reluctance. If teacher attributions of students' performance lead to different consequences for different students, then teachers influence students even more than has been taken for granted.

Teachers cannot do anything directly about ability because it is a durable characteristic. But they can alter self-beliefs about ability. Schunk (1985) demonstrated that student self-efficacy and skill is enhanced when teachers deliver feedback about ability (e.g., "You're good at this!") as students progress. Teachers can also try to ensure that students understand that they can control the internal, unstable component of effort. Simple enough? No, it is more complex than it sounds. Internal and external factors interact to produce students' beliefs about success and failure. For example, difficult tasks set up by the teacher and therefore externally controlled require ability *and* effort for the student to succeed. For a student with a learning difficulty, all the effort in the world may produce a substandard result. With simple tasks it is possible to succeed on the basis of either ability or effort, so learning-disabled students are not at peril if they put forth effort. Or giving a GLD student a complex task with accommodations to help them succeed can reinforce the idea that they do have the ability and that their effort can help them achieve in spite of learning difficulties.

Consider another example of the complexity of internal and external attribution factors: Learning-disabled students sometimes think that effort is not very important as a cause of school success or failure (Licht, 1984). What would convince them that increased effort can make success more likely? Schunk and Cox (1986) showed that learning-disabled students profit from effort feedback (e.g., "You've been working hard.") This feedback will improve their self-efficacy and performance because it helps them understand the importance of effort. On the other hand, the same sort of feedback with non-disabled students may be ineffective or even backfire. Weiner, Graham, Taylor, & Meyer (1983) pointed out that when students see a task as easy, they interpret praise coupled with effort feedback as a suggestion of low ability.

This interaction of internal and external factors has direct implications for teaching. The teacher should set tasks that are moderately difficult (so that some ability and some effort will be required), but because ability varies considerably among students, teachers should individualize tasks as much as possible. Any task assigned to all students may be meaningful and interesting to some and dreadful to others, and the range of student interest will produce a mix of successes and failures. As failures occur and continue, you will invite student misbehavior (as misbehavior is students' alternative means of arousal and motivation).

One problem in dealing with students who are prone to failure is that they may not react in the way that reinforcement theory predicts. Covington and Omelich (1977) have observed that some students do not respond to praise with increased effort and others actually reduce effort. Why? Because they have become inured to failure and expect it. Covington and Omelich hypothesized that when students have low efficacy beliefs about a particular task, they turn to protecting their self-esteem. To that end they pose as capable-but-not-trying, which is the opposite of what impresses teachers, trying-but-not-capable. To protect their self-esteem, they take refuge in excuses. When such a student flunks a test, she does not quietly accept the mark; she explains with a straight face that she had not been able to study because her dog chewed up her notes, her reference books had been stolen, the electricity in the house had been off for two days, and the computer hard drive failed. GLD students are familiar with this ploy. In the past, their effort has frequently predicted failure. To protect a fragile sense of ability, they refuse to expend extra effort.

Can teachers reduce failure and unhealthy attributions? Covington and Omelich think so. They assert that the structure of most classrooms (in which students compete with each other for grades) promotes excessive failure. They recommend changing competition between students to self-competition, shifting focus to mastery learning, or employing cooperative learning teams where no one need fail. And, as mentioned earlier, transforming large assignments into a series of more manageable subgoals should promote success. Finally, contracting with students (i.e., explicitly detailing student responsibilities and deadlines) can give youngsters a less defensive sense of responsibility for schoolwork.

## Shyness in the Attribution Pattern

In her study of GLD elementary children, Baum (1985) coupled an attribution measure with an academic self-efficacy instrument. The instrument asked the child how skilled he or she felt (self-efficacy) in various academic behaviors, such as doing a science project or taking important tests. If a child admitted ineptness, he or she responded to a second question: *Why aren't you very good at this?* The student had the usual attribution reasons to choose from—not smart (ability), don't try (effort), unlucky, or too hard (task difficulty). On a hunch, Baum included a fifth possible explanation: too shy. The data spoke loudly. Baum discovered that GLD children used "too shy" as an explanation for failure 26% of the time. Their LD peers offered the same attribution 14% of the time, and their gifted classmates only 3%. In other words, this single attribution clearly distinguished these three groups of students. Students view shyness, like ability, as an internal, stable attribute. When a student persists in explaining failure because of shyness (or lack of ability), it may lead to a sense of helplessness and, in turn, to avoidance of the very school tasks that need more practice.

Why should GLD youngsters blame shyness for their sense of school failure? Two reasons, one dealing with the environment and the other with genes, are possible. To preserve feelings of intelligence, GLD students may explain their failures by shyness. This sort of explanation can be a bluff in order to appear smart (or not dumb): "I could do it if I weren't so shy . . ." We have seen shyness—the behavior or interest in it—in a variety of situations. For example, a group of GLD fifth graders was producing a video documentary on a topic that was important to them. The students unanimously chose to focus on being embarrassed. In fact they named their documentary production, "Where Are Earthquakes When We Need Them?" Avoiding situations that may be embarrassing contributes to their shyness. On other occasions, we have noted that some of these students seem afraid to interrupt the teacher to ask important questions, to relay information, or to admit when they do not understand something.

Like arousal, shyness is known to be influenced by heredity. Some children are born excessively timid, and ten to fifteen percent of us may enter life with a predisposition toward shyness. At the other extreme, some infants seem to leap audaciously into the world. These biological differences do not automatically result in behavioral patterns that endure for life. They set the stage on which the environment operates, and environmental influences can modify temperamental style. Jerome Kagan (cited in Asher, 1987) remarked, "It takes more than simply a biological vulnerability to produce a [shy] child. You need a stressor plus the vulnerability" (p. 64).

Whatever the reasons for shyness, social hesitancy strongly influences social transactions and others' impressions. Students need to feel secure enough to ask for clarification when they are confused about an idea or about directions. GLD students especially must be able to act as their own advocate and be assertive at the appropriate times. When working collaboratively with other students, they need to feel capable of interacting and contributing to the group process. For excessively shy students, it probably is better to let them begin group work with a single non-threatening peer.

The GLD child has a wild pattern of strengths and weaknesses. It is a confusing and sometimes maddening combination, for the child as well as for parents and teachers. We speculate that the wild pattern itself is an unusual and enduring stressor that may trigger shyness in the GLD child. The teacher's role, indirectly, is to reduce the impact of such a stressor. As we have said, boosting successes—especially by building on the student's strengths—will help students' develop coping skills, enhance self-efficacy, and lessen timidity. Over the long run, tilting the balance of school experiences toward success will mean that there will be fewer failures for the student to explain.

Regardless of the motivational device, reducing failure should help students establish realistic and productive attributions. Remember, when students finish school, self-beliefs such as attributions and self-efficacy become tools for coping with the rest of life.

# Self-Regulated Learning & Memory

## Self-Regulated Learning and Memory

In Chapter 6, we discussed the paradox of short-term storage in memory: Although its capacity is tiny, it is the mental workhorse. In short-term memory, a person can reflect, evaluate, and plan. Of course, short-term and long-term memory constantly interact. Short-term memory continually retrieves information from long-term storage that is necessary for solving problems. Once solved, a problem's solution—and perhaps the procedure—may be translated into immediate performance or filed away for later reference.

In school, typical problems involve academic learning (i.e., how to store knowledge and skills in long-term memory, retrieve them at will, and sometimes synthesize them into new creations), and competent learners develop strategies for saving and locating information in their mental banks. Those strategies pay substantial dividends when they prompt ideas about how to make learning more efficient. But knowledge and use of strategies, at least initially, depends on awareness. The student must put the strategy in mental view, in short-term memory, and she must predict whether the strategy will work with a particular problem or if the strategy needs modification. While a problem is being tackled, the student must monitor progress to evaluate whether the strategy is

- obviously helping to make progress;

- helping a bit, but needs some revision;
- irrelevant to the problem and is wasting precious short-term memory resources; or
- actually worsening things.

Self-monitoring during problem solving is a difficult metacognitive activity because it happens simultaneously with other cognitive activities and therefore competes for the resources of a very limited short-term memory. Some have argued that this aspect of self-regulation is so demanding that it can rapidly deplete mental energy (Vohs & Heatherton, 2000), putting success farther from reach instead of closer. When a learner senses energy depletion, he or she often feels stress, which prompts even faster depletion. (One simple energy-saving device is to use an *external* monitoring device, such as the monitoring and recording form we show later in the chapter (see Figure 8.1).)

Though it is absolutely essential for effective self-regulation, young students and low achievers do little self-monitoring. Students who do not, or cannot, monitor their progress find themselves at dead ends, spinning their mental wheels, retrying approaches that have already failed, and failing to revise their goals. Later in this chapter, we offer some practical advice for helping students self-monitor.

## Academic Self-Regulation

Self-regulated learning behaviors involve three broad activities: strategy knowledge and selection, use, and self-monitoring (Borowski, Johnson, & Reid, 1987). First, a student must develop a variety of specific strategies for learning various content and skills and for demonstrating such learning. For competent learning and performance, strategies differ depending on the task, For example, taking a history test that requires comparing different concepts, forming a reasonable estimate about a long-division solution, studying for a multiple-choice test, or creating a short skit all require different strategies. Self-regulation demands that the learner make decisions about when and whether to apply a particular strategy and, once engaged, monitor the strategy's usefulness.

Second, the student must be able to use the strategies in various situations and environments. In other words, he must generalize and adapt the problem-solving skill to new areas. For example, having learned how to distinguish apparently similar ideas in geography, she might apply the strategy in an English class.

Third, the child needs a sense of capability—self-efficacy—in choosing and applying the strategies. While the first two areas involve knowledge and skill, self-efficacy deals with motivation. It is self-efficacy that helps transform knowledge and skill into action. Without a feeling of capability, students may acquire strategy knowledge, but it is likely to remain dormant until the student believes the strategy can result in some successful behavior.

When learners are convinced that effort at using a strategy will produce success, they are likely to construct a "cognitive simulation" of a learning activity (Bandura, 1989). Before the task itself, as part of the planning process, the learner will visualize herself using a strategy successfully. That mental rehearsal will help the learner apply the strategy when an actual problem appears. The more a student practices the strategy, in simulation and with actual tasks, the more she will believe that the strategy use is under personal control. Coupled with outcomes that are personally valued, a sense of personal control is a powerful steering wheel in school learning.

In summary, academic self-regulation is built on three requirements: using a repertoire of strategies, generalizing strategies to new activities, and feeling of self-efficacy. These requirements present a tall order for any student, especially when teachers expect students to pay attention to external advice. External advice is required, initially, to help implant self-regulation, but teachers—and parents—frequently forget that the eventual goal is *self*-regulation so that a person can be *self*-educated. The more an external environment prompts, cajoles, persuades, and assists, the less the student will practice internal direction. The external steering must fade away while the learner becomes more competent at driving her own learning (Farnham-Diggory, 1990).

These three broad requirements of self-regulated learning make it hard to succeed. Failure can occur when any of the three parts is deficient. The teacher's job is also more difficult as he must have a keen diagnostic sense about which area is faulty and skill at boosting the weak area. Teachers of learning-disabled youngsters must be especially patient. Although LD students can be deficient in any (or all) of the three areas, they are frequently weakest in the second and third areas—transferring a strategy to a new situation and self-efficacy about choosing and using effective strategies. Even when the task is highly similar to one in which the student first applied the strategy, the LD child often has difficulty understanding that he can reapply the strategy (Douglas, 1981; Gelzheiser, 1984). Transfer of skills is not impossible for the LD student; it just takes more practice and patience.

Strategy generalization is essential in reading, partly because most narrative passages are somewhat novel. Also, reading itself is a fundamental part of learning other content. For the skillful learner, reading becomes automatic after a time, and the brain can concentrate on the meanings of the printed material. But for the child with feeble reading strategies, the challenge has now doubled: The struggle of reading combined with uncertainty about dealing with new information will almost certainly overload short-term memory and create stress. The problem takes a different angle for certain students who have trouble monitoring comprehension during reading. The child may plod through page after page and be utterly baffled when, at the end of the assignment, nothing has been stored in long-term memory.

## Goal Orientations and Self-Regulation

In the past 15 years, there has been considerable study of student achievement goals (Dweck, 1986; Winne, 1995). The consensus is that there are two broad categories of goals (they almost seem like personality types) that students use. One form has been called *learning-* or *mastery-oriented*. Students who are learning-oriented are motivated to improve their skill or knowledge. It makes little difference that others outperform them on tests; they want to learn and understand more. Learning-oriented students believe that ability is not an inherited property, but is changeable: The more skillful they become, the more ability they have. It follows that they are likely to credit their successes to effort. These students find interesting content and activities motivating, and they are interested in challenging tasks.

The second form has been called *performance-* or *ego-oriented*. Performance-oriented students are interested in outshining others on projects, marks, and tests. What they learn is less important than appearing capable to others, or at least more capable than their peers. They tend to think of ability as a fixed trait and tend to attribute classroom successes to ability rather than effort. These students are not much interested in the challenge of new material, but they are willing to memorize isolated facts if it will help them score better on tests. When a whole classroom environment is performance-oriented, students with low academic self-efficacy are in big trouble. Because they tend to be toward the bottom of the performance pile, they will show increasing aversion to the learning material and will withdraw or make only feeble attempts at solving problems.

It does not take much insight to guess which sort of student is generally better at self-regulated learning. Research consistently shows that the learning-oriented student is better at goal setting, has stronger self-efficacy about learning, monitors the problem solving process more carefully, seeks out more challenging activities, and creates more useful internal feedback about progress (Meece, 1994; Winne, 2001). Although the deck looks stacked in favor of learning-oriented environments, we need to admit that no published research has examined what happens when classrooms contain a fair mixture of *both* learning- and performance-goal structures (Locke & Latham, 2002).

## What Teachers Can Do

### General Ideas

Teachers, you can imagine, are important in setting the stage for different goal orientations. A learning-oriented atmosphere is cultivated when teachers

- emphasize student progress and attribute progress to effort rather than ability;
- de-emphasize student competitions (which are likely to reward a handful of students (or a single one) at the expense of the "losers");
- model problem-solving approaches to challenging tasks;
- avoid public posting, comparisons, or remarks about student accomplishment;
- encourage student discovery of information and principals; and
- allow students considerable leeway in their choices.

In short, students may profit when teachers help them learn self-regulation strategies, but teachers can sharply undermine those skills if their classroom environments are performance-oriented. The teacher is the cultural director of the classroom and needs to be conscious of that role. When well-meaning teachers concentrate heavily on standardized test scores rather than creating self-educating students, the culture may evolve into a competitive, cutthroat atmosphere that offers limited benefits to only a precious few.

### Encouraging Self-Monitoring

Self-monitoring, we have suggested, is a fundamental aspect of self-regulated behavior. But adept self-monitoring is complex and takes practice, and it requires monitoring of the self-monitoring. Naïve self-monitors think that all they have to do is make sure a monitoring strategy gets used, but what they really need is to assess how *well* the strategy fits the task and works. For example, it is one thing to mindlessly fill out a project checklist and quite another to think critically about whether the checklist is enhancing one's learning and performance. Zooming through a checklist because the teacher requires it is not the same as creating a modified checklist that provides better cues for checking one's progress and understanding. The teacher can help by offering gentle reminders to naïve self-monitors to *think about why* they are learning self-monitoring skills and *what will be the result* if they do it well.

One simple suggestion to help students begin thinking about their learning process is to develop basic monitoring checklists and require students to use them. Figure 8.1 shows a worksheet for monitoring and recording reading comprehension. (A useful byproduct of such checklists is that, by virtue of their sequence and structure, they help students stay organized). Notice the prompt for the student to make a performance prediction (item 3) and the invitation to practice some self-evaluation (items y and z). Although monitoring by itself can elicit self-evaluation, there is good reason to make self-evaluation an obvious performance for students who are just learning to self-monitor. Even students who seem wise at self-monitoring may be surprised at what they discover when they do overt self-evaluation. Most students are vulnerable to the "planning fallacy" (Buehler, Griffin, & Ross, 1994). They grossly underestimate the time and effort required to master or complete a specified task. When students using the form in Figure 8.1 observe that their planning (item 3) was far too optimistic, they may begin to adopt more realistic goals for similar activities in the future.

---

**What Am I Understanding?**

Date:

1. Name of reading assignment:

2. Number of pages in the assignment:

3. How many minutes I think it will take for me to finish (including answering all these questions):

4. Clock time I began reading:

5. One-sentence summary for the first paragraph:

6. One-sentence summary for the next paragraph:

(Continue with as many paragraphs as are in the passage; with secondary students and longer assignments, it is probably better to write one-sentence summaries of each page rather than each paragraph.)

w. Clock time I finished reading:

x. Total minutes spent:

y. How many of those minutes I think I spent fooling around (not reading)?

z. How well do I understand the whole reading assignment?

---

**Figure 8.1.** Form for monitoring and recording reading comprehension.

Teachers can create other forms of self-recording worksheets, such as quality control checklists for complex and multi-faceted projects (Ley & Young, 2001) (which corporate and industrial sectors have used for decades).

## Helping Students Set Goals

Goals are central to self-regulated behavior for several reasons. First, they help direct the learner to focus on a task and avoid distractions. Second, they stimulate energy to get moving and keep moving toward the goal. Finally, carefully using goals often leads to insights about what works while progressing toward a goal: What self-regulating activities have helped me get where I wanted?

Although we have just asserted that goals are motivating, there are conditions attached. One of the important principals of social cognitive theory is that important personal goals are often too large and too distant to be meaningful motivators (Bandura, 1986). Important personal goals (getting a B for a semester grade, graduating in the top 10% of the class) are often so remote that more immediate goals that offer small but almost certain reinforcement (talking on the phone, watching television, playing video games) easily usurp them. One answer to this problem is to carve up long-term goals into a series of smaller subgoals. Four things result:

1. It is nearly impossible to visualize the long process of getting from where you are now to a distant goal. For example, if a long-range goal is to quit smoking, you would have to imagine all the possible smoking contexts and cues between now and, say, six weeks from now. The next step is to visualize yourself not lighting up in this situation and the next one, day after day. It is vastly easier to imagine yourself moving toward a proximate goal, such as avoiding a cigarette over the next hour.

2. Learners progress rapidly from small success to small success instead of waiting and waiting for the BIG ONE.

3. Because of more and faster success experiences, students' self-efficacy grows more quickly.

4. Students learn an important self-regulation skill—the task of splitting up large goals into sequenced small ones.

High achievers, who also tend to have high academic self-efficacy, may already be doing such goal splitting. They already know to set more challenging but realistic goals, whereas poor achievers are awful at goal setting. They seem to be clueless about the usefulness or purpose of goals in self-regulation, sometimes setting them impossibly high, sometimes foolishly low, and other times simply failing to set them at all.

Choice is also related to goal setting. Schunk (1985) found that learning-disabled sixth graders improved their math performance when they used short-term goals, and their performance improved even more when they had a say in goal setting. Participation in goal setting also seemed to enhance their self-efficacy about math skills. It is likely that when students select their own goals, they perceive them as more personally relevant and feel more committed to them than if they are handed down from the front of the classroom.

In a review of 35 years of research on goal setting, Locke and Latham (2002) restate a well-known finding: Challenging goals produce more intense effort and better performance up to the limits of the learner's ability. Challenge, of course, is in the eye of the beholder, and a student may or may not agree with what a teacher views as challenging. It is best, then, to let a student declare what he or she perceives as challenging. With low achievers or learning-disabled students, who may not be very adept at goal setting, teachers may have to gently nudge self-set goals into more realistic challenges.

Locke and Latham (2002) also reviewed the principal of goal specificity. Regardless of whether goals are self-set or announced by the teacher, specific goals are invariably more motivating than vague goals. It is easier to understand "Finish the four problems correctly on page 66" than to "Do your best." However, even vague goals produce better results than no goals.

## Promoting Imagery

For many years, sports psychologists have suggested that athletes mentally picture themselves succeeding at upcoming performances. The data are fairly clear that practicing such imagery can improve skill (Feltz & Landers, 1983; Orlick & Partington, 1986). Why should peering into these little mental windows be effective? There is good reason to think that it works because it strengthens self-efficacy. Conceiving a possible future in which you see yourself moving properly, swishing a free throw, or hitting the baseball solidly creates a personal vision of success. (Smart coaches and athletes also know the corollary: If you dwell on flubbed performances, efficacy beliefs will probably shrink.) Likewise, pulling off a great mental performance shortens the imagined distance to the goal. It shifts a distal goal to a proximal one. Imagery may also help a learner break a large performance into subparts, and thus subgoals, so that she can direct more attention to improving inept pieces of performance.

Mental simulations are not automatically and always a good thing. As we have implied, ruminating about a distressing performance will likely have negative effects. And creating implausible fantasies may be amusing, but they don't help create realistic appraisals about skill (Oettingen, 1995). The challenge is to imagine oneself doing *somewhat better* than a recent past performance.

So what does imagery have to do with the routines of learning and performing academic work? Recent studies (e.g., Pham & Taylor, 1999) show that students can learn to visualize themselves studying for an important exam that they would ace. In Pham and Taylor's study, they gave students some suggestions to visualize—imagine studying at their desks, reading lecture notes, turning the stereo down (or off), doing less chitchatting on the phone, etc. Then the students promised to spend five minutes each day before the exam visualizing an activity and keep a log of their mental simulations. Compared to a control group, the visualization group studied about 60% more days, 38% more hours, and improved their exam scores by 12%. A replication study showed similar, but smaller, benefits in favor of the visualization group.

## Encouraging Student Choice

Awareness and personal control of learning, the core of self-regulation, become vastly easier if a student desires the outcomes of learning and believes the learning is useful. In the end, self-regulation is about personal choice, having some say in

- whether to participate or not,
- how much energy and time to spend on an activity,
- which activities come first or last,
- which learning strategies to use,
- which environments aid learning, and
- which performances best display one's learning.

One option underused in many classrooms (and unacceptable in others) is to let students decide *where* to work on problems or projects. Except for collaborative work, students are usually expected to stick to their assigned seats. But if the assigned seats are surrounded by distractions, they may be some of the worst places for concentrated effort. Good self-regulators know where and when they can find distraction-free areas, and if it is allowed, they will rearrange that aspect of their learning environment (Ertmer & Newby, 1996). If not, the assigned seat becomes an extra and unnecessary barrier to effective self-regulation. Letting a student choose where to study or work delivers two additional benefits. First, it signals to students that they hold some responsibility and can participate in instructional decisions about themselves. Second, it requires students to identify potential distractions and consciously consider how they can minimize them to improve learning. Both of these outcomes are important contributors to self-regulation in the classroom.

Philosophically, all schooling concentrates on two things—teaching people to be independent learners and transmitting the values of the culture(s). Adults face daily demands to make meaningful choices, and schools should help students practice such choosing behaviors. What does it benefit students to be denied choices? Defenders of an autocratic teaching style argue that children and adolescents are not wise or mature enough to make intelligent choices for themselves. Our response is that prohibiting classroom choices creates persons unaccustomed to, and unskilled at, making decisions. Given new freedoms of choice (in college, or as young adults in the workforce), many people are sadly deficient in the wisdom to make useful choices because they have had so little practice at it.

We are not the first ones to make the observation about how important student choice is. Abundant evidence shows that allowing students opportunities to choose enhances their self-regulation, mastery orientation, academic self-efficacy, and attributions of success to effort (Meece, 1994; Zimmerman, 2000). Choice also improves the odds that students will perceive learning activities as relevant and meaningful and, thus, more enjoyable. To the extent the classroom atmosphere emphasizes competition for grades, rote memorization and rehearsal, individual rather than collaborative work, public evaluations and justifying lessons' relevance "because they are in the textbook," students will drift toward a performance goal orientation. They will be happy when they appear smart and miserable when they don't, uninterested in what they have been learning, and unable to self-regulate their learning.

Students who have not been properly guided in self-regulation strategies or who do not have choices about how to demonstrate their learning are likely to have trouble perceiving value in the usual classroom fare. Learning-disabled students, and gifted learning-disabled students in particular, may be the most at risk when choices are shut down. If they lack self-regulation skills and are compelled to perform (or compete) in an area of disability, they are likely to falter. The predictable outcomes are lowered self-efficacy and aversion to the subject matter. Given a choice in performance, the GLD student may not just succeed, but also improve self-efficacy, self-esteem, and interest in the subject area (Grolnick & Ryan, 1987; Meece, 1994).

It is a stiff challenge to the teacher to convert the entire curriculum into something tasty, especially when twenty-two classroom customers have different tastes! As we have suggested, the problem lessens when the teacher offers choices. Yes, it creates new demands on the teacher. She must be flexible enough to entertain the importance of student choices, creative and energetic enough to invent legitimate choices, and willing to struggle with how to fairly grade students who use different kinds of performances for the same instructional objective. Such efforts are by no means impossible. Carole Ames (1992) developed and tested an intervention for a comprehensive shift in classroom goal orientation. She used strategies that we stress throughout this book:

- offering students many opportunities for choice;
- praising and pushing individual improvement rather than outscoring others;
- minimizing public comparisons of student performances; and
- striving to make lessons and content meaningful.

As time went on, Ames found that the culture became less performance-oriented and more learning-oriented. Who seemed to profit the most? The lowest achievers, which likely included a number of gifted learning-disabled students.

What about students who already have good self-regulation skills? When educators teach and promote self-regulatory strategies for an entire class, won't this be old-hat and boring to kids who are self-starters? Interestingly, Young (1996) found that such whole-class instruction did not dampen those youngsters' productivity. Instead, as the classroom culture evolved to a learning-oriented structure, it reduced the achievement gap between the haves and the have-nots.*

Deficient self-regulation does not suddenly burst upon people in adulthood. We speculate that children learn poor self-control by default, partly because schools (and teachers) have not considered it part of their

---

*Intense study of student self-regulation and instructional contexts that teach and support self-regulation has translated into quite a few resources for the classroom teacher. For example, Dale Schunk and Barry Zimmerman (1998), two leading self-regulation researchers, have edited a volume packed with success stories about exemplary classroom practices. In addition to general ideas, many of Schunk and Zimmerman's examples are targeted at specific areas and specific students (e.g., writing, math, reading, secondary students). One chapter (Butler, 1998) focuses specifically on promoting self-regulation in learning-disabled students.

job to teach such skills. Many educators believe that self-regulation is simply part of the baggage students bring to the classroom. Some have it, others don't. We argue that helping students learn self-regulation skills is every bit as important as the usual goals mirrored in standardized achievement tests. Self-regulation helps students realize that if certain strategies work in one setting, then they might work in another. For example, if self-monitoring and recording is useful in memorizing Spanish vocabulary, then maybe it will work with nail biting or squabbling with Sis? In other words, schools can help students form a repertoire of self-regulation skills that they can transfer to the rest of life.

We wish to convey optimism about teaching and learning self-regulation. However, there are boundaries on what people can accomplish with self-regulation. Polivy and Herman (2002) discuss the astounding rate at which individuals with addictive habits fail to change. They observe that most people quit, relapse, quit, relapse, and keep on and on in the same unhappy cycle, victims of the "false hope syndrome." Brute persistence may be commendable in some aspects of life, but it is not much help in self-change attempts. People are often falsely optimistic, believing they can effect more change that is feasible and in shorter time than is required. They also tend to exaggerate the supposed benefits of the ultimate goal: "If I were thin (or didn't smoke, or weren't sex-addicted), I'd have a great social life, a better job, and strong self-esteem." It is also more ego-attractive to shrug off failure by attributing it to effort rather than ability, which implies that all I need to do to make something work is try a little harder next time. The answer to distorted self-assessments, Polivy and Herman say, is to distinguish between a difficult but possible goal and a virtually impossible one. Students, especially GLD students, are often confused about this distinction. Teachers must be sensitive to students creating unattainable goals. If they pursue such goals, they will fail as no amount of self-regulation in the world can overcome an utter lack of ability. Similarly, teachers should not plant false hope by promising that self-regulation will answer all of a student's academic problems. A happy medium may be to help a student downsize a project in scope or duration and apply self-regulated behaviors that offer more promise of success. Succeeding on a modest but still challenging project is a better outcome than failing on a big one.

### Case Studies

Returning to Louis, Mike, and Debra, let's examine how their teachers dealt with the needs of these GLD student to help them use self-regulated behaviors successfully.

### <u>Louis</u>

Louis, the young storyteller introduced in Chapter 5, was willing to expend effort on learning his story. His ability to attend to the task at hand and take responsibility for his own success was evident. In addition, Louis used a variety of self-regulating behaviors en route to success. Table 8.1 lists the personal adaptations of the self-regulation strategies Louis used to complete the project.

Interestingly, the strategies involved in Louis' accomplishment were the very learning skills that GLD students struggle with in school. An important lesson to learn, then, is that teachers may need to convince students that they know at least some of the strategies they need to use, that they can use them properly, and that they are capable of applying them to new learning situations.

### <u>Mike</u>

Mike (also introduced in Chapter 5) designed an explorer vehicle for Mars for his enrichment class. Table 8.2 summarizes the self-regulatory behaviors Mike employed in the pursuit of his goal.

| Table 8.1. Louis' Application of Self-Regulation Strategies | |
| --- | --- |
| **Self-Regulation Strategies** | **Personal Applications** |
| Memorizing sequence and details of the story | Using visual mapping to recall story details<br>Using body movements as kinesthetic cues to link story evens |
| Rehearsing and overlearning | Having high self-set standards for performance<br>Practicing well beyond initial point of mastery |
| Focusing attention | Applying specific tips to avoid distractions, such as focusing on the tops of people's heads while speaking |
| Using feedback during rehearsal | Gauging fit between ongoing speaking performance and goals.<br>Locating rough spots in performance<br>Soliciting and listening to advice<br>Transforming advice into performance |

After Mike finished his project, he discussed with his mentor how he was able to accomplish his goal. Together they devised ways in which Mike could use similar strategies to be more successful in the required school curriculum. Mike thought about picturing projects and concepts in his mind as the teacher described them. Perhaps instead of initially taking notes, he could tape the teacher's lecture and sketch out the ideas in storyboard fashion. Another idea was to see a movie about the topic before it was discussed or even visit a museum or historical site related to the topic under discussion. Mike remembered how his parents had taken him to Gettysburg the summer before and how that visit had made the concepts and details in the unit on the Civil War much easier to grasp and remember. Mike realized that when he had the goal clearly pictured in his mind, many of the details would fall into place naturally. It was like first imagining a picture of an event with details missing. Reading the assignment and listening to the lecture then filled in the missing pieces.

### Debra

Recall Debra, our young historian described in Chapter 1. Early in the GLD program she attended, the class explored several self-regulation strategies such as mapping, visual exposure, and choice. She applied these strategies as she conducted her research study. Debra used mapping to organize her ideas (strategy for organization: visual mapping), she visited the Noah Webster House several times to remember details (strategy for memorizing details: repeated oral and visual exposure), and she chose

| Table 8.2. Mike's Application of Self-Regulation Strategies | |
|---|---|
| **Self-Regulation Strategies** | **Personal Applications** |
| Understanding what is required in the problem | Reading the material for specific details<br>Creating a visual image of what the vehicle looks like |
| Goal setting | Sketching out the model |
| Planning steps | Listing materials needed<br>Setting due date<br>Establishing a visual time line that lists the steps and estimated target dates |
| Seeking feedback | Asking his dad for advice before initiating a plan |
| Allocating time | Setting aside activities not absolutely necessary until project is done |

to assume the role of Jerusha Webster and to portray her life in a slide and tape presentation (strategy for communication: using her talent in dramatic expression). Finally, she asked if she could practice her narrative at home where there would be fewer distractions and where she could rehearse until she was pleased with her effort (strategy for focusing attention: finding an environment where there were fewer distractions).

———

These three scenarios show how enrichment activities can help students identify self-regulating behaviors that they employ naturally when they are achieving in an area of strength and interest. However, because school life requires sustained effort and the application of self-regulatory behaviors on far less exciting tasks, we must teach GLD students how to apply their brand of self-regulatory behaviors to the usual classroom fare such as studying for a test or memorizing the Periodic Chart. In Chapter 12, we discuss how to use self-regulation strategies with more typical curriculum requirements.

# Part III

# Developing Individual Educational Programs for Gifted Students with Learning Disabilities

Developing an Individual Educational Program (IEP) for gifted students with learning disabilities presents unique issues. Traditional IEPs focus on the disability only, but failing to consider a student's gifts seriously compromises any program designed for these youngsters. To attend effectively to the gifted, learning-disabled profile, educational programming must address a number of different components, including the identification system, attention to the student's gifts, the environments in which the student is placed, classroom intervention strategies, and social and emotional support (see Table 9.1). Selective attention to only some of these elements undermines the effectiveness of programs designed to nurture individual development of gifted students with disabilities.

## An Appropriate Identification System

The first component in developing an effective IEP is appropriate diagnosis. Accurately diagnosing Alphabet Children, especially gifted learning-disabled students, is a tremendous challenge. Although the Individuals with Disabilities Act (IDEA) does not specifically address the identification of gifted students, it does argue for a free appropriate public education for all students and includes a mandate to identify students with disabilities. This mandate includes gifted students with disabilities. Unfortunately, school philosophy and policy concerning identification

| Table 9.1. Essential Components of Comprehensive Programming for Gifted Students with Learning or Attention Difficulties |
| --- |
| 1. An appropriate identification system |
|        Identification of giftedness |
|        Evidence and description of academic performance discrepancies |
| 2. Attention to the student's gifts |
| 3. Placement in, and assurance of, the least restrictive supportive environment(s) |
|        Physical |
|        Intellectual |
|        Social and emotional |
| 4. Classroom intervention strategies |
|        Alternate approaches to curriculum and instruction |
|        Accommodations and modifications |
|        Self-regulation and compensation strategies |
|        Remedial support |
| 5. Social and emotional support |
|        Role of counselor |
|        Role of parents |
|        Self-advocacy |

and entitlement to specialized educational services can contribute to under-identification and inappropriate programming for these youngsters. Given that gifted learning-disabled students do not necessarily perform below grade level, the usual discrepancy analysis procedures can obscure identification. For GLD students, the discrepancy should be based on their potential compared to their classroom performance. Assessment should take into consideration the time these youngsters require to complete routine tasks, the support needed from others to complete each task, and the student' predicted achievement levels based on measures of potential.

Conservative and rigid identification procedures make identifying a learning-disabled student's abilities and gifts more difficult. Identification of student's gifts should be based neither on usual classroom performance nor on total test scores in achievement or intelligence. Rather, to identify students' gifts, schools should analyze individual subtest scores and patterns on tests of intelligence in addition to student products, auditions, interviews and other authentic assessments of talent within specific domains. Chapter 10 elaborates on identification issues and practical strategies for identification.

## Attention to Students' Gifts

An extremely important, yet often overlooked component of a GLD student's IEP is the student's gift. GLD students require opportunities to display and develop specific gifts or talents. Historically, remediation of basic skills has been the single-minded focus of efforts to serve students once they have been classified as learning disabled. Few opportunities exist in which bright LD students can demonstrate gifted behaviors. In our experience working with these students, ignoring these students' gifts thwarts their ability to overcome learning challenges. Once their talent or gift is identified and nurtured, these students often show dramatic improvements in self-regulation, perceptions of their ability, and academic achievement. For example, one fourth grade GLD student gained four years in reading achievement during the single year he participated in a special enrichment program for LD/GT. Another young man discovered how to compensate for his weaknesses while participating in a special program for gifted underachievers. This program used creative production as an intervention for bright students who were not producing in school. His delight at his finished product renewed his feelings of self-worth. With positive perceptions of his ability, he recommitted himself to his education. In fact, he advocated for more support in math so he could bring up his grades (Baum, Renzulli, & Hébert, 1995).

Helping students develop their gifts has many advantages. Perhaps the most important is the students' need to find a niche so that they can lead productive and rich lives. Recent views on personal attributes that promote well-being and satisfaction with life suggest that the happiest people make life and career decisions that align with their individual strengths, interests, and passions (Gardner, 1999; Goleman, 1995; Sternberg, 1996). If no one brings attention to the development of budding talents, many GLD students will remain unaware of their gifts and their novice talents may never develop, leaving them ill-prepared to compete successfully in life.

Consider the case of Samantha Abeel, a published poet at the age of 15. Her collaboration with a local artist resulted in an award-winning publication, *Reach for the Moon* (Abeel & Murphy, 2001). If her mother had not insisted on developing Samantha's writing talent in addition to making sure she received remedial help in mathematics, she would have lacked the credentials to enter the college of her choice.

### Samantha's Story*

"It started with a dead fish," explains Elizabeth Abeel, Samantha's mom. "While walking the beach one fall day, I turned to see my twenty-two month old daughter, Samantha, carefully studying the rotting remains of a salmon. When I went back to urge her on, she looked up at me and asked, 'Is this what is going to happen to us?'"

Later, when she was four, she surprised her family while traveling together on a trip when Samantha recited an hour-long cassette story tape of Star Wars. She repeated the whole tale verbatim including tonal inflections. Her mom thought that these episodes boded well for Samantha's success in school. However, when she began school, the happy, bright youngster came home frightened and sad. During second grade, her teacher began to voice concern with her Samantha's progress in math and asked if her parents could provide some extra help at home: "I will never forget that night in February. A simple flash card, 5 − 3 = 2, changed our lives. My bright and verbally agile daughter had no idea of 5, of 3, of 2. As a result of my frustration to 'make her see,' we were both in tears."

It took until seventh grade before the school was willing to identify Samantha's math disability and provide her services. By this time, she had a pronounced difficulty in telling time, counting money, and with language arts skills such as spelling and punctuation. She was under severe stress. There were many trips to the doctor for stomach aches; panic and anxiety attacks began to surface. While all breathed a sigh of relief that Samantha was finally getting the support she needed in math, no one had been focusing on her gift.

That same year her seventh grade language arts teacher recognized her

---

* Quotes from Elizabeth Abeel excerpted from Abeel, S. & Murphy, C. (1993). *What once was white.* Travers City, MI: Hidden Bay Publishing.

gift in writing and provided accommodations to help her be successful. Her teacher describes what happened next.

"Slowly her confidence grew and she bloomed. At the end of her seventh grade year we didn't want to lose the momentum we had. I was getting the message from her mother that writing was Samantha's lifeline. That is when the idea of a summer spent writing was born. Her mother called me one day with a proposal. Would I be willing to give her writing lessons? Her logic was that if Samantha were interested in piano she would encourage piano lessons. The confidence she had built through her writing during her seventh grade year needed to be sustained."

Her mother and teacher thought a collaboration with a local artist would give Samantha a structure and purpose for her writing. Her teacher explained, "Charles Murphy was eager to encourage Samantha because he felt an empathy with her. He knew what it was like to be different, what it was like to be constantly discouraged. As a high school student, he had been denied art classes because he was on the college preparatory track. He had also been discouraged from pursuing an art career because the chances for successfully earning a living were so minimal. Thankfully he followed what he knew was right for him; he pursued what he did well. Art was the key that unlocked the door."

Samantha's teacher felt that Samantha's gift for imagery-rich writing was perfect for writing poetry. The actual painting or slides of Murphy's work for inspiration, Samantha's words poured forth. Poetry was finally the creative outlet she needed to freely express what had been locked inside.

Samantha continued to make gains in math but not enough to pass the state math test required for graduation. However, her published book of poetry was the credential she needed to be admitted into a college well-known for its writing programs.

———

In addition, activities that focus on talent development are intrinsically motivating. When purposeful and challenging talent development activities fit with the students' cognitive strengths and learning styles, the students are more likely to succeed. And because talent development allows students to pursue self-determined goals, they are more receptive to strategies that will help them compensate for problematic weaknesses. In short, when they are motivated to accomplish a goal, GLD youngsters learn how to succeed in spite of their disabilities. Their achievements are substantial, and they begin to feel smart. These experiences lead to improved academic self-efficacy and a positive identity (see Figure 9.1 below), and their positive perceptions of ability encourage GLD students to put forth increased effort to overcome their problematic difficulties.

Focusing on GLD students' strengths also allows professionals and parents to observe students at their personal best. Too often educators base recommendations on what the students cannot do, not what they can do. Snapshots of students' achievements reveal more useful and relevant information about how students learn than their failures. In these situations, students are self-regulated, on task, and performing at high levels. These observations uncover elements, both cognitive and environmental, that are vital to achievement and can be applied to other aspects of the students' academic pursuits. We discuss this topic further in Chapter 11.

---

Wings Mentor Program

- Spellbound by their guest speaker, the 2nd graders asked Sarah, a 5th grade expert on whales, to return and teach them again.
- Matt's mother and teachers could not believe that this was their shy fourth grader who was delivering an outstanding presentation on math concepts such as exponents, algebra, and square roots.
- With tears in his eyes, Jackie's dad confided that this mentorship experience in horses was the most wonderful thing in the world for his third grade daughter.

Programs that pay tribute to students' special gifts, interests, and talents can be fundamental in helping students with disabilities find success. All three of these youngsters are bright students with learning disabilities who participated in a special mentorship program designed to nurture their talents and interests. All three were experiencing low self-efficacy and meager self-esteem and were not happy or motivated in school. This special mentorship experience, however, transformed them into confident young learners.

The Wings Mentor Program, designed for gifted and underachieving or learning-disabled students, is coordinated by the Division of Accelerated and Enriched Instruction in Montgomery County, Maryland Public Schools. It offers a profound experience to bright students who find it difficult and frustrating to have learning problems that interfere with their success in the regular classroom. Through a special one-to-one relationship, mentors assist students pursue an exciting topic while helping them develop skills necessary to succeed in school. (Baum, 2001)

---

**Figure 9.1.** Talent development program for gifted students with learning disabilities.

## Placement In and Assurance of the Least Restrictive Supportive Environment(s)

To establish a setting that offers the GLD student her finest chance for success, you must consider various factors, including the severity of the disability, the nature of the gift, and the age of the student. According to Maslow's (1962) hierarchy of needs, individuals must feel they belong and are valued in order to reach their potential. GLD students are no different. But they often feel like second-class citizens in school because what is rewarded most are the very tasks they find difficult. They view their successes as minimal because either they are taking advantage of accommodations or the teacher has watered down the curriculum in an attempt to meet their disability needs.

However, if teachers considered their talent to troubleshoot computer software, create a winning science fair project, or build a three-dimensional model of working gears as worthy as a well-written report or term paper, these bright but challenged students might feel more like contributing members of their classroom community. GLD students claim they can be themselves in the resource room or a talent development program. In both settings, they receive the assistance or challenge they need and are able to associate with like-minded peers.

These students can succeed in the regular classroom, especially if educators provide opportunities for talent development as well as resource room support. The regular classroom environment coupled with time in the resource room for academic support and time in a talent development program to nurture gifts can work effectively for many of these students, especially if the learning environments value individual differences.

In addition, teachers who adopt a multiple intelligences approach and provide options for learning and communicating knowledge provide appropriate settings for gifted, learning-disabled students.

However, if these GLD students' reading levels are considerably below grade level and their ability to write is greatly impaired, or if the attention problems demand settings with fewer students, success in the regular classroom is doubtful, especially as the students get older and reading and writing dominate the academic setting. Particularly problematic is that these students are sensitive about their disabilities and prefer to hide their differences. They may be unwilling to accept a particular accommodation if they feel it makes them look stupid or disabled in the eyes of their peers. One bright high school student explained, "I dread walking into the classroom to get my test so that I can complete it in the resource room. I wish the teacher would just give the test to my resource room teacher so no attention would be drawn to me."

If these gifted youngsters are considerably brighter than most of the students in the class, they will also have trouble. Under these conditions, behavior problems may arise, as in the case of Blaine (see Chapter 4), where more time in a program for highly able students would have made a difference. Schools that create individualized programs serve these students well. In Blaine's case, his private school accelerated him two grade levels in math. He spent the rest of his day with his age mates where the teacher made accommodations for everyone as needed. She provided a comfortable chair with a reading lamp for those students who found reading under fluorescent lighting difficult and created several "offices" within the classroom, complete with computers, that students could use if they needed a more quiet setting for learning.

Some students simply need smaller class sizes where they are more comfortable asking questions and actively engaging in the curriculum. Others may elect to take on-line courses where the challenge, pace and, environment can easily be controlled. Several districts have self-contained programs for gifted students with severe disabilities, and private schools for GLD students may offer unique programs that nurture the students' gifts and provide appropriate instruction and compensation techniques (see Chapter 11).

## Classroom Intervention Strategies

How do teachers develop educational experiences that respect the abilities of Alphabet Children while helping them overcome their learning problems? To address this fourth component of IEPs, teachers must acknowledge and understand the duality of the GLD students needs, find appropriate curriculum and instructional strategies to accommodate these needs, and develop problem-based or contextual curricula that allow students to express individual talents and interests.

Gifted students with learning or attention deficits have learning needs that resemble those of students who are gifted and those who have learning difficulties. Therefore, teachers must dually differentiate curriculum and instruction for them (Baum, Cooper, & Neu, 2001). Well documented in the literature, characteristics of gifted students include a propensity for advanced-level content, a desire to create original products, a facility with and enjoyment of abstract concepts, creative learning styles, and task commitment in areas of their talent and interest (Renzulli, 1978; Tannenbaum, 1983; VanTassel-Baska, 1992; Whitmore, 1980). Gifted students also identify with others of similar talents and interests, and they possess a heightened sensitivity to their own failures.

The deficits that typically impair the learning-disabled student's school performance frequently offset or complicate the strength of these characteristics. Of these deficits, the most commonly reported problems are limited reading skills, poor spelling and handwriting, difficulties with expressive language, and lack of organizational skills. In addition to these problems, LD students often show an inability to sustain focus, inept social interaction, low self-efficacy, and poor self-esteem (Baum & Owen, 1988). Because GLD students frequently display both sets of characteristics, accommodations that work well with average-ability, learning-disabled students might backfire. Likewise, offering exactly the same provisions to gifted, learning-disabled students that gifted students receive without considering the learning disability may overwhelm GLD students. Table 9.2 lists these contradictory characteristics and sample accommodations that take into consideration both sides of the equation: gifts and learning disabilities (Baum, Cooper, & Neu, 2001).

Gifted, learning-disabled students respond well to contextually-based learning—authentic learning within a discipline taught within a meaningful context. Providing accommodations such as more time on tests and use of technology can greatly increase the students' prospects for high achievement. Equally important are appropriate remedial support and compensation strategies. While a teacher provides accommodations to help students circumvent their lack of reading ability in the classroom, someone must help these students learn how to read and write. Educators also need to help students develop self-regulatory skills that assist them in compensating for problematic weaknesses. Coordinating these needs demands close collaboration among teachers, learning specialists, and the students themselves. Gifted, learning-disabled students must become aware of how they learn best so that they can design effective personal

| Table 9.2. Fundamentals of the Dually Differentiated Curriculum | | |
|---|---|---|
| Characteristics of Gifted Students | Problems Associated with Special Needs Students | Curricular Accommodations |
| Propensity for advanced-level content to accommodate the gift or talent | Limited skills in reading and math | Alternate means to access information |
| Producers of new knowledge through authentic products | Difficulty with spelling and handwriting | Alternate ways to express ideas and create products |
| Facility with and enjoyment of abstract concepts | Language deficits in verbal communication and conceptualization | Visual and kinesthetic experiences to convey abstract ideas concretely |
| Creative learning style | Poor organization | Visual organization schemes, e.g., timelines, flow charts, webbing |
| Need for intellectual challenges based on individual talents and interests | Problems with sustaining attention | Interest-based authentic curriculum |
| Need to identify with others of similar talents and interests | Inappropriate social interactions | Opportunity to identify with others of like talents |
| Heightened sensitivity to failure | Low self-efficacy and poor self-esteem | Recognition for accomplishment |

compensation strategies and succeed as life-long learners. Educators can teach these strategies in the learning resource center and weave them into the practices and procedures in the classroom. (We explore these ideas in greater depth in Chapters 11 and 12.)

## Social and Emotional Support

The fifth component of an IEP for gifted, learning-disabled students focuses on the social and emotional support necessary to help them cope with their strange mix of abilities and disabilities. Because of histories of failure, many LD students lose their confidence in their ability to succeed, and their academic self-efficacy continues to diminish over time. The situation seems even more precarious for gifted LD students. These students often have a heightened sensitivity to failure and are troubled by the vast discrepancy between what they can and cannot do. They may suffer, like Neil (see Chapter 1), from depression and a feeling of hopelessness. One GLD high school youngster, having a particularly tough time in school announced on her birthday that it should be her death day.

Group counseling with gifted learning-disabled students can be helpful. Encouraging students to discuss their concerns within the safety of a group of students with similar problems provides social and emotional security. During these sessions, students must acquire and rehearse skills that enable them to be their own advocates. Topics for such groups might include self discovery, stress and time management, communication skills, perils of perfectionism, and self-advocacy. (For a more detailed discussion on group sessions, see Chapter 13.)

Once parents believe that their child's needs are being addressed in the school, they need to focus on their child's gift, as we saw in the case of Samantha. They should seek family counseling if the student is becoming depressed and if group dynamics of the family are increasingly tense because of the issues surrounding their twice exceptional youngster.

With the appropriate support, GLD students can develop a good sense of who they are and how to advocate for what they need to be successful. As they mature, they need an increasing sense of self-responsibility to help them take charge of their lives. The last stanza of Samantha's poem "Self Portrait" (Abeel & Murphy, 2001) signals that she gained this understanding:

> Now I've written out their shadows
> like the wind collects its secrets
> to whisper into receptive ears, and I
> will leave them at your doorstep,
> a reminder of what others cannot see,
> a reminder of what I can and cannot be.

## Conclusion

When an individual educational program (IEP) addresses the full range of GLD students' needs (all five components), the chances for success greatly increase. As we saw in the case of Samantha, when the needs of her gifts and disabilities were met, her confidence grew and she became a self-assured young woman. As her teacher explained, " . . . the Samantha who sits in my ninth grade classroom is a much stronger, confident person than the girl I saw the first day two years ago. Because she has been given appropriate remediation in her problem areas and encouraged in her strengths, she has the self-confidence to confront her weaknesses" (Abeel & Murphy, 1993).

The August 2000 issue of the *IEP Team Trainer* newsletter includes a training session entitled "How to Ensure a FAPE [free appropriate public education] for Gifted students with Disabilities." The excerpt in Figure 9.3 provides a sample of the language you can use in writing an IEP for twice exceptional students.

---

### Sample Language for IEPs for Gifted Students with Disabilities

The following examples, taken from "How to Ensure a FAPE for Gifted Students with Disabilities" (*IEP Team Trainer*, 2000), present the kind of language that addresses identification of giftedness, academic performance, and placement when writing and IEP.

IDENTIFICATION OF GIFTEDNESS
Austin has been identified as a gifted student in accordance with district policy. On his evaluation he scored 130 on the performance scale of the Wechsler Intelligence Scale for Children and 90 on the verbal scale. He also possesses special talent in music and art, as demonstrated by his work portfolio.

ACADEMIC PERFORMANCE
For the past six months, Austin's academic performance has fallen below his aptitude. Austin's ADHD and other learning disabilities make it difficult for him to progress in a regular ed classroom. He has difficulty sitting for long periods of time in a regular ed classroom, has difficulty getting along with other students in the class, and has manifested disruptive tendencies.

PLACEMENT AND SUPPORTIVE ENVIRONMENT
Austin will be placed in the gifted program for three morning s a week. The rest of the week he will be placed in a sixth-grade classroom, with accelerated work in math, science, and computer science. Austin will also participate in physical education and will receive extra instruction in art and music.

ACCOMMODATIONS AND MODIFICATIONS
As an accommodation to Austin's disability, the teacher will permit him to take breaks as needed during class.

---

**Figure 9.3.** Sample language for an IEP for gifted student with ADHD. (IEP Team Trainer, 2000)

# Chapter 10

# Identification

This chapter presents a variety of strategies helpful in identifying GLD students. Because the definitions in both domains—gifted and learning disabled—are inconsistent in the literature, this task may at first glance appear complex and tedious at best. However, we will aim to consider procedures that simplify the identification process in a meaningful way.

Putting it simply, identifying gifted, learning-disabled students requires evidence of a specific learning disability on the one hand and potential for giftedness on the other. The sequence of the identification process usually depends on which characteristics are most apparent (see Chapter 3). However, no matter which exceptionality becomes the primary diagnosis, it is essential not to ignore behaviors that may indicate the other exceptionality. It is also important to look more deeply into other diagnoses associated with gifted students at risk to make sure that behaviors resembling other syndromes (such as ADHD or Oppositional Defiant Disorder) are not the result of an undiagnosed learning disability or lack of attention to the child's gifts or creativity.

Because much has already been written on identifying learning disabilities and we are not challenging or altering procedures that are already widely used, we will simply summarize them and identify key issues that obscure the identification of learning disabilities when a student is gifted. However, teachers who can easily detect when children are not achieving or when they are experiencing difficulty in learning (even though the underlying causes of poor achievement may be not so obvious) may be totally unaware of gifts in children who cannot read, write, compute or attend to classroom tasks. Therefore, while we will present general guidelines for identifying learning disabilities, we will focus most on the issues surrounding identifying giftedness.

## Procedures for Identifying a Specific Learning Disability

Informal identification begins when parents or teachers suspect that a student is having difficulty in the learning process. A referral initiates formal assessment procedures, which involves collecting systematic, and possibly standardized, information to help make decisions. Professionals use both formal testing and observational data documented in three areas of performance:

1. Discrepancy between intellectual potential and academic performance
2. Psychological processing difficulties
3. Inappropriate learning behaviors

## Documentation of a Severe Discrepancy

Universally, learning disabilities represent a gap between a student's current achievement and what he or she is expected to accomplish based on intellectual abilities or IQ. Because the term *discrepancy* is somewhat vague, some states have tried to sharpen its meaning by creating formulas to indicate the degree of severity. Connecticut Guidelines (1999) recommends a discrepancy score of 1.6 between ability and achievement accompanied by evidence of a processing disorder. A Hartford youngster with an IQ of 130 and a standardized math achievement score at the fiftieth percentile presents this discrepancy. His achievement percentile in math would be the equivalent of an IQ of 100. The 30 point difference between ability and achievement (130 minus 100) translates into a discrepancy score of 2.0. (The standard deviation on most IQ tests is 15 points, and the 30-point discrepancy represents two standard deviations.) Therefore, the child would meet the first criterion on the basis of the discrepancy score. Table 10.1 lists the individual intelligence tests and achievement tests most frequently used to assess cognitive ability and academic achievement levels.

Currently, however, teams of professionals are considering eliminating discrepancy formula for diagnostic purposes. As described in the 1999 version of the Connecticut *Guidelines for Identifying Children with Learning Disabilities*, the discrepancy formula has not proven to be the final word in identification procedures and has been widely criticized for a variety of reasons (Shaw, Cullen, McGuire, & Brinckerhoff, 1995). Some of the problems stem from inconsistency across districts and states on the meaning and measurement of "severe discrepancy." In addition, calculations of the discrepancy can also complicate diagnosis because scores and standard deviations on different tests are not comparable.

In fact, as this book goes to print, Congress is reauthorizing the federal legislation, IDEA, which will no longer require documentation of a discrepancy between a student's ability and achievement to identify the student for services. Instead the law will insist on early intervention procedures to reverse the pattern of underachievement even before a formal diagnosis is made. In other words, schools will be asked to use the best methods within the classroom, including technology and alternative instructional strategies, to see if classroom modifications can alleviate or

| Table 10.1. Tests Typically Used to Assess Learning Disabilities | | |
|---|---|---|
| **Intellectual Functioning** | **Academic Achievement** | **Psychological Processing** |
| Wechsler Intelligence Scale for Children-III (Wechsler, 1991) | Peabody Individual Achievement (Math, Reading, Recognition, Reading Comprehension, Spelling and General Information) (Markwardt, 1989) | Motor-Free Visual Perception Test (Colarusso & Hammill, 1972) |
| | Wide Range Achievement Test (Jastak & Wilkinson, 1989) | Auditory Discrimination Test (Webman, 1975) |
| | Brigance (Inventory of Basic Skills) (Brigance, 1990) | Auditory Skills Test Battery (Goldman, Fristoe, & Woodcock, 1976) |
| | Key Math (Connolly, 1988) | Detroit Tests of Learning Aptitude (2) (Hammil, 1985) |
| | Durrell Reading Test (Durrell & Catterson, 1980) | |
| | Slosson Reading (Slosson & Richardson, 1990) | |

minimize the learning difficulties.

This approach to identification and the elimination of the discrepancy documentation may be both a blessing and an obstacle in identifying and meeting the needs of students who are gifted and learning disabled. The positive aspect of eliminating the discrepancy documentation is that students can receive support without an official diagnosis of a learning disability. Because these students often use their high levels of intelligence to compensate for problematic weaknesses, a severe discrepancy may not appear until very late in a school career. Likewise, if parents spend an enormous amount of time supporting their youngsters so that they succeed as best they can in school, the discrepancy can remain under cover until middle or high school when the school curriculum may become too much for parents to keep up with. By that time, students may already feel like failures and often have problems with self-efficacy, esteem, and behavior. Early intervention without the diagnosis may ease this situation.

On the other hand, for the same reasons as stated above, classroom teachers who are unaware of the nature of the needs of gifted students may not recognize early signs of difficulty and ignore both the student's gift and subtle disability. If the problem is identified, early intervention will most likely focus on remediation only. The implications of these policies are yet unknown, especially for identifying and meeting the needs of Alphabet Children.

To assure that students receive the support they require, we recommend identifying discrepancies informally (without a specific formula) in performance. Noting these patterns will provide valuable information about how the student learns and where he or she requires support. We recommend examining discrepancies *among* subtest scores on the WISC, especially when considering patterns of scores and the discrepancy among the different patterns (see Chapter 5). Understanding the patterns reveals information about how a particular child learns and what his or her strengths and challenge areas are.

Another area where student performance represents a discrepancy is when the student achieves at grade level, but estimates of his or her ability predict superior performance. This underachievement could be due to a subtle learning disability. In addition, evaluating the amount of time and assistance a students needs to complete assignments can reveal evidence about how this youngster learns compared to other students with high abilities. Gifted students with learning disabilities may take more time to complete tasks or receive extra support (e.g., from parents) when compared to their non-disabled intellectual peers.

## Evaluating Psychological Processing Difficulties

Definitions of learning disabilities strongly imply that discrepancies between potential and performance are due to problems in how students perceive or process information. Tests, as usual, provide information on such neuro-psychological processes. Predictably, some critics have expressed concern with the reliability and validity of these measures (Shaw et al., 1995). They argue that some of the tests purported to measure a process such as visual perception may instead measure other related processes, such as visual memory and visual motor integration. A stronger approach involves looking at learning in terms of an information processing model and examining executive functioning (Denckla, 1989; Hammill & Bartel, 1996).

## Learning Behavior Assessment

Historically, behavioral characteristics have been important in distinguishing LD students from non-LD students. Typical characteristics cited in the literature include hyperactivity, mood shifts, general coordination deficits, impulsiveness, short attention span, acting-out or withdrawn behavior, and distractibility. Although some norm-referenced behavioral scales are available to document these characteristics, we think that informal techniques are more informative and practical. Anecdotal observations, teacher-rating scales, and samples of students' work give important information about students' learning behaviors. Observing the student in the classroom and at home can reveal evidence about how this youngster learns compared with other students with high abilities. When using informal observation and anecdotal information, it is important to note the frequency and magnitude of the behavior, whether it corroborates test information, and, most importantly, whether the behavior interferes with the student's classroom performance. In addition, recording the amount of time and assistance a student needs to accomplish assignments is essential.

Many states will not consider a learning problem unless achievement is at least one year below grade level. For very bright children who are

---

### Connecticut State Guidelines

Large differences between ability and achievement scores commonly occur for students in the above average range. Therefore when identifying a severe discrepancy, the team should assure that the statistical data used to determined a severe discrepancy have been adjusted for regression to the mean and measurement error. . . . If a student who is functioning at or above grade level meets the criteria for having a learning disability, the next critical question is whether the student needs special education and related services.

The following issues should be considered when making this determination:

- For some students of high ability who have a learning disability, the severity of the discrepancy may be corrected through regular education accommodations or services; and
- Some students of high ability who have a learning disability may be spending extraordinary amounts of time and effort or may be receiving substantial in and out of school assistance, to achieve success in the classroom. For such students special education services may be appropriate.

---

**Figure 10.1.** Connecticut State Guidelines (1999, p. 28) for service eligibility.

having learning problems, this stance can create a major problem. Often such children are performing at grade level when estimates of their ability predict superior performance, and this underachievement could be due to a subtle learning disability. However, the state will probably ignore this discrepancy because the student is achieving at grade level and, thus, is ineligible for supportive services.

Professionals working with bright students must ignore such policies when considering appropriate programs for gifted but disabled students, as they are not in compliance with current law as stated by 1997 version of IDEA. IDEA allows districts to consider discrepancies in terms of the level at which the child is predicted to perform based on his or her *ability* rather than in terms of grade level performance. In other words, a learning disability can be argued if "the child does not achieve commensurate with his or her age and *ability* levels in one or more of the areas" (CT State Dept. of Education, 1999 p. 4). If a child is gifted and has the potential for performing above grade level but is struggling to stay at grade level, he or she can be diagnosed as having a specific learning disability.

The Connecticut State Guidelines (1999) state specific eligibility considerations for students with high ability. These guidelines (see Figure 10.1) can serve as a model in developing local policy involving gifted students with disabilities. In addition, a flow chart (see Figure 10.2) offered by the Connecticut Guidelines outlines procedure for identifying a learning dis-

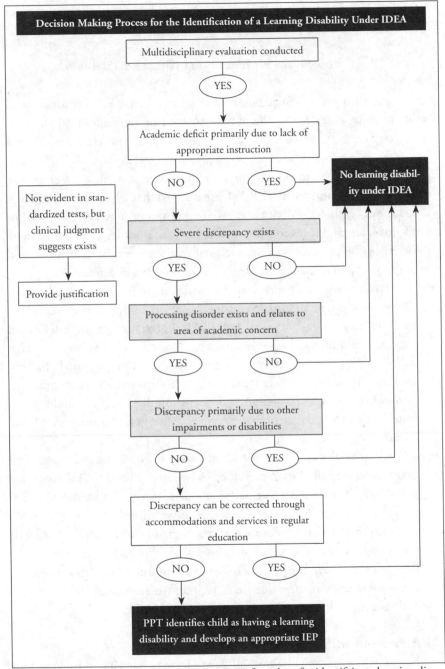

**Decision Making Process for the Identification of a Learning Disability Under IDEA**

Multidisciplinary evaluation conducted

YES

Academic deficit primarily due to lack of appropriate instruction

NO    YES → No learning disability under IDEA

Not evident in standardized tests, but clinical judgment suggests exists

Provide justification

Severe discrepancy exists

YES    NO

Processing disorder exists and relates to area of academic concern

YES    NO

Discrepancy primarily due to other impairments or disabilities

NO    YES

Discrepancy can be corrected through accommodations and services in regular education

NO    YES

PPT identifies child as having a learning disability and develops an appropriate IEP

**Figure 10.2.** Connecticut State Guidelines (1999) flow chart for identifying a learning disability.

ability. The diagram reveals alternate ways to document discrepancies for students who don't meet the requirements in traditional ways.

## Procedures for Identifying Gifts and Talents

How do we recognize potential for gifted behavior in students who are learning disabled? In Chapter 2, we describe Renzulli's (1978, 1997) conception of creative-productive giftedness as an interaction of three clusters of behaviors: well-above-average ability, creativity, and task commitment brought to bear upon a specific interest or field of endeavor. Renzulli, Reis, and Smith (1981) further stated that while ability estimates are mostly stable, creativity and task commitment may be situational or environmental. Professionals are more likely to uncover evidence of these behaviors by exploring a student's total environment, both at home and at school, than if they look solely at the school environment.

Traditional assessment strategies and stereotypes may impede identification of potential gifts in learning-disabled students. For example, a total IQ score on a WISC-III will likely underestimate the intellectual potential of a learning-disabled student. An analysis of subtest patterns will provide a more accurate picture of the student's conceptual abilities. In addition, some odd behaviors (such as 50 reasons for *not* handing in homework or a preoccupation with a consuming interest) might be irresponsible or avoidance behaviors rather than signs of creativity and task commitment.

We generally approach the identification process in two ways. The first, which we call *a priori identification*, entails collecting and analyzing test data and interview information about students. The second, which we refer to as *dynamic identification*, involves using activities purposely designed to elicit creative responses and signal possible areas of student talent and interests. Dynamic identification is akin to the authentic audition process used in the performing arts. The purpose of both approaches is to obtain convincing evidence of well-above-average ability, creativity and task commitment in areas of students' strengths.

### A Priori Identification

*Using Test Scores.* The work of Lewis Terman has guided the development of gifted education for many years. One of Terman's legacies has been a strong emphasis on intelligence testing as the basis for determining which children are gifted and which are not. Although this is still a dominant feature of many gifted education programs, the approach has come under considerable criticism in recent years because intelligence tests are consistently found to be fairly weak predictors of the adult accomplishments of gifted people. In other words, having an above-average IQ test may forecast the *possibility* of significant accomplishment, but it doesn't guarantee significant accomplishment. There are so many intellectually capable people who do little with their abilities and others who through sheer effort overcome deficiencies that there can only be a modest correlation between measured intelligence and accomplishment.

Nonetheless, performance on an IQ test is a carefully controlled sampling of a child's intellectual performance. Though this sampling is not a definitive indicator of potential, IQ information can be a valuable starting point for predicting what a child might do in challenging situations. Dependable IQ information can also tell a valuable story about the particular strength and weakness patterns common among GLD children if the IQ test includes an assortment of subtests within which professionals can observe patterns of strength and weakness (such as the WISC-III).

We believe that IQ tests should not be the sole determinant of giftedness in children; the IQ cut point should not be set so high that other information becomes irrelevant, nor should the diagnostician become fixated on IQ information just because it might be the first information collected. It is a potentially valuable source of information, but it should not be the only information gathered.

### Interpreting the WISC-III

When examining WISC-III scores, it is most important to look for areas of distinct strengths that are logically connected, such as the subtest groupings suggested in Chapter 5. For example, if a child has high scores on all three of the spatial manipulation subtests (Block Design, Object Assembly, and Picture Completion), this could indicate talent in this particular area. At the same time, you should not be overly dependent on these particular categories. For example, the Patterned Sequencing subtests tend to correlate very strongly with the Spatial Manipulation Subtests, so a combination of strengths in the two areas is entirely predictable. However, a conceptual foundation must support the strength pattern you are observing. Any child with average intelligence is likely to have two or more subtests that are somewhat above average. If you take a random group of students, many of them will show a couple of high subtest scores, which by itself does not qualify them as gifted. You should be able to say exactly what the area of strength is, or it is possible that there is none.

On the other hand, areas of weakness should not prevent you from asserting that there is a strength. Many GLD students have particular subtest scores that are one or more standard deviations below the mean.

---

### Case in Point

Brad is a 16-year-old student who wasn't diagnosed as learning disabled until high school, even though he didn't read until sixth grade when he became interested in Tolkien's *Trilogy of the Rings* books. His WISC-III profile is typical of a learning-disabled student who demonstrates strengths and weaknesses in both verbal and performance areas. He was able to compensate for many years because of his strengths, but began to lag notably when he began high school.

A WISC-III subtest score of 10 is average, and the standard deviation on these subtests is 3. One standard deviation below average equals a score of 7, which is at the 16th percentile. Going the other way, a score of 13, equal to the 84th percentile, is one standard deviation above the mean. Below are Brad's WISC-III subtest scores and a legend to help interpret where Brad stands.

| Brad's WISC-III Information | |
|---|---|
| Information: 10 | Verbal: 112 |
| Similarities: 13 | Performance: 121 |
| Arithmetic: 7 | Full Scale: 118 |
| Vocabulary: 15 | Verbal Comprehension: 118 |
| Comprehension: 15 | Perceptual Organization: 128 |
| Digit Span: 5 | Freedom from Distraction: 78 |
| Picture completion: 10 | Perceptual Speed: 111 |
| Coding : 8 | |
| Picture arrangement: 14 | |
| Block Design: 15 | |
| Object Assembly: 19 | |
| Symbol Search: 16 | |
| Mazes: 16 | |

**WISC Scores and Corresponding Percentiles**

| Subtest Score | Percentile Rank |
|---|---|
| 4 | 2 |
| 7 | 16 |
| 10 | 50 |
| 13 | 84 |
| 16 | 98 |

**Figure 10.3.** Brad's WISC profile.

This result should be expected and not hinder the assertion of a talent.

Most of the time, the talents of the GLD child will appear across the Intelligence areas (Spatial Manipulation, Patterned Sequencing, and Abstract Conceptualization), with one or another of these areas being slightly stronger. The weaknesses of these children are most likely in the Dispersive Intelligence areas (Detailed Memory, Quick Information Processing and Patternless Sequencing). More often than not, this broader distinction will be the basis for identifying the talent.

In looking for the difference between Integrative Intelligence and Dispersive Intelligence, you should be careful not to substitute the distinction between verbal and performance tests (and discrepancies) just because test information is often reported in these terms. The strengths of GLD children often cross the line between verbal and performance scores, as do their weaknesses. The verbal-performance discrepancy will, therefore, muddle more authentic discrepancies sitting in the subscore data. Brad's test information in Figure 10.3 illustrates some of these points.

Among Brad's subtest scores, the most impressive is his Object Assembly score of 19. He also did well on Block Design (score of 15), Picture Arrangement (score of 14), Comprehension (score of 15), and Vocabulary (score of 15). The Similarities score is somewhat elevated at 13. Brad's strengths appear across many areas of intelligence. On the other hand, he shows substantial weaknesses are in Dispersive Intelligence—Arithmetic (score of 7), Coding (score of 8), and Digit Span (score of 9). If in evaluating the discrepancies for this child, you lumped Verbal test scores together separately from Performance test scores, the discrepancy between these two areas would be nearly hidden. Using a Verbal/Performance discrepancy would not have been a useful assessment plan for Brad. Likewise, if you based identification on any of the IQ scores (Full Scale, Verbal, Performance), Brad would not look that distinguished. However, an examination of Brad's subtest scores suggests that he is quite spatial and somewhat abstract. His verbal comprehension and perceptual organization skills are also good.

Considering Brad's test pattern, you might ask how high test scores need to be in order to be considered evidence of talent. We believe that, in the area of defined strength, the child will have scaled scores of 13 or above, with at least one score of 15 or more. This guideline meets

Renzulli's criterion of showing distinctly above-average ability, while not putting the standard so high that students with strong motivation and unusual creative potential are automatically eliminated.

### Using a Structured Interview

Once you have documented well above average intellectual ability, you can collect information about task commitment, interests, and creativity. A structured interview with adults who are well acquainted with the student is one way to get at the information. The interview format presented in Figure 10.4 was adapted from items on Scales for Rating the Behavioral Characteristics of Superior Students (Renzulli, Smith, White, Callahan, & Hartman, 1976) (see Appendix B for blank interview form), and Brad's learning disability resource room teacher provided the information. This information, along with his profile on the WISC-III, clearly confirms his potential for gifted behavior (see Figure 10.5).

Adults who are not sensitive to behaviors indicative of giftedness might view this child as clever, but irresponsible and manipulative. It is important to step back from presumed intent to assess behaviors as potential intellectual strengths, which, if redirected, can contribute to the child's ability to become a productive adult.

## Dynamic Identification

The Javits Act (described in Chapter 2) encouraged practitioners and theorists to collaborate in finding strategies to identify gifts in a range of disciplines for students with diverse talents. However, before talent can be identified, students need exposure to and some instruction in a targeted area (Renzulli, 1978; Tannenbaum, 1983). Only then can we assess their ability, interest, creativity, and commitment to the specific field or area of human endeavor.

In dynamic identification, we first define the kinds of abilities being sought and then develop corresponding activities that will elicit particular behaviors. The results of open-ended, creative activities using a wide variety of experiences are excellent indicators of potential giftedness. Whole group lessons, interest center activities, visitations, guest speakers, and exploratory activities present fine opportunities to recognize student enthusiasm, a passion for a topic, strengths, and possible talents. Critical, though, is the teacher's ability to notice the potential. Teachers must

| | **STRUCTURED INTERVIEW** | |
|---|---|---|
| 1. | Describe this child's interests. <br> History (Civil War and other wars)--does not read well, but learned a great deal of history. Sports. | |
| 2. | Have you observed situations in which this child | |
| | • becomes totally absorbed in a particular subject area? <br> History. He reads all books on history, biography and on various periods and eras. He spends time absorbed in these books. No school subject interests him as much. Science is another strong interest. Any verbal discussion absorbs him as long as he does not have to write anything down. | (Yes)/ No <br> If yes, <br> please explain. |
| | • has discussed adult topics such as politics, religion, or current events? <br> Yes, all of them. Everything was a topic of discussion for him (for example, his father's college reunion). He is interested in all adult topics, enjoys discussing them with adults and even asks adults about their own lives. | (Yes) No <br> If yes, <br> please explain. |
| | • becomes self-assertive, stubborn or aggressive. <br> Stubborn when he had to turn in a hard assignment. He had a lot of excuses and a lot of righteous-wounded indignation if you did not accept his excuses. | (Yes)/ No <br> If yes, <br> please explain. |
| | • avoided tasks? <br> Ditto as above. Everything involved with his LD he would avoid. He had all sorts of excuses: his dog died, his mother took him out, etc. Very clever avoider (for things he found hard to do). | (Yes) No <br> If yes, <br> please explain. |
| | • was particularly curious? <br> He has an inquisitive mind, questioned everything and asked many times, "Why do you think such and such is so?" | (Yes)/ No <br> If yes, <br> please explain. |
| | • was highly imaginative? <br> Yes. His written (or dictated to LD teacher) stories revealed his imagination. He would take these stories then shorten them and put them on paper. They had complicated plots and many characters. He also wrote a play. | (Yes) No <br> If yes, <br> please explain. |
| | • was humorous or seemed to be aware of nuances of humor? <br> A crooked smile. When you saw that smile, you knew he was getting the humor of the situation. Even his excuses were funny and he said them with humor. | (Yes)/ No <br> If yes, <br> please explain. |

**Figure 10.4.** Structured interview filled out by Brad's resource room teacher.

---

**Brad's Profile**

Well-above-average ability
1. WISC-III profile (subtest scores)
2. Understanding and interest in adult topics
3. Knowledge of history
4. Inquisitive mind, incessant questioning
5. Author of plays with complicated plots and many characters

Creativity
1. Has a lot of excuses (fluency)
2. Clever task avoider
3. Inquisitive mind
4. Imaginative stories, wrote a play
5. Sees humor in situations

Task Commitment
1. Passion for history—learned a great deal of history on his own.
2. Reads many books on history. (Notice that this student does not read well in a traditional sense, but studies print material in area of interest. This is typical behavior of GLD students who will read even though it is difficult if the material interests them.
3. Spends much time absorbed in books in interest area.

---

**Figure 10.5.** Brad's profile confirming his potential for gifted behavior.

observe student behaviors during and after these experiences, noting problem-solving abilities, leadership, original ideas, in-depth questions, elaborate products, and a desire to do more, go further, or continue with the activity or specific topic. Checklists to document behaviors as they occur can be far more dependable than trying to recall events at the end of a long day.

You can use dynamic assessment to identify students for talent development programs within specific domains. Using authentic activities designed by experts within a domain provide opportunities for students to "act like a practicing professional." This type of identification has worked especially well with gifted students at risk (Baum, Cooper, Neu & Owen, 1997; Baum, Owen, & Oreck, 1996; Delcourt, 1998).

We have used dynamic identification in a number of programs for GLD students. (Much of our work has focused on identifying students who have talents in science, engineering, and visual or performing arts, as many gifted adults with learning disabilities have found a home in these disciplines.) In one such program, we sought to identify LD students who demonstrated potential for gifted behavior in spatial design, visual thinking, or dramatic expression. We designed specific activities corresponding to each domain and instructed teachers in learning disability resource rooms how to use them. They administered the activities to all their learning-disabled students and rated their performance using behavioral checklists that we provided. They then provided these students with additional activities within the domains to develop their abilities from novice toward expert.

In 1993, we received federal funding for Project HIGH HOPES, a three-year project to identify and nurture talent in students with disabilities. The targeted students were from all over the diagnostic alphabet: LD (learning disabled), ADHD (attention deficit/hyperactivity disorder), ODD (oppositional defiant disorder) SED (social and emotional disorder), PDD (pervasive developmental disorder), and HI (hearing impaired). To implement the grant, we developed the Talent Discovery Assessment Process (TDAP), a reliable and valid assessment tool to identify talent potential in the domains of visual and performing arts, physical and biological science, and engineering. We based this audition-oriented tool on evidence that the most accurate predictors of potential talent are observations of student behavior over time when they are engaged in authentic, domain-specific activities.

We invited all fifth graders from the participating schools who were classified as having special needs according to federal guidelines to participate in the audition activities, which took place over the course of 3 months. A professional or content expert within each domain designed and administered the activities, and two observers tracked specific behaviors associated with the domain on corresponding observation sheets. We also encouraged observers to take notes on their observations. At the end of each session, the observers and specialist discussed their observations and rated the students holistically with a simple 3-point scale. They recorded these ratings on a student summary sheet. The scale indicated the students' readiness for more advanced development in that talent area. Figure 10.6 displays a student summary sheet with a list of the behaviors for each domain. Figure 10.7 presents a sample note page. The identification activities are included in Appendix A.

The dynamic identification activities described in Appendix A are examples of the creative options you can offer these students. You can

## HIGH HOPES: Talent Discovery Student Summary Sheet

STUDENT:__________ SCHOOL:__________

SITE CODE:________ SPECIAL ED SETTING:________ FREE/REDUCED LUNCH:______

CHILD ID:________ DISABLING CONDITION:_______ ETHNIC GROUP:________

| PERFORMING ARTS | OBS. 1 | OBS. 2 |
|---|---|---|
| Uses facial expressions | | |
| Uses expressive voice. | | |
| Uses body language | | |
| Shows clear communication of intent. | | |
| Creates elaborate movements, characters, or skits. | | |
| Accepts and incorporates others feedback. | | |

| VISUAL ARTS | 2-D OBSERVER 1 | 2-D OBSERVER 2 | 3-D OBSERVER 1 | 3-D OBSERVER 2 |
|---|---|---|---|---|
| Achieves balance in artwork. | | | | |
| Uses form (dimensionally and design to produce the desired effect. | | | | |
| Communicates intent clearly. | | | | |
| Creates a unified design which relates parts to the whole and uses appropriate inclusion/exclusion ratio. | | | | |
| Experiments with different ideas, materials, or techniques. | | | | |
| Combines disparate parts to create a unique solution. | | | | |
| Uses details to show complexity of ideas. | | | | |
| Uses tools and materials effectively | | | | |
| Accepts and incorporates others' feedback. | | | | |
| Is able to talk about work. | | | | |

| SCIENCE | BOT OBSERVER 1 | BOT OBSERVER 2 | ZOO OBSERVER 1 | ZOO OBSERVER 2 | PHY OBSERVER 1 | PHY OBSERVER 2 |
|---|---|---|---|---|---|---|
| Displays curiosity by asking relevant questions. | | | | | | |
| Shows a lot of knowledge related to today's topic. | | | | | | |
| Actively manipulates materials. | | | | | | |
| Communicates clearly the results of the project. | | | | | | |
| Systemically tests hypothesis. | | | | | | |
| Tries to predict outcomes. | | | | | | |
| Represents ideas in the form of a model. | | | | | | |
| Finds means of overcoming obstacles in problem-solving. | | | | | | |

| ENGINEERING | OBS. 1 | OBS. 2 |
|---|---|---|
| Actively manipulates materials. | | |
| Tries to predict outcomes. | | |
| Understands the main concepts of each lesson's topic. | | |
| Creates a product which shows clarity of thought and focused plan of action. | | |
| Puts materials together in a unique way. | | |
| Explains the logic of alternative solutions. | | |
| Shows problem-solving skill by pursuing an unprompted investigation. | | |
| Observes patterns in experi-mentation. | | |
| Finds means of overcoming obstacles in problem solving. | | |

### HOLISTIC RATINGS

| PERFORMING ARTS | | | VISUAL ARTS / 2-D | | | VISUAL ARTS / 3-D | | | SCIENCE / BOTANY | | | SCIENCE / ZOOLOGY | | | SCIENCE / PHYSICS | | | ENGINEERING | | |
|---|---|---|---|---|---|---|---|---|---|---|---|---|---|---|---|---|---|---|---|---|
| OB1 | OB2 | CS | OB1 | OB2 | CS | OB1 | OB2 | CS | OB1 | OB2 | CS | OB1 | OB2 | CS | OB1 | OB2 | CS | OB1 | OB2 | CS |
| | | | | | | | | | | | | | | | | | | | | |

**Figure 10.6.** Sample talent discovery summary sheet.

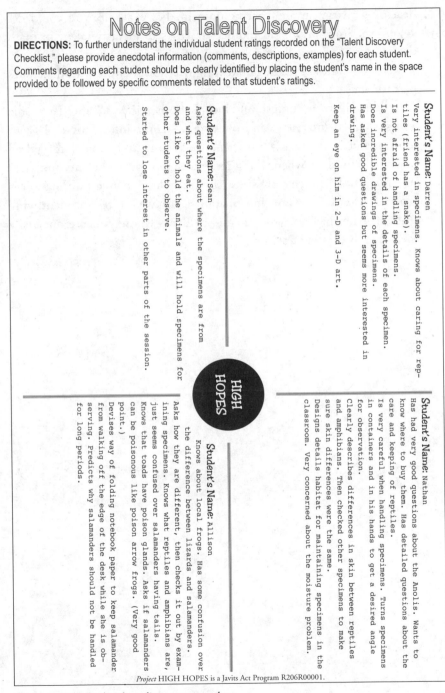

# Notes on Talent Discovery

**DIRECTIONS:** To further understand the individual student ratings recorded on the "Talent Discovery Checklist," please provide anecdotal information (comments, descriptions, examples) for each student. Comments regarding each student should be clearly identified by placing the student's name in the space provided to be followed by specific comments related to that student's ratings.

**Student's Name:** Darren

Very interested in specimens. Knows about caring for reptiles (friend has a snake). Is not afraid of handling specimens. Is very interested in the details of each specimen. Does incredible drawings of specimens. Has asked good questions but seems more interested in drawing.

Keep an eye on him in 2-D and 3-D art.

**Student's Name:** Sean

Asks questions about where the specimens are from and what they eat. Does like to hold the animals and will hold specimens for other students to observe.

Started to lose interest in other parts of the session.

**Student's Name:** Nathan

Has had very good questions about the Anolis. Wants to know where to buy them. Has detailed questions about the care and keeping of reptiles. Is very careful when handling specimens. Turns specimens in containers and in his hands to get a desired angle for observation. Clearly describes differences in skin between reptiles and amphibians. Then checked other specimens to make sure skin differences were the same. Designs details habitat for maintaining specimens in the classroom. Very concerned about the moisture problem.

**Student's Name:** Allison

Knows about local frogs. Has some confusion over the difference between lizards and salamanders. Asks how they are different, then checks it out by examining specimens. Knows what reptiles and amphibians are, just seems confused over salamanders having tails. Knows that toads have poison glands. Asks if salamanders can be poisonous like poison arrow frogs. (Very good point.) Devises way of folding notebook paper to keep salamander from walking off the edge of the desk while she is observing. Predicts why salamanders should not be handled for long periods.

HIGH HOPES

*Project* HIGH HOPES is a Javits Act Program R206R00001.

**Figure 10.7.** Sample talent discovery note sheet.

develop activities in any specific domain. For example, you could develop experimentation and inquiry activities to identify talent in math or the social sciences. Remember to offer a variety of hands-on activities so that difficulties in reading or writing will not interfere with the child's performance.

Ideally, identification should include both *a priori* (WISC-III profile and structured interview) and ongoing, dynamic information. *A priori* information is frequently sufficient to document potential for gifted behavior. However, when trying to understand specific talents and areas in which these students are most comfortable, dynamic information is especially useful. Dynamic information is also well suited for identifying students who may not test well and students whose gifts are not easily measured by existing tests.

# Attending to the Gift

"Neglected or suppressed strengths are like infections under the skin; eventually they cause serious damage" (Levine, 2002, p.300). Particularly poignant for gifted students with learning, attention, or behavior difficulties, Levine's comment demands that we attend to the development of these students' gifts or talents. Too often the strengths and interests of GLD students are either unrecognized, seen but ignored, put on hold, or are irksome because they are the wrong talents for conventional school achievement. Such reactions compromise the students' motivation, academic self-efficacy, and self-esteem, and thereby inhibit their growth and chances for success.

Bryan's story, below, illustrates how a talent development approach was instrumental in reversing Bryan's pattern of chronic underachievement and in providing a window into his learning difficulties. Without focused attention on his gift Bryan probably would have been placed in a highly restrictive environment for students with social and emotional disorders.

### Bryan

A bright, creative youngster, Bryan had performed well during his elementary school years. He showed particular talent and interest in the areas of language arts and music. Bryan had less success in the areas of math and science but managed to get by. When he entered middle school in sixth grade, Bryan's performance, even in language and music, deteriorated. He seemed to lose all ability to focus on tasks. He became disorganized, failed to complete most assignments and showed a variety of attention-seeking behaviors. His grades dropped from A's and B's to B's and C's. His teachers were concerned with his downward trajectory and referred him for testing. They suspected that he had a learning disability or an attention deficit disorder.

In the fall of seventh grade, a comprehensive psycho-educational evaluation revealed that Bryan was highly intelligent, but had some problematic weaknesses. His scores on the *WISC* hit the 99th percentile on the verbal scale, but only the 40th percentile on the performance scale. On the *Woodcock Johnson Cognitive and Ability Test* Bryan was at the 99th percentile on overall cognitive ability. His only weaknesses were in motor and perceptual speed (74th percentile) and math (26 percentile). Despite these discrepancies and the accompanying behavior patterns, the pupil personnel team did not feel that Bryan had a learning disability or attention deficit. They decided that his behaviors were more symptomatic of behavioral problems and classified him as emotional or behavioral disordered (EBD). They also felt that his profile did not indicate a need for direct services at the time. Instead, they suggested that Bryan and his teachers establish behavior contracts and weekly monitoring by his parents.

Throughout the seventh grade Bryan still showed attention problems and immaturity. His teachers reported that he was "inattentive, restless, impulsive, lacked perseverance and had trouble following directions." They complained that he did not exert sufficient effort in his studies and often handed in work late, if at all. He was frequently in trouble, especially on the school playground. His academic performance slid into the C/C- range in most subjects. Although his parents thought that their weekly monitoring efforts had some minor effect, they voiced their growing concern that Bryan did not appear motivated and lacked self-discipline. They feared that his on-going underachievement would sharply restrict future academic options.

**Talent Development Opportunity**

During Bryan's eighth grade year, the teacher of the gifted happened to be participating in a national study on reversing underachievement in high-ability students (Baum, Renzulli, & Hébert, 1995). She asked her colleagues to nominate students who were achieving significantly below their measured potential as indicated by scores in the superior range on tests of intelligence or cognitive ability. Bryan's profile met the criteria perfectly, and he was invited to participate in the study. The intervention was based on Type III Enrichment (Renzulli, 1977). Type III Enrichment opportunities are an individual or small group investigations of real world problems. Students selected for the study would become involved in an investigation of a problem in an area of interest using authentic means of inquiry and would ultimately report their results to a real audience. This type of project is not an independent study, but an inquiry conducted with the assistance of an adult facilitator or mentor.

### The Process

Bryan initially met with the enrichment specialist two periods a week to work on his project. At their first meeting, Bryan complained about his social studies curriculum. His eighth grade class was pursuing a mock trial that Bryan found hokey and frustrating. He argued that he could write a better court case for the eighth grade courtroom simulation: "I don't like the old one. It's got some stupid character named Candy Cane in it, and I think I could do a better job. My friend and I already have some ideas for the case. Can we work together?" Although his friend soon lost interest, Bryan stayed committed to the task and decided to continue the project on his own even though he thought the project seemed overwhelming.

Bryan and the enrichment teacher negotiated a management plan to assist Bryan in organizing the project. First they defined the problem at hand (the inappropriate law simulation), the projected solution (an original simulation), and the anticipated audience (eighth grade students in civics class). Next, they identified the information needed, the available resources, the steps needed to complete the project, and a projected timeline. Brian then was ready to begin his inquiry. When Bryan began to see the amount of work the project required, he convinced his social studies teacher to compact his curriculum so that he could have more time in the enrichment center to work on his project. Curriculum compacting consists of pretesting a student on concepts or skills to be mastered during a unit of study and then excusing the student from assignments on material already mastered (Renzulli, Smith, & Reis, 1982). Bryan tested out of the unit on "How a Bill Becomes a Law" and was able to use this time with the enrichment specialist to complete his project. Figure 11.1 presents a copy of the management plan, which also served as a contract between Bryan and the enrichment specialist. The plan helped Bryan see the bigger picture, pointed him in the right direction, and offered unique and authentic strategies to gain knowledge about the subject.

---

### Management Plan for Individual and Small Group Investigations

Name(s) Bryan
School MJH                    Grade 8

Beginning Date 10-6-89
Estimated Ending Date 2-89

**What idea do you plan to investigate? Why?**
Jury Trials. Because we want to write a better one for the 8th grade.

**What form(s) will the final product take?**
Role play for class use.

**List some possible intended audiences:**
8th grade classes
Social Studies Publisher

**How will you communicate the results of your investigation to an appropriate audience?**
Devise role play situations and rules that simulate a jury trial.

**Getting Started: What types of information or data will be needed to begin your project?**
Packet of information on court room procedures from Civics teacher.
Court room procedures.

**Where can you find that information?**
Media Center, Attorneys, Court observations

**How-to-do-it books/written materials: Use bibliography format**

---

**Figure 11.1.** Management plan developed for Bryan.

Following the structure of the management plan, Bryan met with small successes right away, and the project continued to enlarge. He worked on the court trial script over the course of the entire academic year. The enrichment specialist offered suggestions, shared in his excitement when the plot began to take form, and acted out parts Bryan had written to allow him to critique his own clarity. In addition, he asked two civics teachers to critique his work and then willingly returned to the drawing board to edit his draft.

Check the boxes below ?typing at top of copy is illegible? to complete your project and list the specific sources:

☐ Viewing TV, videos, films, etc. (which?) _____

☐ Interviewing people (who?) Jo Marie Alexander/attorney, Mrs. Rosenbaum
                            Court room-Hampton Court
☐ Observing/collecting data (what?) Court Justices interviews _____

☐ Surveying (who?) _____

☐ Taking a class or working with a mentor (specify)_____

☐ Attending a performance (specify)_____

☐ Other (specify)_____

List all materials and equipment needed:
Computer

TASKS: List in the order necessary to complete your project     To be completed by:

1. Get info, talk with people about how it works.    Oct.
2. Examine other role play simulations.    Oct.
3. Decide how we want to design the format for
        our role play.    Nov.
4. Decide on plot and characters.    Dec.
5. Skeleton of drama.    Dec.
6. Divide responsibilities for roles and directors.   Jan.-Feb.
7. Write.    Jan.-Feb.
8. Conference with teacher and attorney.    April
9. Edit/Copy/Put together    May
10. Evaluate performance    May
11. Revise and submit for publication.    May

Adapted from Renzulli, J. S., & Reis, S. M. (1985). *The Schoolwide Enrichment Model*, p. 439. Mansfield Center, CT: Creative Learning Press

**Figure 11.1** *continued.*

## Overcoming Obstacles

During the course of the project, the enrichment specialist became fully aware of Bryan's strengths and weaknesses. His lack of organizational skills was apparent from the start. The enrichment specialist described him as "totally disorganized at all times," even though he had the management plan to use as a guide! Together they invented simple strategies to help keep Bryan's materials organized. There was a box next to the computer labeled "Bryan's Stuff" and a file folder on the bookcase where he kept all draft copies of the script. Because Bryan did his writing directly on the computer, he taught himself to make back-up files on a disc in case his file was erased. He even e-mailed his files to himself at home so he would be able to work on the draft at his own computer. Bryan began to consider how these strategies could be useful in organizing assignments and materials for all his other courses.

At first, Bryan was put off by the feedback he received on his work, which required him to rewrite sections for clarity and authenticity. He explained that rewriting wasn't all that hard, it was just "plain monotonous." However, he observed that his attention span, focus, and attention to details greatly improved when he worked on the computer, especially when he listened to rock music through a headset. He even amazed himself with his level of concentration when he got "in the flow" and spent over three hours at home one night editing his draft. Bryan used this insight and self-awareness to convince his language arts teacher to allow him to leave the classroom during the writing process time because he found the classroom environment too noisy and distracting. The teacher allowed him to complete his writing assignments in the computer lab plugged into his favorite music.

## Reflection and Metacognition

The final phase of the intervention was to reflect on insights gained over the course of the journey. The close interactive relationship between the enrichment specialist and Bryan was a catalyst to uncovering new understandings about his learning style, self-regulation, and other ingredients crucial to Bryan's success. To initiate this kind of reflection, the enrichment specialist asked Bryan how he felt about the project now that it was completed. Bryan was excited that the social studies teacher agreed to read the court case to the sixth grade for the class' reaction before actually using it with the eighth grade. He hoped that the students would have a better understanding of courtroom procedure after using his simulation and perhaps even become interested in studying law or the court system.

The enrichment specialist asked him what he thought he had learned about himself while completing his project. Bryan mulled over various aspects of the process. He commented that he learned how disorganized he was and that the box and file folders helped him stay organized, as did the management plan (even though he didn't always stick to the deadlines). He realized that he loved planning the simulation and developing creative ideas, but following through on it and adding all the details were difficult for him. In the past he would have given up, but not this time, namely because he was determined to finish the project and because he was given school time to work on it..

As Bryan explained,

> I think it would have helped me more if I paid attention to deadlines. I would have been done a lot sooner. I know that. I guess I would recommend using a schedule more than just keep going. I get bored easily and want to quit and switch to something else. The schedule helps you break the project down into manageable pieces so you don't have to do it all at once. Probably the best thing I learned from writing this trial is just to keep going and no matter if it bogs down, you've just got to stick with it. Eventually it will be done, and then you can go on to something else. You just keep looking forward, not like "Thank God it's over," but to see the project put to use is just overwhelming.

The enrichment specialist, too, analyzed her own growth in understanding how Bryan learned, what motivated him, and what hurdles plagued his progress. She was regularly surprised at Bryan's level of productivity, his task commitment, and his courage to attempt activities that demanded skill in areas previously identified as severe weaknesses. She recalled one incident as pivotal to her understanding and appreciating the role that motivation and self-confidence play in student productivity and achievement:

> Bryan was finishing up doggedly on his court simulation because it was going to be piloted in a 6th grade classroom as a preview before the eighth graders used it. In the midst of his

project completion, he started writing a novel—actually he began 2 novels simultaneously. He had written about 40 pages, came into my room, threw it on my desk, and said, "Here's a new novel and it's on Norad." Enclosed within was an intricate diagram of an underwater installation, visually a perfect graphic, and this is done by a student tested as having poor spatial abilities! He said it came to him as a visual image after a 14-hour stint at the computer working on his novel.

It appears that productivity begets more productivity. I hadn't seen Bryan as excited and eager to work in the years we've known him at this school. I guess he needs multiple projects to keep him focused. And, when he is motivated, he finally finishes them all.

### Turning Point

Bryan completed his project in June. His report card, still erratic, began to move toward As and Bs, especially if Bryan was interested in the subject. His year-end testing revealed a gain of two years in math, an earlier area of weakness. More important, he began to self-regulate his own learning. At the end of the year, he initiated a discussion with members of the pupil personnel team and requested support for the following year from the special education teacher in math and science—subjects he dodged previously because he found them so difficult. No longer was Bryan depressed and unmotivated, nor did he lack self-discipline. For the first time in years he expressed a desire to improve academically, and he was now confident that he could accomplish his goals.

## Lessons Learned from Bryan's Story

Why was the focus on student interests and talents more effective than the behavior modification techniques employed initially? To understand the complex dynamics involved, let us review the scenario and identify and what actions contributed to and lessened the problem.

### Factors Contributing to the Problem

When we first met Bryan in middle school, his performance had been spiraling downward each year. He had become a behavior problem and seemed uninterested in reversing his pattern of poor achievement. He ultimately became an Alphabet Child and labeled as EBD—emotional and behavioral disordered. This label directed the intervention toward extinguishing poor and inappropriate behaviors. To this end, a behavior modification program was instituted in which Bryan was expected "to shape up and be rewarded."

The classification of "emotional and behavioral disordered" and its subsequent treatment was a significant contributor to Bryan's continuing underachievement. There is no question that the team misdiagnosed Bryan's problems. The results of his testing, coupled with observations of his behavior, provided strong evidence that Bryan had subtle learning disabilities in the areas of math, spatial abilities, organization, and time management. This profile is typical of many high ability youngsters with subtle learning disabilities. Because elementary grade levels don't put tall demands on these particular skills, high ability students with subtle disabilities can usually use strengths to compensate for weaknesses in organization.

As assignments became more difficult in middle school, however, Bryan was no longer able to keep up the charade. His frustration turned into depression, aggression , and discouragement. Because he lacked the skills necessary to perform well at this level, his achievement and behavior worsened. Strong extrinsic rewards may have reduced acting out behaviors, but they did little for the fundamental problem, which was a mismatch of abilities and environment. The attention-seeking behaviors and lack of focused effort to complete assignments were Bryan's ineffectual strategies for coping with his undiagnosed learning problems. A behavior contract didn't provide him with new skills or strategies needed to overcome his learning difficulties.

The second problem, layered on top of the first, was the teams' decision that Bryan did not need any direct services. In truth, with every poor mark he received, Bryan became less confident in his abilities and his behavior deteriorated. A more careful look at what was happening to Bryan's motivation, confidence, and lack of skills might have steered the team in a different direction.

As discussed in earlier chapters, several mediating variables are precursors to achievement (Bandura, 1989; Zimmerman, 1989). In Chapter 7 we highlighted the importance of self-efficacy, or a person's belief that he can organize and carry out some behavior (Bandura, 1997). Compared to those with weak self-efficacy, people with a robust sense of efficacy spend more energy at a task, pay more careful attention to the task, work harder at planning how to go about the task, persevere longer, set more challenging goals, and persist in the face of barriers and occasional failure. Success becomes more likely for them, which in turn boosts self-efficacy. Self-efficacy translates into a "can do" attitude, as opposed to resistance, avoidance, or anxiety about performing some task.

Other characteristics of competent learners, are that they have a collection of effective learning strategies stored in memory and they know how to select particular strategies for particular purposes (see Chapters 6 through 8). The learners' knowledge about, use of, and confidence in their strategies enables them to seize control of their learning (Levine, 2002; Mooney & Cole, 2000; Zimmerman, 1989). Bryan, similar to many underachieving or learning-disabled students, lacked these essential prerequisites to achievement.

Without a sense of self-efficacy, a repertoire of successful learning strategies, and some self-regulation skill, students feel powerless in their efforts to learn. Kaufman (1991) argued that such students are severely discouraged and what they need is encouragement not punishment or remediation. When an intervention focused on Bryan as a capable student with talents and interests, a different learner emerged. Motivated to write a law simulation, Bryan was willing to overcome problematic weaknesses to reach his goal. Thus, the journey provided a context for change—an opportunity to achieve success by engaging in an enriching and meaningful experience where the end (his goal) justified the means (learning and applying strategies).

## Factors Contributing to Success

Bryan's talent development experience suggests a set of issues that support success. Embedded in his program were several components essential to any program that is to meet the needs of GLD students. These factors include a relationship with a caring adult, an emphasis on pursing talents and interests in an authentic manner, and integration of self-regulation strategies.

**1. Relationship with a caring adult.** Bryan developed a relationship with a caring teacher who respected him for what he could do. The enrichment specialist played a vital role in helping Bryan believe in himself. She offered emotional and cognitive support as he pursued his self-determined goal. Her feedback was constructive, and she continuously conveyed a belief that he could write the court case. Students who reverse their pattern of underachievement often attribute their turn-around to a special teacher or mentor. These adults possess specific qualities. They show respect for the student, hold high expectations, and demonstrate a belief that the student is capable and can succeed (Baum, Renzulli, & Hébert, 1995; Emerick, 1992).

Many kinds of talent development experiences, such as internships mentor programs and small group interaction with a teacher facilitator, offer opportunities to develop these special collegial relationships.

**2. An emphasis on pursuing students' talents and interests in an authentic manner.** The enrichment specialist encouraged Bryan to pursue an area of interest in an way that resembled how a professional would go about it. He was emotionally committed to solving the problem of a goofy and immature court simulation. The project had a real purpose; it was not just one more school assignment to be graded. In other words, Bryan was engaged in learning for intrinsic reasons rather than for factors imposed upon him by others. Previously, the school had focused only on helping Byran overcome his learning deficits. Contracts, meetings with teachers, and parental monitoring, all well-intentioned, were aimed at helping Bryan complete school tasks. These methods, based on extrinsic rewards, often have limited success with high ability students who lack the motivation and organizational skills to achieve at a level commensurate with their ability (Clinkenbeard, 1994).

In any instructional design, programs that capitalize on students' talents and interests are more likely to result in cognitive and emotional gains. The Enrichment Triad Model (Renzulli, 1977) is a particularly appropriate approach to talent development, especially for students who have difficulty reading and writing. This model incorporates skill development to produce new knowledge through the pursuit of independent or small group investigations that are based on the student's own interests and strengths. Students identify an area of interest and then focus on a real problem to be investigated and solved. Important or impressive solutions are not guaranteed, of course. Sometimes the outcomes are feeble or downright dumb. But the important issue is that, in the process, the student is learning *how* to address problems and *how* to self-regulate learning behaviors. And, thanks to self-evaluation during the process, the student comes to understand that he or she is capable of focusing, persisting, and coming to some closure on a worthwhile problem.

The model consists of three sequenced activities: general exploratory, group training, and individual and small group investigation. General exploratory activities (Type I Enrichment) offer exposure to potential areas of interest not necessarily found in the regular curriculum. Students with learning deficits may be introduced to ideas through lectures, demonstrations, movies, interest centers, or other approaches that bypass weaknesses in reading. These are no-fail activities meant to expose students to new ideas in a non-threatening atmosphere where they are given free rein to explore.

The next step—Type II Enrichment activities—provides training in such areas as critical thinking, creativity, and problem solving, using authentic strategies of a discipline. Because GLD students often perform better on experiential activities using higher-level thinking skills, these types of activities engage the students and allow them to investigate problems using the methods and tools of the practicing professional.

In Type III activities, students become investigators of real problems that are relevant to them. They are mentored in the development of a product that should have an authentic impact on an audience, preferably outside the school setting. Students focus on original solutions to problems and proceed as a "practicing professional" using methods of inquiry to solve a chosen problem.

**3. Integration of self-regulation strategies.** Another contributor to Bryan's success was introducing specific self-regulation strategies as they were needed to complete the project—organizational boxes and folders, a computer for writing and editing , background music, and a management plan and deadlines. Bryan learned these strategies in the context of the project as well as the ability to identify obstacles to success and learning strategies that fit his learning style.

Gifted learning-disabled students learn better within meaningful contexts, especially when they are interested in the topic. When students are committed to a project, a remarkable assortment of study behaviors step forward. They seek more information about a topic, set about organizing information, and strive to create a meaningful product. Experiencing success and then reflecting on the strategies used to get there builds their self-efficacy about what they can do (Bandura, 1997; Zimmerman, 1989). Our work dependably shows that the students begin to transfer these learning strategies to other areas of their curriculum and their lives (Baum, Renzulli, & Hébert, 1995; Oreck, Baum, & McCarthy, 2000)

## Talent Development Opportunities

It is fundamental to the development of Alphabet Children to identify and nurture their special gifts and talents. Usually a program designed for gifted children provides this kind of nurturing. However, simply plopping GLD students into an existing program for gifted students may be inappropriate and lead to negative results. These students may not readily fit into existing programs for several reasons:

1.  The programs may be content-centered with little regard for individual strengths or interests.
2.  The program orientation may place heavy emphasis on reading and writing.
3.  If the gifted curriculum is built around an honors theme, it adds to, instead of replaces, existing curriculum requirements.
4.  Some programs lack sufficient structure and guidance because it is assumed that students can produce independently.

Programs for GLD students should serve to validate individual gifts and help the students understand who they are. As we saw in Bryan's case, the teacher must create an environment where students feel appreciated and where their gifts are both recognized and valued. Such programs

1.  encourage students to gain information and communicate their ideas in creative ways based on individual talents and interests;
2.  convey sophisticated content through guest speakers, demonstrations, active inquiry, visitation, films, or mentorships;
3.  use experts, equipment, and modes of inquiry of the practicing professional;
4.  acknowledge and reward students' individual differences by offering options that align with the strengths and interests of the students; and
5.  include a metacognitive approach where students reflect on the compensation strategies that enable them to succeed in spite of

learning differences.

In short, programs appropriate for GLD students should include personnel who welcome individual differences and feel comfortable highlighting student strengths. These adults should communicate their belief in these students' ability to create or accomplish great things. They must also help students identify strategies that assist them in compensating for weaknesses in pursuit of their goals. Such teachers understand that advanced reading and writing skills are not a necessary prerequisite for learning and creative productivity.

Various administrative program designs have shown success in offering appropriate opportunities for talent development. The choice of program will depend on the students' talents and learning needs.

### Placement in Existing Programs

There are many documented cases of GLD children doing exceptionally well in existing programs. These are typically students who have been recognized for their giftedness first, and their disabilities are more subtle or do not involve reading or writing. Below are examples of common alternatives already found in most school districts.

**Acceleration.** Accelerated programs in a particular area of student strength help the GLD student cultivate specific talents. Advanced courses could challenge a student with a strong aptitude for math if the methodology, motivation, and product are aligned with the student's gift. The student can remain in regular or remedial classes for areas requiring a different kind of attention.

In Montgomery County, Maryland, GLD students with talent in math or science participate in Advanced Placement (AP) or honors classes. According to program director Richard Weinfeld (personal communication, May 19, 2001), these students are competitive and achieve at a level commensurate with their gifted peers. For the remainder of the day they attend a special class for GLD students.

**Established Enrichment Program.** These programs have been especially successful when the student is allowed to pursue a specific interest, such as computers. The opportunity to interact with peers of similar intellectual abilities and interests encourages the GLD student in developing a positive self-image. Focused attention is given to an area of strength to balance the disproportionate amount of time and energy expended on overcoming weaknesses. Odyssey of the Mind, storytelling festivals, debate teams, mock trials, Model U.N. History Day, Science Fair contests, Math Counts, and, of course, arts and athletic programs within the school offer breadth and depth for developing talents and interests.

**Schoolwide Enrichment Model (Renzulli & Reis, 1997).** Programs based on this model have been found to be particularly effective for GLD students for several reasons. First, flexible identification allows these children to become part of the talent pool or participate in an enrichment cluster on the basis of interest. Second, the program exposes students to a wide variety of activities that are purposefully designed to ignite student interest and encourage creative productivity. In contrast to other enrichment paradigms where individual students are asked to conform to a challenging but prescribed curriculum, the educational experiences in this model evolve from the strengths and interests of the student.

**Mentorships.** Another program option offered in many schools is the opportunity to use mentored tutoring. The benefits accruing from the special relationship between mentor and mentee have been well documented. Learning-disabled students perform better in one-to-one settings, partly because such an environment maximizes the students' observational learning. In addition, the student gains feelings of satisfaction and self-worth when working side by side with an expert or professional in an area of common interest. One such program is the *Mentor Connection,* a summer opportunity for gifted students described in Figure 11.2. One GLD high school student, Lara, was experiencing severe depression at the end of her sophomore year. Sacrificing her social needs, she often spent considerable time studying to maintain high grades in her academic program. Lara's parents had been considering sending her to a summer program for study skills sponsored by a university interested in students with learning disabilities. However, concerned about her depression they agreed that she needed a positive educational experience and enrolled her in *The Mentor Connection.* Lara was assigned to a female biologist. She and two other gifted young women worked together as research assistants with the biologist, helping her study communication among mice. Lara found the experience very positive, especially because it enabled her to form meaningful relationships with her mentor and peer researchers.

Another talented high schooler, Welles, explained how this program raised his feelings of self-efficacy:

---

**The Mentor Connection: An Inquiry-Based Summer Program for Talented Teens**

UCONN Gifted Education and Talent Development

University of Connecticut

Neag School of Education

UConn Mentor Connection is a summer program for rising high school juniors and seniors located at the University of Connecticut, Storrs, CT. We believe students' interests, abilities, and motivation are very important talents. We also believe that it is essential for students to have opportunities to manifest their talents in high levels of creative productivity.

As a participant in UConn Mentor Connection, you will:

- Take on the role of the practicing professional.
- Experience real-world problem solving.
- Develop a collaborative relationship with a researcher in your area of interest.
- Enhance your awareness of your talent areas and career opportunities.
- Create a photographic essay of your involvement in research to share with students and teachers.
- Interact with students who share common interests.
- Experience college life and the nature of research in your selected field.
- Have fun under the supervision of a specially trained staff of high school teachers and resident advisors.
- Earn University of Connecticut credit, providing certain requirements are met.

---

**Figure 11.2.** A description of The Mentor Connection program.

I was told in sixth grade that I was smart and had a learning disability. I had a lot of trouble organizing myself. Since that time, I doubted myself until I attended UConn Mentor Connection. When I went to Mentor Connection, I worked in one of my favorite subjects: medieval literature. A special mentorship site was created for me, and I loved working with my mentor, Mr. John Sexton. John was a doctoral student in the medieval studies department. He was so enthusiastic about his work, and he took a very personal interest in me.

I worked one-on-one with John, and we translated parts of *Sir Gawain and the Green Knight* and *Beowulf*. I never thought I could do this, but I did, and I know that I did a great job. John told me that I was doing work that graduate students complete. I was truly motivated because I loved what I was doing.

Throughout my three weeks in the program, I was pretty much on my own. I learned that I could do anything I put my mind to. I can recall saying to myself, "Oh yes, I did all that, and I can be really proud."

John really influenced my life, and I have kept in touch with him. He made me believe in myself. I helped him to create parts of the mentorship site the year after I attended the program. We still e-mail each other once in a while.

## Specially Designed Programs

Sometimes it is necessary to design special programs and opportunities for GLD students. Because of learned behavior patterns, repeated failures, learning and attention deficits, or the nature of existing programs, the GLD student may not fit into any established program. In this section we describe three specially designed programs. The first, Project HIGH HOPES, was a three-year talent development program within the school setting especially for Alphabet Children funded by the Javits Act. Project HIGH HOPES served students with special needs who were identified as talented in the arts or sciences. This three-year project was highly successful in nurturing extraordinary talents of these special Alphabet Children. Not only did this project incorporate elements described previously, but gave us the opportunity to study in depth how these talented youngsters learn and the kinds of learning environments that allow them to be successful. The second program, Montgomery County's Center Program for GLD students, focuses on self-contained classrooms for GLD students within the regular school setting. This comprehensive elementary, middle, and high school program serves gifted students with severe learning disabilities. The final description is a special school for gifted boys with learning problems. The Greenwood School is especially appropriated for learning-disabled boys who also have strong spatial abilities. It provides remediation and talent development opportunities especially in developing spatial and artistic talents.

**Project HIGH HOPES: Identifying and Nurturing Talent in Students with Special Needs, Javits Act Program (1993-96)\*.** We designed this program to identify and nurture artistic, scientific, or

---

\* Contributors for HIGH HOPES descriptions made by Dr. Carolyn Cooper, Project Administrator, and Dr. Terry Neu, Project Coordinator.

engineering talents in students with special needs. The sequence of activities followed typical talent development models (Bloom et al., 1985; Csikszentmihayli & Whalen, 1993, Renzulli, 1977). The first step was to expose students to a variety of domains in order to uncover talent potential. Once students were identified as talented within a particular domain, they participated in talent development activities within that domain. These lessons taught students the skills of the discipline through authentic activities and learning experiences. During the final stage, activities encourage students to further their abilities by becoming creative producers within their talent areas.

This project served 130 students in grades 5 through 8 at 9 sites in Connecticut and Rhode Island, including six public schools, a private school for the learning disabled, and two schools for the deaf. Of the 130 students, 72 (55.4%) attended a special school, 19 (14.6%) received resource room services in their school, and 39 (30%) were mainstreamed within the regular school setting. We selected students from the special education population at each site who had been identified as having one or more of the following: learning disabilities, attention deficits, emotional and behavioral disorders, pervasive developmental disorders, or hearing impairments.

Activities during the first year involved the domains of visual and performing arts, biological science, physical science, and engineering design. These activities were part of the Talent Discovery Assessment Process (see Chapter 10) and served as audition sessions where students' potential talent in these domains could surface.

During the second year of the project, activities focused on teaching students the skills and methods of the discipline of their talent. Dr. Joseph Renzulli's Enrichment Triad Model (1977) guided the skill development curriculum, and we designed activities to elicit specific cognitive, creative, and affective behaviors characteristic of practicing professionals in each discipline. Content specialists, such as zoologists, botanists, a biological illustrator, physicists, engineers, visual artists and actors, taught bi-weekly, 90-minute lessons that engaged students in learning authentic skills of those professionals. The types of activities conducted within each domain were advanced well beyond the actual grade level of students participating in Project HIGH HOPES, and the dually-differentiated curriculum (see Chapter 8) addressed both the students' gifts and their special needs. Table 11.1 lists sample topics.

During each session, students were engaged in authentic content and advanced-level skills. For example, over the course of several engineering sessions, students learned how to use a transit to measure the gradations of their auditorium. From these measurements, they constructed a topographic map and then a scale model. In biology, students assumed the role of scientist as they discovered what constitutes an owl's diet. They carefully dissected owl pellets and, using anatomy charts, identified parts of skeletal structures of the owl's prey. One group of students reconstructed an entire vole skeleton, learning about the structure of the food chain and the carrying capacity of the owl in the process. By comparing and contrasting the skeletal remains, students determined important facts about what the owls had consumed, and probing questions led to higher-level extrapolation, inference, and deduction.

The next phase of the project helped students apply their new skills in an interdisciplinary context. Project HIGH HOPES conducted an extremely successful one-week summer residential program on the campus of the American School for the Deaf in West Hartford, Connecticut. Twenty-seven identified students worked in research and development (R&D) "companies" to solve a genuine problem associated with the pond there. This intense problem-based learning experience gave these middle school students a rare educational opportunity to become bona fide real-world problem-solvers. The students were assigned to interdisciplinary teams comprising engineers, scientists, artists, and actors to collaborate on the problem. Their goal was to develop a proposal containing a creative solu-

| Table 11.1. Project HIGH HOPES Talent Development Curriculum | |
|---|---|
| Engineering | Topography, Model Rocketry, Android Anatomy, Leonardo's Wagon |
| Physical Science | Liquid Surfaces, Qualities of Air, Hard and Soft Water, Purification of Water |
| Zoology | Microscopes, Cells Alive, Predatory Behavior of Hydra, Pond Organisms, Animal communication, Food Webs, Social Behavior, Human Heritable Traits |
| Botany | Carnivorous Plants, Experimenting in Physiology, Genetic Variation in Plants |
| Visual Arts | Composite Creature, Optical Illusion (design concepts), Linear Perspective, Still Life Drawing, Chiaroscuro (light and shade), Impressionism: Painting Landscape, Metamorphosis (drawing), Wire Sculpture, Clay Modeling, Carving, Construction (assemblage/mixed media), Metamorphosis (clay modeling) |
| Performing Arts | Basic Elements of Movement, Movement and Space, Using Voice and Expression, Developing Character Roles, Tableau Technique |

tion for reconstructing the pond (see Figure 11.3).

Students worked in an advanced laboratory environment in which specially selected and highly qualified teacher-facilitators coached the individual research and development companies in the creative problem solving process. When needed, content-area specialists (mentors) in the four domains—engineering, performing arts, science, and visual arts—furnished technical advice on tools, techniques, and materials used by practicing professionals in those specific domains. Both teacher-facilitators and mentors taught students to capitalize on their talents and strengths to create a relevant proposal with supporting products, data, and budget considerations.

For 3 days, student R&D companies were fully focused on the creative problem solving process. Which species of animal life had once inhabited the pond? What degree of stress had the existing bridges tolerated? Student companies then began to finalize plans for their presentations to the Board of Directors and eagerly sought advice from the mentors as to how to polish their presentations creatively and professionally.

At the Presentations Forum, held on the final day of the week, each R&D company presented its proposal to a simulated Board of Directors

---

### Pond Problem

As you are about to see, the American School for the Deaf has a water feature. The feature has some problems. You will visit the site and be provided with resources and information about the site. Once at the site your group will be asked to gather information about the site and use resource people to help develop your plan for improving this water feature.

Original, creative, innovative useful solutions are encouraged. There is no one right answer to this problem. Groups will be recognized for excellence in their plans. Your group's task is as follows:

1. Identify the existing problems and future potentials of the site.
2. Review the resources.
3. Decide on additional information that you might need.
4. Brainstorm solutions to the problems.
5. Develop an action plan to fix the problems.
6. Prepare a presentation of your plan. (It is important to note that plans will be presented to a panel of people, some of whom have the authority to consider and implement your plan.)

---

**Figure 11.3.** Project HIGH HOPES activity involving students in real-world problem solving.

for the school. In addition, another 300 people sat in the audience. The students introduced themselves as the professionals they had become in the course of the week's work; "I'm Joseph, and I'm the botanist in this firm!" one proclaimed to the audience.

Each company presented its proposed solution for reconstructing the pond using an innovative approach that reflected the creative problem solving techniques the students had been using all week. Combining artistically-enhanced overhead transparencies, video clips, 3-D models, and dramatic performances, students illustrated both the deteriorating pond conditions they had analyzed and their companies' recommendations for correcting them. Most of the companies redesigned the existing structures; one team built a scale model of the pond and constructed prototypes of a new bridge and dam (see Figure 11.4). Another team began their presentation with a skit in which the team's actors portrayed elements of the pond environment, including the animals, plants, and garbage floating in the water. The scientists then described why the pond was in its current condition, and the engineers explained their solution using visual sketches designed by the artists. They ended their presentation with a return of the actors who now portrayed the pond as the clean, healthy environment their rehabilitation plan predicted.

In every aspect of the students' presentations, their integration of basic skills was evident. For example, one company calculated the cost of implementing its proposal and included an itemized budget in its presentation. This budget was not just a list of basic costs; the team used higher-level skills of comparison and contrast, forecasting, and evaluation to develop their budget. Similarly, students had learned the

**Figure 11.4.** Student-constructed model for the Pond Problem

basic skill of classification to identify insects. But they went well beyond merely identifying insects. They chose to apply the scientific method and develop original experiments that tested the effect of temperature on various pond creatures.

Modern technology helps students expand their basic communication skills. Several companies integrated videotaped segments in their presentations. Their videos reflected thorough planning and organization, creative and artful photography from many perspectives, a polished and smooth-flowing script, and clever sound effects.

Students also learned organization skills. The teams had to carve up the big problem into little sequenced tasks, determine who was responsible for each task, and decide on the time needed to complete the tasks. The challenge of solving authentic problems within a given time required the students to organize their efforts efficiently, effectively, and economically.

Collaboration of the sort expected in Project HIGH HOPES is an important skill for students with learning disabilities to acquire. In one company, two students, as their company's scientists, worked together to write the script for their presentation. One of these students used her superior verbal skills, while a deaf classmate signed the message for non-hearing members of the audience.

The students remained focused on their tasks over the course of the week. Often they ignored scheduled free time to continue working on their projects. Students who had few social skills bonded around similar interests and purposes. On the final day, there was no doubt in anyone's mind that each of these youngsters was highly talented. For the week, they seem to have left their disabilities at home.

During the final year of HIGH HOPES, students engaged in activities where they could continue to solve problems and develop their talents at levels commensurate with talented peers without disabilities. These students, who had been regarded as losers in fifth and sixth grade, were gaining entrance into the districts' traditional gifted programs and advanced science and art classes. Table 11.2 summarizes these students accomplishments as they evolved from students with special needs to students with gifts and talents. Some had entered art contests, others auditioned for roles in their school plays, and some entered advanced science classes. One young woman conducted a study on animal behavior

| Table 11.2. Project HIGH HOPES Student Accomplishments. | | |
|---|---|---|
| **Domain** | **Opportunity** | **Results** |
| Engineering | Odyssey of the Mind competitions | Five teams participated in Connecticut; two second-place awards and one third-place award |
| Engineering | Egg-drop competition | Two students had award-winning entries in the school's egg drop contest |
| Performing Arts | Auditions for school plays | Five students were selected by an audition process for leading roles in their schools' productions |
| Visual Arts | Student regional juried art shows | Ten students had art work selected in juried competitions in Massachusetts, Rhode Island, and Connecticut |
| Visual arts | District gifted art program | Three students selected for advanced art class |
| Science | Science fair competitions | Seven students entered science fairs and one received a written commendation for high quality |
| Science | Physics Day Competition | Twelve students participated in district science completion. Nine received recognition for their problem solving ability. |
| Science | Acceptance to science advanced classes | Two students accepted into their districts' advanced science class for gifted students |

and won a commendation at a science fair competition.

During the talent development lessons, Project HIGH HOPES staff had the opportunity to observe the students succeeding. Under the learning conditions created during these sessions, students appeared motivated, in control of their learning, and confident in their abilities. More specifically, they displayed a variety of self-regulatory behaviors known to underlie learning and achievement (Zimmerman, 1989). These included focus and sustained attention, perseverance in overcoming obstacles, active participation in the activity, willingness to extend learning both in and out of school, and cooperation and teamwork. Interestingly, these same learners seldom showed such behaviors in their traditional classes.

**Self-contained classrooms.** Some districts have established full time, self-contained programs for GLD students. Montgomery County, Maryland Public Schools offers this option for high ability students with severe learning disabilities. There are three elementary programs that serve approximately 50 students, three middle school programs, and two high school programs. These programs are unusual because they simultaneously addresses giftedness and the academic needs of each student by offering gifted curriculum and appropriate accommodations to compensate for learning difficulties. We had the opportunity to visit this program and observe students actively engaged in a challenging curriculum especially designed for high ability students. Small class sizes and opportunities for hands-on learning with accommodations served these students well. One student bragged, "I love coming to school now. Classes are exciting. We have great discussions and are always learning new and interesting things. My writing has improved because we are allowed to use the computer and we even have voice sensitive computers. I speak my first draft into the computer and then edit it."

There are many advantages to this kind of program. First, students are not embarrassed by their poor reading or writing abilities. Second, students work with their intellectual peers as they engage in sophisticated content. Third, all students use accommodations in some form, so no one stands out as different. Finally, the school aligns instructional strategies with students' learning strengths. As a staff member summarizes, "Careful attention is given to both the physical and social climate of the classroom in which needs are supported and abilities are recognized and nurtured." (Weinfeld, Barnes-Robinson, Jeweler, & Shevitz, 2002). Similar programs exist in southern Westchester County, New York and Albuquerque, New Mexico.

**The Greenwood School.** Sometimes the needs of these students are best met in a private school setting where a more comprehensive support program is offered. The optimal setting is one that offers both remedial support and opportunities for talent development. We found one example of this approach at The Greenwood School in Putney, Vermont. We visited this creative environment designed for boys ages 10-15 who have special needs in reading, writing, spelling, or mathematics, but who possess average or superior intelligence. The school seems best suited for GLD students with spatial talents, and we have recommended this site for several youngsters who have since thrived in this environment. Greenwood is described on its web site (www.greenwood.org) as an enriching and challenging pre-preparatory school for a specific population, rather than as a clinically modeled "special school." As the director explains,

This distinction is important to us, both because it accurately expresses our identity as a comprehensive educational institution in a field of mainstream junior boarding schools, and because it helps our students to form a positive image of themselves now and in the future.

The breadth and richness of the Greenwood curriculum has set a standard in the profession. Students succeed at Greenwood because the program is designed to address the needs of the whole student: intellectual, emotional, creative, and physical. A full pre-preparatory academic program, including language tutorials, science, history, literature, mathematics, art, music, drama, public speaking, and athletics assures that our students are intellectually challenged, creatively inspired, and factually informed.

Our visit to this picturesque learning environment gave us the opportunity to see students in their tutorials and engaged in enrichment and talent development activities. We were especially impressed with the school's unique offerings in engineering and design as well as visual and performing arts. Figure 11.5 includes a description of the Village Program (The Greenwood School, 1997-2003, www.thegreenwoodschool.org/academics/village.cfm).

### Lessons Learned About Teaching and Learning for Talent Development

As mentioned previously, talent development activities are fertile ground for observing how bright students with disabilities learn. In each of the opportunities described in this chapter, common themes emerged that reinforced students' abilities to perform as gifted rather than disabled. Using examples from Project HIGH HOPES, we summarize these themes here and then apply them to classroom practice in the next chapter.

Successful curricula for GLD students must incorporate advanced concepts and authentic skills of the domain. Many Project HIGH HOPES lessons were adapted from college-level texts. Because professionals within the domain conducted the sessions, students gained authentic knowledge of the discipline and used first-hand the methods and tools of the practicing professional. Students' successes depended not on the traditional reading-then-discussing motif but rather on authentic activities of constructing and applying knowledge within meaningful contexts.

---

### Enrichment at The Greenwood School

**THE VILLAGE PROGRAM**

Greenwood's unique Village Program demonstrates the practical application of mathematics, social studies, science and other subjects. . . . Co-developed by a Greenwood faculty member, Village is a simulation of the essential elements involved in constructing a town, complete with social structures and an economic system. Students model miniature inhabitants (complete with fantasy "persona"), obtain loans, plan a town center, and purchase construction materials. Each student designs and builds a model house in the school's carpentry shop, and 1/24 acre of school campus is set aside for his personal use during the game. In mid-May all properties are value assessed by a visiting architect and "bought back" by the school. Students invite their parents to a miniature Village fair and spend their profits at a fantastic and often zany final auction.

An additional dimension of Village is that other academic studies are often explored by, and coordinated with the Village program. For example, when students study the Middle Ages,
- They construct a medieval village
- Learn medieval music
- Dramatize a medieval play
- Read medieval-themed literature

The Village program offers an ideal means of showing creative students how practical knowledge is a necessary foundation for the expression of creative ideas.

In addition to accomplishing educational objectives, Village fosters
- A sense of community responsibility
- The study of environmental concerns as the development of the Village site expands
- Exploration each year of a different environmental issue is highlighted, although many may be explored

Excerpted from The Greenwood School Web Site, www.thegreenwoodschool.org/academics/village.cfm.

---

**Figure 11.5.** The Village Program at The Greenwood School  (The Greenwood School, 1997-2003, www.thegreenwoodschool.org/academics/village.cfm).

- Talent development activities de-emphasized reading and writing. Downplaying reading and writing directly reduces those areas of weakness most common in students with special needs. Remember that students with learning disabilities spend much of their cognitive energy each day trying to decode information or write down their thoughts, leaving little opportunity or energy for exploration and invention. When educators push reading and writing limitations into the background, domain-specific talents such as problem-solving become more prominent.

- Observing the mentors or other professionals as they worked with these youngsters revealed that none of them spent much time lecturing, especially at the start of an activity. These facilitators placed far more emphasis on observational learning: Mentors modeled what the students were to do and quickly allowed them to proceed with the task. For example, the visual artist gave verbal instructions only while she was simultaneously showing samples of the technique under study. To illustrate a technique, she provided a demonstration as she described the process.

- Mentors often used visuals to get a point across. For example, engineers used an inverted colander as a model to represent dimensionality of concentric circles on a topographic map. Verbal exchanges between students and mentors occurred individually as students engaged in an activity. Once students completed an activity, lively discussions ensued. It appears that, for gifted learning-disabled students, discourse was more meaningful *following an experience* than preceding it..

- Mentors broke complex learning tasks into several manageable parts that culminated in a final product. For example, students performed a series of improvisational pieces separately at first and then as a whole at the end of the class. Likewise, students combined sketches of individual still life representations into a more complex piece for their portfolios. As a result, students began to understand that many sub-tasks made up finished products.

- Clear and consistent communication about expectations was essential to students success. Those mentors who experienced the least amount of difficulty with student discipline tended to be clearest about their expectations. They presented to the group the activity's objective, simple and specific directions, and what each student was expected to do to achieve the objective. Mentors also prompted students to ask questions to clarify any confusing directions. For students who needed to see precisely what was required of them, the mentor modeled the activity. Mentors also explained to the students that, since the youngsters were being regarded as professionals, they must act professionally. For example, when students were observing animals or using instruments and tools (microscopes, transits, drills) or materials (clay, props, motors), they needed to be extremely careful and respectful of them.

It is significant that there were no accidents or incidents of misbehavior during these lessons. Unemotional, verbal cues for behavior seemed effective in reminding students of their responsibility and accountability. When one young artist once left the work area to browse through some art books before cleaning his space, the mentor whispered a gentle reminder that artists clean up their areas when their work is finished. The youngster smiled and willingly complied.

- The experiential activities that promoted problem solving benefited students in three ways. First, because the students were actively engaged, their attention span increased. Second, this approach allowed students to think and act in modes commensurate with their strengths. And third, learning in a personally meaningful context allowed for improved memory and transfer of skills to novel situations.

- Alternative assessment procedures incorporating experiential activities and product-based learning were important in gauging student learning. Communication options other than reading and writing provided opportunities for students to demonstrate domain-process skills. In addition, using assessment via experiential activities allowed content specialists to encourage students to find ties to other real-world situations and problems. This bridging not only anchored learning but encouraged transfer to other problem-solving situations as well.

From the outset, Project HIGH HOPES sessions had been designed around culturally worthwhile problems rather than merely a series of "hands-on" activities. For example, the performing arts mentor frequently set up a scenario and challenged the students to figure out how to have the characters convey the meaning. Divided into two groups, the students performed for each other. As they alternated roles, the audience group critiqued the other group's performance and suggested strategies to improve it. In zoology, students tackled the question, "Why do you think temperature affects the metabolism of reptiles?" Students formulated a hypothesis and designed an experiment to test it. During the process, these budding scientists soon deduced that they needed to control for alternate hypotheses and revised their experiment accordingly.

## A Talent Development Plan

We conclude this chapter with encouragement that you will begin to provide opportunities for bright youngsters to develop their special talents. To help you organize these activities, Figure 11.6 includes a sample Talent Development Plan developed by Rick Olenchak (see Appendix B for a reproducible copy).

**PERSONALIZED TALENT DEVELOPMENT PLAN**

F. Richard Olenchak, Ph.D.

Beginning ________ and Ending ________

Student ______________________ Date ________

Classroom Teacher(s) ______________________ Grade ________

Mentor ______________________ Updates ________

Current Interests ______________________

| TALENT DEVELOPMENT ACTIVITIES | FREQUENCY & LOCATION | GUIDING ADULT | PROPOSED OUTCOMES & DATES |
|---|---|---|---|
| | | | |
| | | | |
| | | | |
| | | | |
| | | | |
| | | | |
| | | | |

Student's Signature ______________________

Parent's Signature ______________________

Mentor's Signature ______________________

Signatures of School Faculty Involved

______________________

______________________

______________________

Signature of School Administrator ______________________

**Figure 11.6.** Personalized talent development plan.

# Chapter 12

# Effective Classroom Practices

So that bright students with attention or learning difficulties can meet with success in school, learning environments must be sensitive to the unique needs that these struggling students present. These students typically have difficulties in reading, writing, and attending to the task at hand. They often have negative attitudes about self, school, and learning, and little motivation for school-related tasks. As described in Chapter 9, they need a dually differentiated curriculum, but too often, these bright students are frustrated by pressure to learn in ways that highlight their disabilities.

By definition, remedial efforts highlight weaknesses and emphasize the simplest tasks, which hold little interest for a bright child. When remediation is the main entrée on the educational menu, these challenged gifted learners have little to hunger for and begin to regard school as distasteful, perhaps even unhealthy. They may generalize feelings about specific areas of weakness into a broader feeling of depression or hostility, and their self-worth may begin to dwindle.

To bring their appetite back, the total educational environment must address the unique needs of these students—physical, intellectual, and emotional. Students must be allowed to engage in a challenging curriculum that is tailored to how they learn, receive appropriate accommodations, and find opportunities to feel respected and valued in the school community. This menu requires a collaborative effort among families, students, teachers and specialists. The following case study concerns Melanie, a dyslexic young artist, and demonstrates both the spirit and the strategies needed to forge a collaborative model for optimizing the learning environment.

## Melanie*

The art room was filled with a collection of student displays, all interesting and indicative of budding talent. As I glanced about I was suddenly drawn to a very unusual piece of art—an old door that had been used as an inviting canvas for creative artistic expression. The art teacher said that many students had taken their turn at transforming this door into a powerful piece of art, but none were so accomplished as this piece. Asking more about the artist, Melanie, I learned that she was severely dyslexic. But, the art teacher revealed, Melanie was doing well in school because of the support she received from her mother, friends, and teachers.

My interest was now sparked about this positive and seemingly successful collaboration; I took the time to interview some of her teachers, the learning specialist, and Melanie herself. Their stories painted a picture of what an inclusive model should look like. The account of Melanie's academic journey captures the essence of what can be accomplished when professionals collaborate to educate the whole child through talent development, classroom modifications, and differentiated instruction.

Melanie entered this school in the third grade. Earlier, she had attended a school where no one seemed to understand her problems, talents, or unique academic needs. She had been diagnosed with dyslexia and was having extreme difficulty learning. Melanie described a particular incident:

> I had been absent the previous day when the other second graders wrote their poems. The teacher said I was to write mine that day about spring. I had no idea what to do. The only thing I could think of was to copy the first line of everyone else's poem and turn it in. My teacher loved the poem. I got an A and she never realized what I had done. I could not even read the words I had copied. The A only made me unhappier about school. No one knew I couldn't read and I was too ashamed to confess.

Her parents, sensitive to her anguish and lack of genuine accomplishment, enrolled Melanie in her current school. The school empha-

---

* Written by Susan Baum

sized art and students took art classes several times each week. Melanie soon discovered that she had an interest in and talent for art. She received help from the learning support team and, for the first time in her life, felt valued in the school setting. Melanie's mother read to her and became her scribe so she didn't fall too far behind in her school assignments. Reading came slowly and writing was painful. But little by little she began to read and write, although with great difficulty. By the time she entered high school, she knew how to work hard and could advocate for what she needed from the environment in order to be successful.

Her lack of reading and writing skills did not keep her from being successful within the curriculum because the teachers in the school tended to integrate art projects in their classrooms. For example, the language arts teachers offered art activities to all students in every literature unit. On one occasion, after reading Joseph Conrad's *Heart of Darkness*, the students chose from a variety of projects, including creating a mural that illustrated the characters' attributes. The students were required to justify their visual depictions of the characters—including color and facial expression—with relevant text from the book. Melanie opted to work with the mural group. She told me that her group's lively discussions during the planning process gave her much deeper insight into the book. As she explained, "I knew there would be a question on this novel [on the final exam]. When I read the question, I just closed my eyes and visualized the mural, and the words just came!"

Melanie, her teachers, and her learning specialist collaborated to develop modifications for assignments that required writing. One such modification allowed Melanie to use her artistic abilities to express her understandings of targeted concepts. For example, instead of the traditional English class essay, Melanie often chose to produce intricate mind maps showing abstract and mature insights about characters and plot development. An illustration of her drafts and final piece appear in Figure 12.1.

On some occasions, though, Melanie decided to write the essay and refused the offered accommodations. During those times she worked with the learning specialist who would help her to organize her ideas into a thoughtful written piece. Using a computer program, *Inspiration*, that uses mapping as a prewriting exercise, Melanie was able to transfer her visual ideas to the computer. Spelling and grammar checks on her computer helped her turn in well-written assignments.

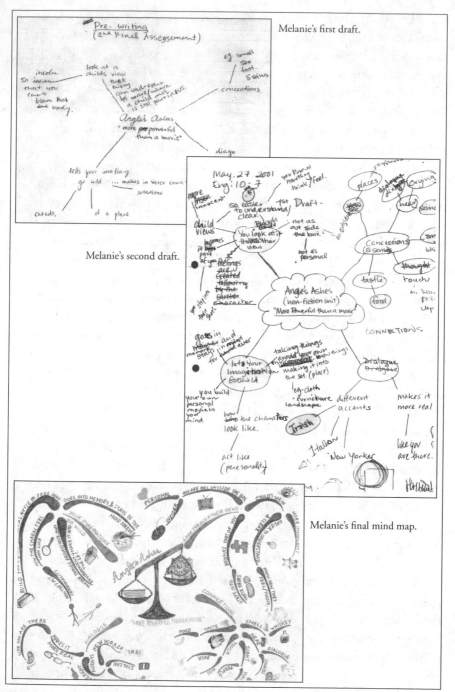

**Figure 12.1.** Melanie's mind maps.

Melanie's first draft.

Melanie's second draft.

Melanie's final mind map.

Melanie was not always as confident as she is today. Looking back, she attributes her ever-increasing sense of efficacy to her art experiences: "Art is my therapy. Through my art I can explain who I am and how I feel. Art is where I am to reveal and represent, often metaphorically, the pain, anguish and isolation I often feel. When I painted the piece that hangs in the art room of the green chair in the red room, I was trying to show how I don't blend in. The green chair almost clashes in this setting. That's how I can feel at times. That's what being different is all about."

Melanie hid the fact from her peers that she couldn't read until she was in ninth grade. The accepting atmosphere at this school empowered her to reveal to her friends that she was dyslexic. Since then, her friends have become additional collaborators. They take notes for her and help her read difficult material. It is not a one-way street, though. Melanie remarks, " I could not accept help from them if I could not reciprocate. I help my friends see the bigger picture. They often count on me to give them the structure for their writing. We bounce ideas off each other, and they know I will give them different points of view."

## Learning Environments That Promote Success

The happy ending of Melanie's story underscores the need to attend to the intellectual needs of these bright but struggling students. We need to deliver curriculum to students in ways that honor their intelligence and provide windows of opportunities for them to be successful. Her teachers were able to optimize her strengths in delivering the curriculum while supporting her in areas of weakness. Melanie's experience is unusual, but it is not unique. Her teachers never watered down her curriculum or lowered their standards. Instead they found ways to help her succeed in spite of her disability. For Melanie to feel successful, her performance had to meet her internal standards on tasks she deemed important and relevant. It is precisely for this reason that we have emphasized approaches typically encouraged for gifted students. A curriculum that respects intelligence and offers sophisticated challenge and personal relevance will afford Alphabet Children opportunities to achieve high quality success.

Just as important as addressing intellectual needs, it is essential to arrange the physical environment to facilitate learning. Room arrangements, class size, and resources within the classroom need to align to the learning styles and characteristics of the student. Likewise, it is important to provide an emotional climate that is attuned to the esteem needs of these students. To assess the climate in the classroom, teachers should ask themselves the following questions:

- Is my instruction and the curriculum appropriate to the intellectual levels and learning styles of my students?
- Have I provided choices for learning and communication?
- Have I provided a physical environment where the child can focus and attend?
- Do I focus and honor the gifts and talents each of my students brings to the classroom?

Table 12.1 highlights the important aspects of curricular and classroom structure. The remainder of the chapter provides a detailed discussion of each area.

## The Intellectual Environment
### Providing Appropriate Instructional Activities

As we pointed out in Chapter 6, learning follows a somewhat predictable cognitive sequence. The sequence begins with some stimulus or event getting a child's attention, then senses transfer the information into working memory where it gets interpreted, manipulated, rearranged, and elaborated upon. In the best cases, the information is eventually stored in long term memory, retrieved, and communicated as needed. For too many students, learning breaks down at the very beginning because we fail to capture and hold students' attention. For others, reading and talking about a topic in a non-meaningful context restricts memory and retrieval. And, of course, many gifted students with learning and attention problems have been able to attend to and store much information, but poor writing and organizational skills prevent them from expressing what they know. To overcome such hurdles to learning, teachers need to engage students at the outset, allow them to learn by doing, and encourage them to communicate in ways that fit with their strengths.

We have identified four kinds of instructional strategies particularly successful in helping these gifted students achieve within the classroom:

1. using appropriate entry points,
2. using project-based learning with a variety of exit points,
3. investigating authentic problems, and

## Table 12.1. Supportive Learning Environments

**Instructional Aspects**
- Curriculum is engaging, respectful, and makes use of students' strengths, interests, and talents.
- Instruction incorporates careful and purposeful sequencing of lessons.
- Teaching strategies de-emphasize teacher talk as a primary means of delivering the curriculum.
- Short, intense activities are used, with opportunities for reasonable movement and quiet conversation.
- Lessons are oriented toward a problem-solving approach that results in creative products or discoveries.
- In respect for their learning needs and styles, students are offered choices about accessing information and communicating their understandings.
- Compensation strategies empower students to achieve success across the curriculum.
- Individual and small group instruction can be settings for remediation of basic skills where appropriate.

**Physical Aspects**
- Physical space is arranged to help students focus on the task.
- Quiet places for concentration are provided.
- Technical aids are available, including video or DVD players, computers, calculators, headphones, and lamps for reading.
- Space and opportunities are offered students requiring movement to assist their learning.
- Students are given choices of seating for listening purposes—rug, beanbag chair, at desk, standing quietly in back of room.

**Emotional Aspects**
- *All* students are respected.
- Risk-taking and creativity are valued.
- *All* students have choices for how they learn and how they communicate their ideas.
- Students are aware of their talents and are encouraged to use them.
- Teachers expect students to succeed and they communicate those expectations clearly.
- Teachers organize environments to improve the likelihood of success.

4. using creative problem solving approaches.

In addition, teachers need to teach students compensation and self-regulation strategies, provide them with appropriate accommodations, and offer remediation as needed.

1. **Using appropriate entry points.** Gaining students' attention at the start of any lesson is critical. Many of us do exactly what our own teachers did: automatically jump into a discussion or lecture without

evaluating the motivational value of these triggers. We have learned from Project HIGH HOPES (see Chapter 11) and other experiences that "teacher talk," especially lectures or giving directions, is rarely successful in engaging and holding students' attention. It can even interfere with learning during the attentional phase for gifted students who are not strong in linguistic intelligence. Think of how typical lesson starters—classroom discussions, assessing prior knowledge, vocabulary review, and reading the text—can inhibit these special youngsters from engaging in the lesson. Initial activities must *invite* students into the lesson by creating meaningful contexts where these learners can successfully connect ideas to prior understanding and form new concepts.

Howard Gardner (1999) devotes considerable attention to using a multiple intelligences approach to form appropriate entry points to learning. He argues that teachers should initiate lessons in ways that grab students' attention. For an artist it might be using a painting or movie; for the block-building crew, it might be creating a structure or figuring out how something works. Some of our students who are strong in the personal and bodily-kinesthetic intelligences come alive when drama introduces a lesson.

Teachers can use entry points in two ways: to develop skills or to introduce concepts within a unit (Baum, Viens, & Slatin, in consultation with Gardner, 2003). For example, using improvisational drama to develop and write about a character can be an important bridge for students with strengths in performing arts. We worked in a seventh grade classroom with students experiencing learning, attention, and emotional difficulties. Their teacher had described how it was nearly impossible to get the students to put their ideas in writing. We decided to use character interviews as an entry point. We started with some warm-up activities to set the stage for creative drama. (An excellent source for these and other drama activities is *Live On Stage* ( Blank & Roberts, 1997). The teacher took the role of a brilliant taxi driver and one of us interviewed him. The students were then invited to ask the driver their own questions. (Interestingly, the students who had never said much before posed the most intriguing queries.) Next, we asked students to volunteer to play different characters and we repeated the activity. One young man became a mad scientist, another a lazy dragon-slayer with a Scottish brogue.

After these warm-ups, we brainstormed and listed questions we would want to know about any character. We then provided a list of interesting characters for the students to become (e.g., David the dangerous dentist, Lucky Lucy the hairdresser, and Clarence the exhausted clown). Asking the students to work in pairs, we explained that one would become the character and the other would assume the role of interviewer. We gave the students five minutes to conduct the interviews—no writing, just role-playing. At the conclusion of the "interview," we asked the students to write about themselves (if they were the character) or about the character they interviewed. We told them that they should just start writing and let the words flow without fretting about punctuation, spelling, or grammar. Over the course of a week, the students worked on polishing their drafts. Working with the draft on the computer made editing and revising a much simpler task.

In Figure 12.2 includes the first drafts from one pair of students. The teacher was amazed at the quantity and quality of work from these two students. (We were also surprised.) The mad scientist character had never written more than a few words on any essay assignment.

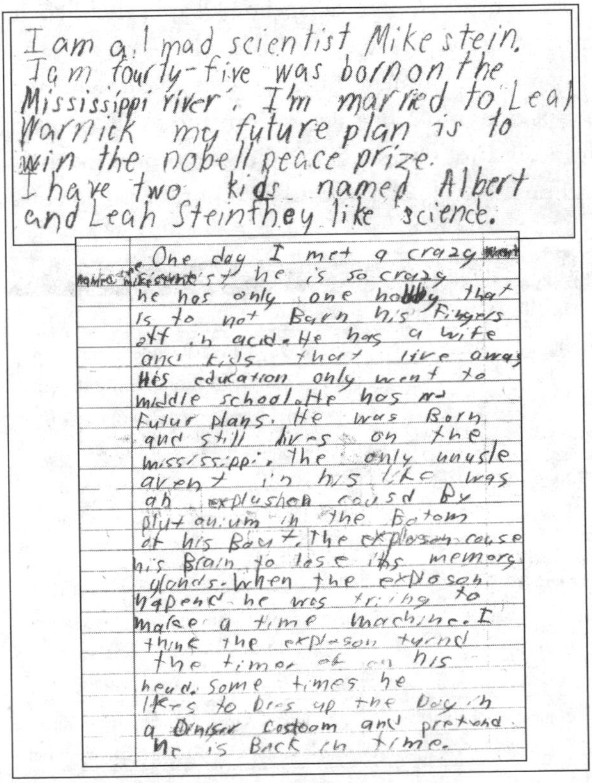
I am a mad scientist Mike stein. I am fourty-five was born on the Mississippi river. I'm married to Leah Warnick my future plan is to win the nobell peace prize. I have two kids named Albert and Leah Stein they like science.

One day I met a crazy scient'st he is so crazy he has only one hobby that is to not Barn his Fingers off in acid. He has a wife and kids that live away His education only went to middle school. He has no Futur plans. He was Born and still lives on the mississippi. The only unusle avent in his like was an explushon causd By plutaunium in the Botom of his Bout. The explosen cause his Brain to lose its memory glands. When the exploson hapend he was triing to make a time machine. I think the explason turnd the timer of on his head. Some times he likes to dres up the Day in a Draiser costoom and pretend he is Back in time.

**Figure 12.2.** First drafts of a writing assignment introduced by an entry point appropriate for GLD students

Table 12.2 shows other examples of entry points to literacy. Note that the entry point itself sets the context and is meant to engage the students. However, essential to the success of any entry point is the teacher's skill in

guiding the students from the experience to the targeted goal. In this case, we brainstormed questions anyone would want to know about a character and presented a list of interesting characters for the students to describe. These prompts provided students with the structure that allowed them to develop and write about a character. Finally, using computers, students developed their first drafts into a credible piece of writing.

In addition to using alternative entry points to teach specific skills, teachers need to consider how they initiate a unit of study. When activities align with students' strengths and interests, they engage reluctant students and provide them with access to content that does not rely heavily on reading as the primary source of information. Gardner (1999) has identified a variety of approaches, summarized in Table 12.3.

We have been very successful using a multiple intelligences approach with Alphabet Children. Consider the problem of beginning a unit on genetics with a group of bright seventh graders who had attention deficits and were severely learning disabled. We started the unit using an experiential entry point in which we simulated the random assignment of X and Y chromosomes. One of us took the role of Mom and held Post-It™ notes with X written in bold to represent the X chromosome given by females. The other assumed the role of Dad and held notes with an equal

| Table 12.2 Entry Points to Skill Development | | |
| --- | --- | --- |
| **Instructional Strategy** | **Intelligence(s) Tapped** | **Example** |
| Movement and dance | Bodily-kinesthetic | First grade bilingual students moved to song "Monster Mash." Their monster movements generated descriptive vocabulary in English to use in writing. |
| Character interviews | Bodily-kinesthetic Personal | Seventh graders used improvisational techniques to develop characters for a story they were writing |
| Storyboarding | Spatial | Fifth graders developed visual stories using a filmmaking technique to understand how to focus their ideas and use topic sentences and paragraphs. |
| Logic puzzles | Logical-mathematical | Third graders used deductive reasoning puzzle to improve reading comprehension. |
| Playing musical pieces and learning how to transcribe melodies onto a written musical scale. | Musical Bodily-kinesthetic | Fourth graders practiced writing music to learn and understand graphing. |

**Table 12.3. Howard Gardner's (1999) Entry Points.**

| Entry Point | Description |
|---|---|
| Foundational/ EXISTENTIAL (Aligned with the existential intelligence, for people who ask "big questions" or questions with philosophical overtones) | Starting a unit with a big question: Why are humans drawn to war? Why do humans allow other humans to starve? Why should we spend money on space exploration? |
| NARRATIONAL (Aligned with linguistic intelligence, for people who like learning about topics through stories) | Presenting a story to introduce a unit. |
| AESTHETIC (Associated with spatial and perhaps naturalist intelligences, for people who like to see a visual representation of an idea) | Using works of art to analyze some aspect of the topic to be studied. . |
| QUANTITATIVE/NUMERICAL (Connected with Logical/Mathematical intelligence, for students who are attracted to numbers, who observe the world quantitatively) | Describing numerical aspects or perspective of topic such as the amount of money lost during the stock market crash of 1929 to introduce a unit on the Great Depression. |
| EXPERIENTIAL (Connected with bodily-kinesthetic, perhaps personal and spatial intelligences, for students who prefer hands-on experiences) | Using hands-on activities like performances and experiments. (Introducing a unit on molecular bonding with a movement exercise or experiment.) |
| SOCIAL (Aligned with personal intelligences, for students most attracted to simulations, role playing, working in groups to solve social problems) | Beginning a unit on Westward expansion by simulating the trip. Students take roles of the pioneers and solve problems daily concerning resources and relationships. |
| MUSICAL (Aligned with musical intelligence) | Beginning with musical metaphors such as listening to the message of the music in the Battle Hymn of the Republic to get a sense of the urgency of the Civil War or comparing and contrasting music of a period to get a sense of the rhythm or tempo of the era. |

number with X and Y markers to represent male contributions. The students drew a Post-It™ note from each parent and affixed it to their shirts. Predictably, students found it hilarious when boys got to be girls and vice versa. But on top of the humor, they very quickly understood the random nature of heredity. And in the process they absorbed new vocabulary and principles during the experience—"chromosome," "inherit," "females carry the X chromosome," and so on.

The next engagement used a narrational entry point, and through a slide show we introduced the students to one of our families in which red hair was passed down from grandmother to daughter to grandchildren. Further into the topic, we told a story of the gene for hemophilia that also existed in the family but had remained hidden until the son was born. The students were very curious about the disease and paid close attention as the story of the young man unfolded through the slide show. We then explained how the gene for hemophilia is carried on the X chromosome. It only remains hidden if another X chromosome is present *without* the gene for hemophilia. We marked some of the X Post-Its™ with an *h* to represent this concept. The students used cards to generate all the possibilities of random combinations of X and Y chromosomes with some of the X chromosomes carrying the gene for hemophilia. We repeated the initial demonstration experience with the Post-Its™ where, as before, they received their genetic make-up from Mom and Dad. This time, however, using the chart shown below, they identified whether they had hemophilia, were a carrier, or did not have the gene at all.

During the second lesson, the students continued to learn new terms—

| | |
|---|---|
| XX | Female with no hemophilia |
| X/hX | Female with no hemophilia but is a carrier |
| XY | Male with no hemophilia |
| X/hY | Male with hemophilia |
| X/hX/h | Female with hemophilia |

*sex-linked genes, carriers, genotype, phenotype.* At the end of the sessions, they developed a chart predicting the outcome of the grandchildren's children should they marry someone with no hemophilia. For homework they read a brief summary of the concepts covered in the lessons as a review. The teacher remarked that she had never seen this group so attentive and who could remember the language and principals three weeks later on an exam.

We consistently find that when we present advanced content through alternate entry points, learners are thoroughly engaged and demonstrate that they understand the targeted concepts. Note that when using entry points to initiate learning, reading *follows* the lesson rather than precedes it. Students learn vocabulary in the context of the experience and review it at the end of the session.

**2. Using project-based learning with a variety of exit points.** Another problem for students who have writing, organization, or attention difficulties is how teachers assess mastery of curricular objectives. Evaluating learning through conventional written tests and assignments may not be valid for this population of students, as illustrated in the Desert

Storm political cartoon in Chapter 5. Performance and product assessment are usually better evaluation tools. (In truth, we believe this type of assessment is better for all students.) According to Gardner (1997), to demonstrate whether a concept is understood, individuals should be able to represent their knowledge in more than one way using more than one symbol systems: "We have to put understanding up front in school. Once we have that goal, multiple intelligences can be a terrific handmaiden because understanding involves a mix of mental representations entailing different intelligences" (p. 11)

The group mural described in Melanie's story signaled how powerful that choice of medium was in conveying meaning. Compared to a multiple choice test, having students construct a working model of a complex machine is far more likely to tap their understanding of gears, levers, and pulleys. Instead of merely applying a formula when certain terms appear in a word problem, most students would profit more from constructing a model of the Pythagorean theorem. Similarly, choreographing a dance sequence representing good vs. evil in a particular novel allows the performing artist to creatively articulate these conflicting forces.

By tapping into the students' strength from a curricular perspective, we can generate many choices for students to develop products to show their understanding. The products described in the examples above parallel specific, real-life disciplines. Artists design murals, engineers build structures and models, and choreographers create movement stories. Thus, by concentrating on the talents of Alphabet Children, we can generate many choices for acceptable products. Table 12.4 offers more examples.

The most important aspect of discipline-related activities is that the knowledge and understandings that result from authentic experiences provide a foundation or schema for writing and taking traditional tests. Melanie was able to write about the characters in *Heart of Darkness* by visualizing the mural, and after using a simulation to introduce the genetics unit, the 7th graders' were successful on their test. For these students, active learning and authentic products readied them for more traditional writing assignments.

**3. Investigating authentic problems.** Ben and the students in Project HIGH HOPES show us that Alphabet Children often thrive on problem-based learning and investigating real-world problems. When students act as first hand inquirers and develop authentic products, they

| Table 12.4. Discipline-Related Products (Nicols & Baum, 2002) | |
|---|---|
| **Discipline** | **Products** |
| **Writers** <br> Communicate with words | Poetry, Stories, Editorials, Speeches, Scripts, Song lyrics, Letters to the editor |
| **Artists** <br> Use visual images to communicate ideas | Paintings, Sketches, Photography, Film, Cartoons, Digital art |
| **Engineers** <br> Make models to explain or design how things work | Architectural Models, Working models, Prototypes, Three-dimensional models |
| **Performing Artists** <br> Communicate ideas and feelings through performances | Skits, Monologues, Choreographed pieces including dance or music, Gymnastic or other rhythmic stunts |
| **Mathematicians and Economists** <br> Express ideas using mathematical representations | Formulas, Tables, Charts, Graphs, Timelines, Equations |
| **Social Activists** <br> Focus on bringing about awareness of social problems and creating change through action-oriented events | Public services, Letter writing campaigns, Legislation, Speeches, Demonstrations, Media events, Effective use of the arts |
| **Historians** <br> Recreate the past through documenting and analyzing primary sources and communicate their findings using appropriate products | Storytelling, Photo essays, Video documentaries, Interviews, Timelines, Historical essays |
| **Leaders** <br> Use their inter- and intrapersonal intelligences to organize others to accomplish goals | Lead an event, Chair a committee, Organize a trip |
| **Scientists** <br> Design and carry out research and summarize findings | Hypothesizing, Interviews or surveys, Graphs, Statistical summaries |

use their strengths and aptitudes naturally as they are applied in the real world. Solving authentic problems makes learning relevant and highly contextual—conditions of learning essential for bright but challenged youngsters. Such experiences encourage students to address problems just as professionals do in their work, using methods of inquiry, materials, and strategies unique to real world domains. Using professional methodologies and equipment helps students see that individual gifts are valued and respected.

Students, of course, are not professionals, and their problem-solving approaches can be naïve and ineffectual. But that is OK! Even when students' solutions turn out badly, they are still learning important skills:

- How to think and act like a professional
- How to work collaboratively, giving and receiving assistance and constructive criticism
- How professionals go about modifying solutions to improve them
- How to get back on your feet after hitting a stone wall
- How to take advantage of talent
- Appreciation that creative productivity is a realistic and socially useful objective
- Appreciation that failures happen to everyone, and failures can offer good advice about what *not* to do in the future

Many of these incidental learnings are related to aspects of self-regulation. In that sense, they do not address learning about content but rather learning about learning.

Many how-to books detail the real world methods practicing professionals use to create new knowledge or products. An excellent resource for teachers is the "Mentors in Print" section of the Creative Learning Press catalog and web site (www.creativelearningpress.com). These books provide youngsters with the knowledge of how to be, for example, a photographer, investor, scientist, cartoonist, or toy inventor.

As we said, an important incidental benefit of using authentic problems is that they allow students with different talents to work together. Students can collaborate and create by relying on each other's talents and contributions to solve the problem and communicate results. They learn from one another and come to value each other's unique abilities. Compare this approach with some widely used cooperative learning arrangements in which students with challenges in reading and writing work with "experts" to reap the benefits the more advanced learners can offer. In these arrangements, the challenged students often perceive that they do not have an equal opportunity to contribute.

In short, using authentic problems allows students to contribute according to their strengths, apply basic skills within a meaningful context, and engage cooperatively in active inquiry and problem solving. Table 12.5 outlines these components with respect to the Pond Problem described in Chapter 11.

**4. Using critical and creative-thinking strategies.** Simulations, debates, and role playing are instructional strategies that encourage

| Table 12.5. Developing Authentic Problems Guide (based on the Pond Problem) (adapted from Baum, Viens, & Slatin with Gardner; in press) | |
|---|---|
| **1. Selecting the problem:** | |
| PROBLEM | Polluted pond on school property |
| PURPOSE | To suggest ways to bring the pond back to life |
| AUDIENCE | School community, Town council, Board of Education |

**2. Relating problem to basic curriculum:**

| | Curricular areas /activities | Targeted concepts and skills |
|---|---|---|
| Science | Conduct pond study | Observing and recording pond life and conditions<br>Looking for ecological patterns |
| Language Arts | Developing a plan | Finding background information<br><br>Developing a persuasive written argument |
| Math | Preparing a budget for proposal | Estimating costs to implement plan |
| | Making models and murals | Constructing models or drawing plans to scale |
| Art | Photography | Using close-up lens, photographing nature |
| | Sketching observations | Observing carefully |
| | Creating models or murals | Practicing design technique; communicating a point |
| Performing Arts | Developing skit to portray life in the pond | Using improvisation techniques, character interviews, and tableau |

**3. Deciding on the professional roles needed.**

| Possible Roles Needed | Associated talents (probable related intelligences) |
|---|---|
| Photographers | photography (Spatial, naturalist) |
| Environmentalists | Observations, looking for patterns (spatial, naturalist) |
| Scientists | Chemistry, ecology, field biology, data collecting (mathematical/logical) |
| Financial experts | Accounting (mathematical/logical) |
| Artists | Sketching, painting, sculpting (spatial, bodily kinesthetic, naturalist) |
| Performing artists | Acting, singing, dancing (bodily kinesthetic, musical, personal) |
| Writers | Persuasive writing (linguistic, personal) |
| Engineers | Constructing models (spatial, bodily kinesthetic, mathematical/logical) |
| Politicians | Writing or giving speeches, locating funding sources (linguistic, social) |

critical and creative thinking We know that gifted, learning-disabled children have considerable strength in creative thinking as well as higher order thinking. Where more unusual or creative answers are preferred, these students can excel. Such opportunities to contribute original and clever ideas should increase the self-efficacy of these students as well as contribute to their self-perceptions of being smart. Experiences that encourage these higher level thinking opportunities will also empower these students to develop alternate paths to reach goals and solve problems that bypass their learning problems. Programs such as Creative Problem Solving, Synectics, and Talents Unlimited are especially suited to the learning abilities of gifted youngsters with special learning needs. These programs offer a systematic instructional approach that requires critical and creative thinking to solve problems and produce high quality responses. Teachers can easily apply the techniques to both enrichment activities and the regular curriculum. Table 12.6 lists several helpful resources.

All the approaches described here involve experiential learning. Learning occurs through the experience of engaging in the topic at hand. Traditionally, the learning sequence involves mastering content through reading, lecture, and testing *first*, and then, *if time allows*, students can choose interesting projects to complete. The almost suffocating pressures of school accountability and the emphasis on standardized testing means that time for such projects will be in scarce supply. Tight instructional time may force teachers to ask students to pursue creative projects at home (if at all) instead of in class. Unfortunately for Alphabet Children, a more motivating approach is to challenge them *first* with a creative project relating to the topic. Reading and research are then directed toward a specific goal within a context. For example, in a unit on Native Americans, one student talented in drawing might use class time to develop a mural depicting the life of the Navajo Tribes during the 1800s.

**Table 12.6. Resources for Teaching Creative Problem Solving to Students.**

Eberle, B., & Stanish, B. (1997). *CPS for kids: A Resource book for teaching creative problem-solving to children.* Waco, TX: Prufrock Press.

Schlichter, C., & Palmer, W. R. (1993). *Thinking smart: A primer of the Talented Unlimited Model.* Mansfield Center, CT: Creative Learning Press.

Stanish, B., & Eberle, B. (1997). *Be a problem solver: A resources book for teaching creative problem-solving.* Waco, TX: Prufrock Press.

The content needed to complete the project will steer her attention and activity in the learning process. To review content, concepts, and big ideas of the unit, the teacher could have students share their projects. This kind of discussion after students have completed the project helps prepare students for more traditional unit tests.

## Classroom Modifications and Student Compensation Strategies

Learning difficulties connected with Alphabet Children's particular syndromes tend to be relatively durable through life. A poor speller will always have to rely on outside help to check for and correct spelling errors (e.g., spell check program, editor). Students who have difficulty memorizing math facts might need to ensure accuracy by using a calculator. Basic remediation for weaknesses is often not appropriate for the Alphabet Child. Remediation may make the learner a little more skillful, but he will probably not become proficient in areas of weakness. At some point we must decide when to use compensation techniques in favor of remedial strategies. Clarifying the targeted outcome can help guide this decision. For example, we should ask, "To what extent do we help children by teaching them to improve their handwriting before encouraging them to put their thoughts on paper using a word processor?" Is the outcome authoring or being able to use handwriting for communicating ideas?

Let's review the distinction between a disability and a handicap. Disabilities are physical states or conditions that result in impairment of functioning. Disabilities become handicaps when they interfere with the individual's ability to function in specific situations. (Lewis & Doorlag, 1983, p. 50) Learning-disabled children have been found to be capable and productive outside the school environment. They learn, create, and perform well. In school, however, they become handicapped—required to do tasks that are extremely difficult because of a neurological or information processing disorder. In helping the child achieve success in school, we should try to evaluate whether the environment is creating the handicap.

Consider the student who has an excellent understanding of mathematical principals but has great difficulty remembering math facts. What will be in the student's best interest—giving her thirty minutes a day of drill or allowing her to use a calculator? Will a small adjustment to the environment avoid handicapping this youngster's ability to succeed? Is it possible that using a calculator to perform drill exercises will help the student remember the facts? At times, we must make modifications in the educational environment to accommodate specific learning needs. Thus, in this chapter we use the term *modifications* to indicate the specific adjustments we can make to the learning environment to accommodate students' needs.

The modifications we make allow these students *to compensate* for problematic weaknesses. We have learned that effective compensation strategies are often unique to each individual (Mooney, 2000; Reis, Neu, & McGuire, 1995). The success of any strategy depends how well it fits with the student's learning strengths. For students like  , using art as a basis for her writing is successful. Melanie also relied on her friendships and social relationships for support in such activities as note taking and test review. Other students are more comfortable using technological assistance, such as taping class lectures or using a laptop computer to take notes in class. Modifications that match the students' means of compensating obtain the best results.

Optimizing the link between student need and environmental modification requires three elements:

1. Students' awareness of how they learn best
2. A flexible learning environment
3. Mutual planning between students and teachers

An excellent resource for helping older students discover clever ways to compensate is *Learning Outside the Lines* by Jonathan Mooney and David Cole (2000), two severely learning-disabled students who graduated from Brown University at the top of their classes. This resource provides excellent discussion topics for student focus groups (described in Chapter 13).

Table 12.7 summarizes some of the major difficulties these special students face and offers some practical tips for helping students compensate for them. We have already discussed several of these ideas, but will elaborate on some of the more significant suggestions.

## Modifications for Focusing and Sustaining Attention

Remember that for many Alphabet Children students, sitting and listening trigger inattention while movement and active engagement increase attention. Modifications should involve changing the environment to be more engaging or giving students props to help them focus. When we discussed the problem with attention and focus previously, we

| Table 12.7. Modifications and Accommodations | |
|---|---|
| **Difficulty** | **Keys** |
| Focusing and sustaining attention | • Employ environmental modifications<br>• Use alternate entry points aligned to students' strengths and interests<br>• Use technology<br>• Try novelty<br>• Allow attention sustainers: permitting gum chewing, listening to music using headphones, underlining or highlighting text when reading, doodling or playing with clay or silly putty while listening |
| Acquiring information with limited reading skills | • Use a multiple intelligences approach<br>• Reverse the usual sequence, i.e., begin with experience<br>• Teach through projects<br>• Teach through the arts (drama, visual arts, poetry, etc.)<br>• Use seminar instruction, lively discussion groups, simulations, and moral dilemmas<br>• Use primary sources such as interviews, guest speakers, demonstrations<br>• Engage students in discussion using supporting text<br>• Take advantage of multi-media presentations<br>• Use picture books<br>• Employ teaching materials with a visual component<br>• Provide books on tape<br>• Use text-to-speech software |
| Organizing information | • Use advance organizers<br>• Provided skeletal outlines<br>• Use visual models and recipes<br>• Teach and model webbing, storyboarding, using flow charts<br>• Provide software programs that help with writing and organizing<br>• Use inductive teaching strategies |

suggested that teachers use entry points that fit with students' intellectual strengths to engage them more fully in the curriculum and instruction. In addition, adjusting the physical environment by offering different kinds of seating (e.g., a bean bag chair or work stations where there is little noise or distractions) can have a profound effect on students' ability to focus. Other very minor accommodations such as allowing students to doodle during a lecture, hold clay or an elastic band in their hands, or chew gum have helped students' ability to sustain attention, especially during listening activities

## Accommodations for Slower Processing Speeds
Many students with learning disabilities or attention deficits have

| Table 12.7 *continued.* | |
|---|---|
| Remembering details and non-contextual materials | • Provide meaningful contexts for integrating facts and strategies<br>• Use mnemonic devices<br>• Use, and teach how to use, visual imagery<br>• Allow students to use highlighter pens to mark important concepts (if rules permit it)<br>• Encourage students to teach each other<br>• Use word processor and laptop computer for note taking<br>• Provide student with a copy of the information that highlights key facts<br>• Have students sequence activities after a lesson or event<br>• Have students tape directions or information<br>• Provide students with environmental cues and prompts (posted rules, steps for performing tasks, etc.)<br>• Allow students to use resources in the environment to recall information (notes, textbooks, pictures, etc.)<br>• Have students outline, summarize, or underline information to be remembered<br>• Tell students what to listen for when being given directions or receiving information<br>• Have students immediately repeat or paraphrase directions or information |
| Written expression<br>(These suggestions assume that writing does not equate with paper and pencil tasks. When possible, students should complete writing tasks using a word processor. | • Use artistic (visual and performing), scientific, and technological products to communicate knowledge<br>• Use portfolio assessment of products and performances in addition to grading written products<br>• Use technology (e.g., word processing programs with spelling and grammar check, electronic speller, word predictive software, organizational software<br>• Establish writing routine through on-going discussion and practice<br>• Extend time for completing written assignments or test<br>• Instruct students about using graphic organizers<br>• Provide clear written expectations for writing tasks (rubrics)<br>• Enlist writing prompts<br>• Encourage students to proofread for only one type of error at a time<br>• Use writing for real-world purposes |

difficulty processing information. It takes them longer to understand and interpret verbal language. For some, the problem worsens during listening; with others, comprehending written language is more difficult. Complex tasks that require a series of mental operations—organizing the information, thinking about meaning, and producing an intelligent response—are laborious at best. Students with processing problems require more time for completing assignments and taking tests. They need strategies that help them keep track of their thinking, such as having advance organizers for classroom discussions, opportunities to jot down key ideas when asked a question, using appropriate manipulatives, or using self-talk to track their ideas. Perhaps the most important modification, though, is group size. These students perform much better when small group instruction is provided.

### Acquiring Information with Limited Reading Skills

Bright students who have problems with decoding written content should have access to information in ways that minimize reading. Using inquiry methods and primary sources are exciting and sophisticated ways of learning. Instruction that incorporates such entry points as films, television documentaries, live drama, and computer software packages are especially useful in conveying facts and new information to the student. Lectures, taped interviews, books on tape, and text-to-speech software also provide students with alternate means of gaining information. Field trips, demonstrations, and enthusiastic guest speakers can initiate and sustain learning in engaging ways.

Families, too, can provide these experiences for their youngsters. By informing parents of the topics you will be covering during the year, families may be able to arrange outings to a museum, play, or historic site related to the curriculum. These outings can help special students acquire a more useful mental scaffolding to which they can link new information covered in class. When these kinds of experiences *precede* the reading assignment, students can more easily decode the content because they already have some cognitive preparation from the initial experiences.

Picture books are a particularly effective resource for the students who are spatially oriented and prefer images to written words. Picture books are not just geared for 5-year-olds, and they have evolved far beyond the *Comics Illustrated* so common decades ago. High quality picture books exist for all age groups on a wide range of topics and can help introduce students to topics. Capable illustrations can deliver a wealth of content and provides a context, making reading and comprehending the text easier. History buffs, for example, can spend days pouring over visual accounts, such as maps, of Civil War battles. The pictures present welcome invitations for inquiry and further pursuit. Likewise, students can explore original selections from Emily Dickinson, Shakespeare, Browning, Frost , and others in picture books. Table 12.8 presents a number of excellent titles arranged by disciplines. The school media specialist may have additional suggestions.

Another area where Alphabet Children students often stumble is completing assignments on worksheet pages. They may feel over-

---

**Table 12.8. Bibliography of Picture Books.**

**Biology**

Heller, R. (1999). *Chickens aren't the only ones.* New York: Puffin.

Heller, R. (1999). *Animals born alive and well.* New York: Puffin.

Lear, E. with Nash, O. (1968). *Scroobious pip.* NY: HarperCollins.

McCord, A. (1993). *Dinosaurs.* Tulsa, OK: EDC Publishing Co.

**Geology**

McClerran, A. (1986). *The mountain that loved a bird.* Natick, MA: Picture Book Studio USA.

Siebert, D. (1999). *Mojave.* New York: Bt Bound.

**Botany**

Heller, R. (1999). *The reason for a flower.* New York: Puffin.

**Mathematics**

Anno, M. (2001). *Anno's hat trick.* New York: Harcourt Brace Publishers.

Anno, M. (1999). *All in a day.* New York: Puffin.

Anno, M. (1986). *Socrates and the three little pigs.* New York: Putnam.

Korab, B. (1995). *Archabet.* New York: John Wiley.

**Psychology (Social and Emotional Issues)**

de Paola, T. (1983). *Sing Pierot sing.* New York: Harcourt, Brace, and Jovanovich.

Espeland, P., & Waniak M. (1984). *The cat walked through the casserole.* Minneapolis: Carolahoda Books.

Locker, T. (1995). *The mare on the hill.* New York: Puffin.

Steiner, T. (1983). *The original warm fuzzy tale.* Sacramento, CA: Jalmar Press.

**Literature/Writing**

Dickinson, E. (1991). *I'm nobody! Who are you?* Owings Mills, MD: Stemmer House.

Frost, R. with Jeffers, S. (2001). *Stopping by woods on a snowy evening.* New York: Dutton.

Heller, R. (1998). *A cache of jewels and other collective nouns.* New York: Puffin.

Longfellow, W. with Jeffers. S. (1996). *Hiawatha.* New York: Puffin.

Shakespeare, W. (1980) *Under the greenwood tree.* Owings Mills, MD: Stemmer House.

Van Allsburg, C. (1984) *The mysteries of Harris Burlick.* Boston: Houghton Mifflin.

Wood, A. (1998). *I'm quick as a cricket.* Singapore: Child's Play International Ltd.

**Table 12.8.** *continued.*

**Anthropology**

Aardema, V. (1992). *Bringing the rain to Kapiti.* New York: Puffin.

Anno, M. (1985). *Anno's Britain.* New York: Berkley.

Cox, D. (1989). *Ayu and the perfect moon.* Toronto: Random House of Canada.

de Paola, T. (1996). *The legend of the bluebonnet.* New York: Puffin.

Musgrove, M. (1992). *Ashanti to Zulu.* New York: Puffin

**Sociology**

Provenson, A. & Provenson, M. (1987). *Shaker Lane.* New York: Viking Press.

**History**

Aliki. (1986). *A Medieval feast.* New York: Harper Trophy.

Gerrard, R. (1999). *Sir Francis Drake: His daring deeds.* ??: Sunburst.

Goodall, J. (1987). *The story of a Main Street.* New York: Margaret K. McElderry.

Hartley, D. (1986). *Up north in winter.* New York: Dutton.

Hendershot, J. (1987). *In coal country.* New York: Alfred A. Knopf.

Levinson, R. (1995). *Watch the stars come out.* New York: Puffin.

Seawall, M. (1996). *The Pilgrims of Plimoth.* New York: Aladdin.

Winter, J. (1992). *Follow the drinking gourd.* New York: Alfred A. Knopf.

**Fine Arts or Aesthetics**

Clement, C. & Clement, F. (1986.) *The painter and the wild swans.* New York: Dutton.

Fleischman, P. (1988). *Rondo in C.* New York: HarperCollins.

Raboff, E. (1988). *Paul Klee.* New York: Harper Trophy.

Striker, S. (1980). *The great masterpieces—Anti-coloring book.* New York: Holt Rinehart & Winston.

whelmed and anxious by the amount of information on the page and not be able to understand either the written directions or content contained on the page. Teachers should select worksheets with care. These materials should have spare content on a page and be inquiry-based if possible. More importantly, there should be a visual component that can supply content necessary to complete the learning objective.

Consider an activity, taken from a learning kit called *Photo Search*, published by Learning Seed, that asks students to uncover the events surrounding intriguing photographs of different events in history. For example, the caption to the picture in Figure 12.3 is "This is a picture taken on opening night." Students then need to explain where and when this picture was taken.

This method teaches students the research skills of hypothesizing, collecting supportive data, and drawing conclusions. All of these skills can be generalized to other areas of the curriculum.

This activity provides a focused and obvious purpose for reading. When there are specific questions to answer, even poor readers will be able to skim the text to find what they are looking for. The visual cues provides an organizing schema within which words become easier to recognize.

**Figure 12.3.** Photograph from *Photo Search* learning kit.

### Strategies for Accommodating Poor Organizational Skills

Alphabet Children often have difficulty organizing information sequentially. This problem can affect their ability to receive, process, and communicate information, as we pointed out earlier. For example, when they try to take notes during a lecture, they can become confused about organizing the content into major topics and subtopics or about distinguishing core content from peripheral material. Each fact can appear as a separate and equal entity, putting a sizable strain on their capacity to remember. Manipulating ideas in their head can also be difficult. These students succeed much better when they can see the facts or topics preferably in outline form or when they can work with manipulatives while doing activities such as mental math and estimation.

When these students need to organize information to produce a report, story, or other product to communicate ideas or sequences, they struggle with this same confusion in organization. Providing them with visual cues or having them create a visual models of their ideas (such as organizers, storyboards, visual representations, and structured responsive formats) first can help these youngsters organize their ideas.

**Organizers**. Alphabet Children often grasp content faster if they see the bigger picture before they learn details. One way to introduce the big picture is to provide students with copies of lecture outlines (in advance of the lecture), leaving spaces for students to fill in details. If you project an overhead transparency or a slide of this outline and use it to point your students to where you are in your presentation, the students will have an easier time following the pattern and flow of the lesson. Also, an organizer that includes a brief overview of the lesson's purpose and how you plan to cover the information will give these students a better context and overall picture of the lesson.

In addition to having difficulty organizing and understanding information presented to them, many gifted students with learning or attention deficits have trouble organizing information for products and presentations. These students are often holistic thinkers, and their ideas do not emerge in neat, sequential form. When faced with planning a project or a piece of writing, these students simply do not know where to begin. Using webbing or mapping can be a lifesaver to these students.

Webbing is a type of graphic organizer that helps students with processing and organization difficulties sort out their ideas and sequence them into a logical written or oral response. Webbing begins by plop-ping seemingly random and disconnected ideas down on paper and then drawing lines to connect the concepts. Students should place the main topic at the center of the page and then lists ideas related to the topic. Once the ideas are down on paper, students begin to categorize the ideas into subtopics. They can generate new and more focused webs and add details as needed. The visual picture of the aspects related to the topic readily evolves into a more sequential outline. The major subtopics be-come the Roman Numerals, and the details listed under those headings become the letters of the outline.

Pictured in Figure 12.4 is a web Debra, the young historian (intro-duced in Chapter 1), used to generate ideas and organize her research on Jerusha Webster. Debra and her teachers used the web to discuss some ideas that were initially fuzzy. When her teacher had brought in an an-tique photo album to introduce the class to historical inquiry, Debra got the idea of conducting a study about one of the families portrayed in the album. Such a venture would be impossible because it would involve travel and additional resources, but her teacher explored other possibili-ties with her. The web was a "picture" of the discussion.

After generating some tentative ideas, Debra evaluated the possi-bilities to see which one was most the appealing and feasible. The initial investigation included a trip to the Noah Webster House. Debra was enchanted with the artifacts and historical lore all around her. The cura-tor, sensing her excitement, asked Debra if she would be interested in contributing to the collection. He suggested that Debra create a slide and tape show about what it was like to live during colonial times through the eyes of Jerusha Webster, Noah Webster's sister. Debra leaped at the opportunity. After carefully considering possible topics to be included, Debra developed a second web to help her plan her research (see Figure 12.5 ). This format led to some research questions, an outline, and po-tential resources for finding information.

Others graphic organizers include Venn diagrams, flow charts, and matrices. Venn diagrams can be a great way to address the problem of comparing and contrasting particular topics. They require students to consider how classes of information are related to each other. Once the student establishes a picture of relationships, it becomes far easier to describe. (Critical Thinking Books and Software Publishing Company offers many materials that teach students how and why to use Venn diagrams.) Likewise, flow charts offer students a visual means of organizing information in order to get a clearer picture of relationships among facts,

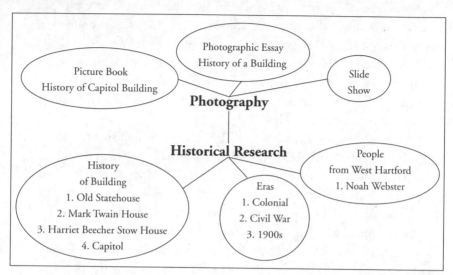

**Figure 12.4.** Debra's first web.

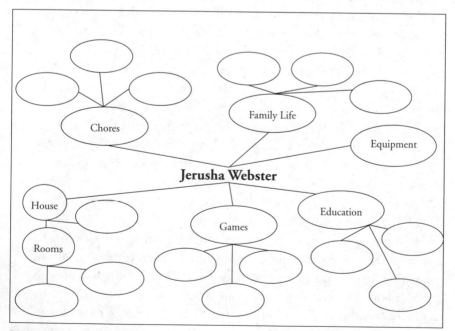

**Figure 12.5.** Debra's second web.

concepts, or events. While these thinking skills activities are excellent tools for teaching students to understand the strategy, it is up to the teacher to help students apply the technique to specific curricular areas.

Software programs such as *Inspiration* assist students in organizing ideas into meaningful categories for both understanding and writing. Many resources are available, and we recommend visiting the web site www.graphic.com for additional information. Table 12.9 lists other resources.

**Storyboarding.** Have you ever read a book or short story in which the author jumps unexpectedly back and forth through time? It may be creative writing, but for most of us who think that things occur in a sequential fashion, it can be confusing. Now consider the plight of a bright student who has trouble organizing ideas and produces such writing unintentionally! One useful strategy for helping students organize a project or story is the storyboard. A pictorial sketch with details added can help GLD students sequence the events in a story, create a mood, and elaborate on an idea just as filmmakers do. Drawing a storyboard can

### Table 12.9. Resources on Graphic Organizers

Black, H., & Black S. (1990). *Organizing thinking : Graphic organizers* (Book II). Pacific Grove, CA: Critical Thinking Books and Software.

Bromley, K. D. (1996). *Webbing with literature: Creating story maps with children's books.* Boston: Allyn & Bacon.

Bromley, K., Irwin-Devitis, L., & Modlo, M. (1996). *Graphic organizers: Visual strategies for active learning.* New York: Scholastic.

Hyerle, D. (1996). *Visual tools for constructing knowledge.* Alexandria, VA: Association for Supervision & Curriculum Development.

Margulies, N. (1991). *Mapping inner space: Learning and teaching mind mapping.* Tucson, AZ: Zephyr Press.

O'Brien-Palmer, M. (1997). *Great graphic organizers to use with any book: 50 fun reproducibles and activities to explore literature and develop kids' writing.* NY??: Scholastic.

Parks, G. (1992). *Organizing thinking: Graphic organizers* (Book I). Pacific Grove, CA: Critical Thinking Books and Software.

Staton, H. N. (1991). *Content connection: How to integrate thinking & writing in the content area.* NY: Scott Foresman.

Tarkin, P. & Walker, S. (1996). *Creating success in the classroom! Visual organizers and how to use them.* Englewood, CO: Libraries Unlimited.

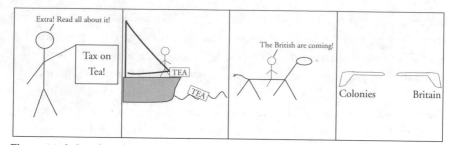

**Figure 12.6.** Storyboard of events leading up to American Revolution.

also help these bright youngsters with memory and sequencing. The storyboard pictured in Figure 12.6 sketches out some of the events leading up to the American Revolution. The student need not be an artist; stick figures with words here and there will suffice. As we mentioned before, any technique in which the student actively interacts with the content can enhance the student's learning.

**Visual representations, formats, or recipes.** Providing an organizational format to steer product development helps gifted students with organizational difficulties communicate ideas. An outline can help students guide or organize their thinking. Another type of recipe is a visual sketch. A model of a display board for a science fair project provides the student with a visual standard of what the final product should look like.

**Structured response formats.** Many Alphabet Children have difficulty organizing responses on simple assignments and worksheets. Their answers do not seem to be in any recognizable order, which creates consternation for the teacher and makes grading the work harder. To help these students complete work that is neatly organized, teachers can provide structured response sheets. These sheets address two vital issues. First, they nudge Alphabet Children to complete work that is neat and easier to read. Second, these materials provide a visual model for organization, and it becomes harder to fail because of scrambled sequences or sloppy construction. Teachers should discuss how the sheet is set up so that information is clear and easily understood, allowing these students to incorporate the strategy into their own repertoire.

It is important to select materials that both stimulate the students' thinking and provide them with a way to organize their responses. Notice the two activity sheets shown in Figure 12.7. They not only offer interesting challenges, but provide students with a structure for recording their answers.

## Deductive Reasoning

A mouse, a rabbit, and a tiger are called Cicero, Ego, and Fred. From the clues below, match the name with the animal.

a. Ego is larger than a mouse.

b. Cicero is older than the rabbit, but younger than the tiger.

c. Fred is older than Cicero

|  | Mouse | Rabbit | Tiger |
|---|---|---|---|
| Cicero |  |  |  |
| Ego |  |  |  |
| Fred |  |  |  |

Ego is the _____.        Cicero is the _____.        Fred is the _____.

Three racing car drivers named Graham, Mario , and Pancho entered cars in a 24-hour race and each won a prize. From the following clues, determine who drove each car and what prize was won by each driver.

a. The coupe won a higher prize than Mario's car.

b. Mario did not drive the Spyder

c. A hatchback won the prize.

d. Graham's car won first prize.

e. The Spyder came in second.

|  | C | H | S |
|---|---|---|---|
| G |  |  |  |
| M |  |  |  |
| P |  |  |  |

| PLACE | CAR | DRIVER |
|---|---|---|
| 1st |  |  |
| 2nd |  |  |
| 3rd |  |  |

**Figure 12.7.** Activities using structured response formats. From Black, H. & Parks S. (1998). *Building Thinking Skills: Book 2*. Pacific Grove, CA: The Critical Thinking Company. Reprinted with Permission.

## Strategies for Remembering Details and Non-contextual Materials

As we noted in Chapter 6, students with learning or attention difficulties may have severe problems with memory. Difficulties in storing, and then retrieving facts and details in isolation present tall hurdles for these students. As a result, many are poor spellers, forget phone numbers, and never master their math facts. One way to help these students with memory problems is to teach them how to invent mnemonics or funny ways to remember little details so easily lost. You probably remember some mnemonic chestnuts from your own school days: The principal is your *pal*, Roy G. Biv cues the ordered colors of the spectrum. These are well tested memory aids, but remember that the mnemonic strategy usually works best when the student invents a personal and original mnemonic.

Another strategy is to use visual imagery to help encode details into a meaningful context. For example, if you are teaching the water cycle in science to primary grade youngsters, you might have your students close their eyes and picture Ronnie Raindrop as he begins his trip. Have them feel the rain and listen to its patter. Ask them what Ronnie might be thinking as he tumbles to the earth. Can they hear the splash as he lands in the puddle? Ask them to tell you what he is thinking as he rests in the muddy puddle. Is Ronnie still Ronnie the Raindrop, or has he become part of the whole puddle? Have them feel the sun peeping out behind the cloud as it spreads its warmth to the ground below. Describe how Ronnie—or what is left of him—is soaking up the sun, feeling warm and content. All of a sudden he feels as light as air. As a matter of fact, Ronnie has evaporated into the air and is swirling up towards the clouds where he rests comfortably. Have them imagine other evaporated water droplets joining with Ronnie. Tell the students to picture all the raindrops holding hands, dancing and playing until there are so many that they form a cloud. Ronnie moans that things are getting crowded and he feels bloated and damp. He is getting so heavy. Watch! He's falling, falling. Listen! Hear him call out, "Here I go again!" Guided images help the students put facts into a story or scene that they can conjure up when asked to recall details. There are a variety of resources available for using visualization techniques with your students. Table 12.10 lists several choices.

Students themselves report that the most vivid memories come from information gained in a lively discussion, an experiment they conduct, or a simulation in which they have participated. In other words, the more

| Table 12.10. Resources on Visualization Techniques |
| --- |
| Bagley, M. & Hess, K. (1998). *Two hundred ways of using imagery in the classroom*. Monroe, NY: Royal Fireworks Press. |
| Bagley. M. (1998). *Using Imagery to develop memory*. Monroe, NY: Royal Fireworks Press. |
| Hess, K. (1986). *Enhancing writing through imagery*. Monroe, NY: Trillium Press. |

active the learning activity is, the more likely information from it will be captured in long-term memory. Students believe it and so do we.

Generations of teachers have used drill and flashcards to help students remember math facts, spelling words, names, and dates. If you step back from this ritual, you might ask, which of these many facts are important enough to memorize, and how can I help students to *overlearn* them? The term *overlearning* describes practice on skills seemingly mastered. For most learners, practice stops when the skills appear to be mastered. The problem is that a sense of minimum proficiency is not the same as automaticity. Automaticity in learning is the ability to respond quickly and efficiently—automatically—while mentally processing or physically performing a task. Automaticity results from experience, performing a task again and again. Think about learning how to ride a bike or drive a car. First attempts are difficult; we often talk to our selves to keep all the facts or steps in mind. Once we've practiced the task over and over again, we find that we can perform it without thinking about it. For Alphabet Children with memory problems, tasks others find pretty easy—sight recognition in decoding, memorizing math facts, forming letters of the alphabet or spelling words—are not even close to automatic.

Some of these students never accomplish automaticity and thus their skills in note taking, reading comprehension, and simple math manipulation is greatly compromised. In our culture, some of these skills are more important than others, such as decoding printed letters, and especially letter-sound relationships. Math facts, too, are important, but they can be done with a calculator. Interestingly, when we allow students to use a calculator to complete math practice sheets, they begin to memorize the facts. Because using the calculator takes longer, and is more actively engaging for simple problems, students will tend to memorize the fact if it is asked frequently. For example, while completing a math problem sheet, the student encounters the fact "9+3" five times. By the by the fourth occasion, most students are motivated to skip the clunky calculator and use the head.

So why would a useful memory shortcut, the calculator, be initially important but lose its attraction for simple math? Using a calculator is multi-sensory. One needs to say or think the numbers, touch them in, see them light up on a screen. And when the answer appears, the students tend to say it to themselves as they write their response.

Eventually, we should wonder where more time should be spent—mastering facts or developing good number sense? Spending time teaching these students *how* to think about numbers, *how* to estimate, and *how* to problem solve will provide the youngsters with strategies for figuring solutions even if they have forgotten (or never learned) their math facts.

## Using Technology to Compensate for Weak Basic Skills

Technology has become vitally important in enabling many students with learning or attention difficulties to reach high levels of achievement. Using technology, these students are able to access and organize information, increase accuracy in mathematics and spelling, and improve the visual quality of the finished product. In short, when these students complete assignments on the computer, they can rapidly produce work that will make them proud and surprise most observers. When these students are denied access to technology, their disability begins to look like a real handicap.

In a world with unlimited resources, every student would complete written assignments on a computer. Students with writing problems who have been fortunate enough to have access to a computer have shown remarkable improvement in their writing. They report a sudden sense of empowerment, as though an evil curse has been lifted. Not only does the finished product look neater, but these students have a much easier time reading and revising drafts. In addition, many spell check programs recognize phonetic spelling, which is a big help to poor spellers. (This fact alone might be reason to teach bright students with spelling problems to spell phonetically, especially when students strong in Integrative Intelligence prefer this approach.) Using a computer bypasses a step for those students who have not developed automaticity in writing. No longer do they have to think about how to form letters while trying to keep a complex idea in mind; instead they simply touch a key. One student we know who had horrible handwriting and began doing his homework on the computer became more willing to sit down to do his written assignments and put substantially more time and effort into his work. He composed more effective sentences and better-organized paragraphs. His restless behavior nearly evaporated.

Technology provides powerful assistance for students with learning disabilities. According to Schwab Learning, a branch of the Charles and

Helen Schwab Foundation (2002) "any item, piece of equipment, or system that helps bypass, work around, or compensate for a specific learning deficit" can be considered assistive technology. These items range from low tech options such as pencil grips, highlighting pens, and dictionaries, to high tech items such as reading systems, voice to text software, and other programs that help students organize and outline their thinking and writing. Schwab Learning offers an online booklet, *Assistive Technology Guide, Third Edition* (2002) (see www.schwablearning.org) that describes how technology can help students with learning disabilities succeed.

When the curriculum is meaningfully challenging and teachers implement appropriate modifications, Alphabet Students are far more like to achieve success. Technical assistive devices, of course, are not magic. Specialists still need to use remedial techniques to teach these students how to read, write, and spell. Reading programs that provide explicit instruction in phonological awareness, phonics, and decoding (Wilson Reading Program, Orton Gillingham techniques, and the Lindemood Bell approach) have met with great success for some gifted students with reading disabilities.

## Physical Learning Environment

Learning style theorists argue that no one learning environment suits all. Depending on our preferred styles of learning, particular contextual attributes enhance our ability to learn. Some of us prefer working in small groups around a table, others of us prefer working independently seated at a desk with a straight back chair. Some can't concentrate with hub-bub or background noises, while other prefer the blabber of a television show or some favorite music in the background. Some of us read better by lamp light, and others prefer bright fluorescent lighting. The point is that in each classroom there should be options that allow students to find their optimum setting for completing assignments, listening to a lecture or discussion, or getting themselves organized.

We have found that Alphabet Children need environments that consider their energetic learning style and need for movement, their distractibility and difficulty in concentrating, and their need for alternate ways of accessing information and communicating their understandings.

We know that many Alphabet Children are packed with energy and have difficulty sitting still for sustained periods. Jonathan Mooney

(Mooney & Cole, 2000) insists that his brain works better when he is moving. Allowing students like Jonathan "a walking corridor" in the back of the room where they can stand up and move about a little is an appropriate accommodation. Some teachers have found that having a writing stand or lectern for overactive students has helped them to focus.

The physical environment needs to attend to the high levels of distractibility found in some Alphabet children. What kinds of accommodations can help filter out extraneous stimulation so that these students can concentrate and attend to the tasks at hand? One consideration might be to allow students to listen privately to music. Yes, it does seem contrary to give a distractable child even more external stimulation. Music, though, is not the usual random stuff; it is rhythmic, predictable, and probably familiar. As we learned from Bryan's story in Chapter 11, some Alphabet Children fare better when they are tuned into their music through headphones. Music being fed directly into the ear seems to supersede distracting extraneous noises.

Concentration for some bright students with learning or attention difficulties requires areas in the room where they can shut out distractions. Some of them need to have a quiet corner that limits both visual and auditory stimulation. A classroom might need several cubicles with a desk and laptop available to students who needs "office" time. Others may gravitate to a reading corner with a comfortable chair and lamp light or a beanbag chair to snuggle into during activities like circle time or class meetings.

Other classroom arrangements can assist learning for special students. We have found that for large group discussions, Alphabet Children usually need to be seated close to the teacher and out of the way of distractions such as windows and doors. Ideally, the classroom teacher encourages small group learning as well. Under these circumstances we have found that small table arrangements work well as students can easily watch the teacher, and the teacher can easily observe each student.

Another important consideration is to make accessible those resources that align with the students' strengths and interests. For example, having blocks available for the young engineer to use for product development or art supplies for the talented artists should enhance their ability to succeed across the curriculum. Interest centers are another way to deliver content and offer a variety of experiences for students to apply basic skills in ways that fit with their learning strengths and interests.

Variety and flexibility are the keys to creating a nurturing physical environment for these special students. Discuss options with your students and experiment with which conditions help students work at their personal best. Listening to your students' suggestions will reinforce the idea that their ideas count and that you are all on the same team.

### Creating a Supportive Emotional Environment

As Melanie's story demonstrates, students must feel emotionally safe and valued to spend optimal energy on mastering the curriculum and overcoming personal obstacles to learning. Abraham Maslow (1968), a humanistic psychologist, argued in his well-known *Toward a Psychology of Being (3rd Edition)* that individuals must feel like they belong and are valued in order to reach their potential or self-actualize. However, learning-disabled students often feel like they are part of a lower caste in the classroom because what is rewarded most in school are the very tasks that bright but disabled students find difficult. If continuous modifications have to be made for them to achieve or assignments watered down to be create phony successes, how can they feel efficacious? To create an environment that is truly dedicated to developing potential in students, we must value and respect individual differences by rewarding students for socially useful behaviors that they do well. The philosophy behind such an environment is one of interdependence, where students work in cooperative groups to achieve goals. Educators encourage all students to develop their talents and are offered options for mastering the curriculum. In this environment a well-produced video production about life in the Amazon is as useful as a written essay on the same topic. As a result, no child will feel like a second-class citizen, and gifted students with learning or attention deficits can indeed excel.

Following are some suggestions to assure that your environment nurtures the emotional needs of your students.

1. Create a buddy system in which the Alphabet Child and a classmate can consult each other about directions, assignments, and feedback about performance.
2. Offer options to all students for communicating knowledge. Book reports, for example, can take many forms.
3. Use cooperative groups to accomplish curriculum objectives.

In forming groups, make sure that these bright youngsters with leaning or attention difficulties are matched with students whose skills complement theirs. For instance, pair a reader with a writer. Make sure the learning outcomes of the group are communicated in a way that allows these bright youngsters to demonstrate their unique talents.

4. Create a bulletin board where students can place "situations-wanted" ads and "help-wanted" ads. All students can then advertise their strengths and seek help in areas of weakness. An ad might read, "Do you need a great cover to put on your social studies report? See Suzy, the local artist." Or, "Help Help Help! I need someone to review what is assigned for homework each afternoon before dismissal. If you have great organizational skills, please apply for the position."

Borrowing an idea from a token economy structure, students may receive a certain number of coupons to use as payment for a job well done. Students can collect coupons to buy more services or purchase free time or other rewards the teacher has listed. For instance, a student might exchange ten coupons for one night with no homework. Students can earn additional coupons for services they render or exceptional behaviors they show.

In a classroom that values the emotional needs of children and expects that each child be respectful and responsible, behavior problems are minimal (Nelson, 2000). Is this also true for students with learning and attention problems? We have found that many of the behavior problems experienced by bright students with learning and attention deficits are responses to an inappropriate or unconcerned environment where their needs are not being met. Misbehavior can also result from unclear and inconsistent expectations. The suggestions offered throughout the text have focused on providing a learning environment that encourages self-regulation, high levels of achievement, and talent development. To set the stage for these lofty goals, we need to help these students become independent learners who assume responsibility for their learning. We conclude this chapter with some summary suggestions. We hope you will find them useful in providing the flexible structure necessary to allow these students to fulfill their promise.

1. Encourage students to assume responsibility for their learning.

Students need to participate in negotiations about what will be learned, how they wish to learn it, and how they will express their understandings. In addition, these students must have a clear understanding of what is expected and by what criteria success will be determined. Contracts and mutually generated rubrics are particularly useful in communicating and recording explicit expectations.

2. Provide management plans to help students organize long-term assignments. Such a plan lists individual tasks to be covered and provides target due dates and possible resources. Initially, these plans should be very detailed and target dates monitored carefully. It is a good idea to sit with students to get them started because frequently students simply do not know how to begin. (See Chapter 11 for a completed management plan.)

3. Provide clear information about what behavior is acceptable. Do not allow these students to blame their misbehavior on the fact that they are overactive or that they are on medication. Encourage them to control behavior. A gentle touch on a shoulder by a classmate served to remind one student to pay attention when the teacher was giving directions. A mentor told another student that if he wanted to be a member of the film production company, he had to control his behavior. The mentor continued to explain what control meant: listen, don't interrupt, and be considerate of others. The student agreed to those conditions. He also negotiated with his mentor that when he felt out of control, he could leave the group for a few minutes to regain control.

4. To enhance motivation, pair activities so that the less desirable task *precedes* a preferred task. This strategy is sometimes called Grandma's Rule, in deference to the often heard "You must finish your [fill in some unpleasant vegetable], then you may have dessert." (Grandma was right. Can you imagine having your dessert first and then trying to face the cold veggie? The payoff is followed by a chore. Ugh.) The student will become task oriented and more focused in working through the first task in order to have time for the preferred activity. This strategy worked particularly well for a group of GLD students who elected to

use rub-on letters to give their project a professional look. Using rub-on letters is tedious and not too exciting. However, the students eagerly attacked the task because they knew the faster they finished, the more time they would have to enlarge some photographs in the darkroom. (It should be noted that they did the lettering task in several small units rather than finish the complete task in one sitting.) Other students gained extra time to work on architectural models they were building with Legos™ *after* successfully completing classroom assignments. Interesting results of this contingency were that not only did the quality of student work improve, but the time needed to complete assignments decreased.

5. Provide plenty of time for involved students to work without interruption. It is extremely frustrating to a student totally involved in learning or creating to have to stop because of artificial time constraints. Contrary to folk wisdom, bright students with attention deficits can concentrate and work for long periods in areas of strength and interest. The potential derived from intensive involvement in creative production might be worth the reduced time for the next activity.

6. Be sensitive to students' frustration levels. Provide legitimate escape routes where GLD students can admit that a task may be too difficult while preserving integrity. For example, one student with poor fine motor coordination had an impossible time using rub-on letters. Totally frustrated with the task, he volunteered to go to the library to survey children's books for possible publishers and record their names and addresses. It took him an hour to complete the job, but this negotiation let him contribute meaningfully to the group effort while avoiding failure.

To conclude, these students spend a considerable time in school each day. If the learning environment does not support them and if these students don't feel appreciated and capable, their learning problems will become severe emotional issues. The suggestions we describe in this chapter should help to support these special students and contribute to their sense of well-being.

# A Community of Support*

In previous chapters of this book, we concentrated on the characteristics of gifted students with learning or attention difficulties and suggested strategies for how schools can best meet their educational needs. However, as implied throughout the book and evidenced in the case studies, these special students often have social and emotional needs that even the best academic programs cannot completely meet. Realistically, we need to look beyond classroom teachers and enlist the support of others—chiefly parents, counselors, and community agencies and resources. As we have seen in many of the case studies, parents play a major role in advocating for their youngsters and are often instrumental in having their children properly identified and served. In addition, without a counselor in their corner, many of these youngsters would not have achieved as they did. The psychological services these students received helped them understand their challenges and become proactive in getting the support they needed. We also recognize the role community organizations play as they offer opportunities and environments in which these students can fit in socially and feel valued for their talents. Sports programs and scouting clubs are prime examples of social support networks with a fine track record of enhancing the self-efficacy and self-esteem of bright but aca-

---

* Dr. Terry Neu contributed both ideas and resources to this chapter.

demically challenged youngsters. Through coordinated efforts, parents, counselors, and community can offer the social and emotional structure vital to the development of Alphabet children. The following story of Rose illustrates a successful collaboration.

### Rose

An attractive, talented, and creative young girl, Rose enjoyed school. She excelled in elementary school, especially when she was learning about a favorite topic or when she had a positive relationship with her teacher. Even though her teachers were a little concerned with Rose's progress in reading, they considered her a fine student with many creative talents. But when Rose entered middle school, her comfortable world started to evaporate. She complained vaguely of problems with her teachers, saying she found them difficult to understand. Her teachers' directions confused her, and she felt insecure during classroom discussion. Instead of engaging in a classroom discussions and activities, she would escape to her books: Even though reading was challenging, it was less confusing than classroom interactions. Rose's parents were somewhat concerned that she was not paying attention in class, but they were pleased that she was reading. They grew alarmed, though, when they received the results of the sixth grade state test: Rose scored far below grade level in reading, writing, and math. Her parents insisted upon having a complete psycho-educational work up. The testing revealed that severe auditory processing problems were at the root of her difficulty with academic skills, and she was diagnosed as having a learning disability. Rose's advanced vocabulary and creative talents had disguised the problem during her elementary years, but the challenges the middle school environment presented proved too much.

After testing, Rose's parents tried repeatedly to convince the school to provide appropriate programming. The school offered minimal accommodations, and it was clear that they understood very little about what students who were simultaneously gifted and learning disabled needed. Rose quickly lost interest in school and no longer wanted to go. She became phobic about many things—catching a disease, being in a car wreck, etc.. With her self-esteem spiraling downward and the possibility of depression setting in, her parents opted to enroll her in a different educational setting and provide her with counseling. The school Rose and her parents chose was less structured than the public school, encouraged creative expression and thought, and emphasized the child's readiness to learn. For example, guest speakers frequently gave presentations on assorted topics from veterinary medicine to pottery making. Students decided which sessions to attend and how deeply—or whether—they would pursue a topic. Through special activities such as performance nights and art shows, the school also provided opportunities for students to display their creative talents.

Meanwhile, Rose's counselor encouraged her to explore her gifts and talents. He suggested ways for Rose to use her talent in writing and the arts for both therapeutic and talent development purposes. He encouraged her to keep a journal, create scrapbooks, and to write her memoirs. These creative outlets were emotionally healing for her, and she purposefully found time to engage in them. Although Rose found writing difficult, sometimes excruciating, she began to develop a love for writing.

The counselor also provided her with the tools she needed to address her feelings of social awkwardness. Rose confided, "My counselor helped me see things differently and to put things in context. For instance, when I would be obsessing over some issue, he would ask me this question: "Rose, next year at this time will this still be important?""

In 9th grade, Rose decided to return to public school. Her auditory processing difficulties resurfaced, and she didn't comprehend or process much oral instruction during the school day. She would work for hours at home to complete her assignments. Her love of learning made her persevere even though the work was difficult. Still, there were days when Rose was simply overwhelmed with schoolwork. Her mother would then step in and declare a "mental health day." This simple gesture gave Rose some breathing room from the regular school day demands and allowed her to complete assignments, which in turn reduced her anxiety about keeping up with her peers. Her journal entries, short stories, and poetry also calmed her anxiety, and of course, the by-product was an impressive body of written material.

High school provided Rose with the opportunity to focus seriously on her strength in the arts for the first time. She took sculpting and jewelry making and excelled in these areas. She spent every free moment in the workshop inventing, crafting, and polishing her pieces and displayed several of her glass sculptures in local art shows. Her art teachers told her about the Arts Academy (a magnet school) and encouraged her to apply. The Arts Academy provided a half-day program in conjunction with local high schools. Students attended academic classes in their local high schools in the morning and then spent three hours in the afternoon in classes at the magnet school. This option excited Rose and she lost no time locating and completing the application forms. The application required evidence of creative talent, and Rose's entry won her a partial scholarship to the program. Her parents gladly contributed the remainder of the tuition because they understood the need for Rose to develop her talent and find like-minded peers who shared similar artistic talents. Attending the magnet school helped Rose regain her social and emotional balance: "I enjoyed the great diversity of students from all walks of life. But I especially liked the environment because every student there *wanted* to be there. That's not the case at the local high school. Students at the Academy are passionate about their art. It makes a huge difference in the environment of the school where creativity is valued."

Although Academy teachers had very high expectations and the classes were challenging and required a great deal of creative and analytic writing, Rose's high school refused to give credits for Academy courses toward the language arts requirements for graduation. Rose felt that she could not put time and energy into two programs simultaneously, and so she chose to drop out of high school, but continue at the magnet school.

With her newly created free time, Rose sought out other experiences in the wider community to augment her education. She had the opportunity to go to El Salvador as part of a university service-learning project with which her father was associated. Rose joined the group of college students and worked alongside local villagers constructing a town meeting center. (Since then, Rose has returned to El Salvador twice more and raised several hundred dollars from high school groups to aid village projects.)

Fueled by a desire to help other communities, Rose discovered the Institute of International Living. This organization provides cultural experiences through service learning projects across the globe. Rose applied for admission to a summer program after her junior year and was accepted with a partial scholarship. Rose chose a Brazilian experience that offered a week-long stay with a local family to learn the culture, followed by a four-week internship at a rainforest research station where she had an in-depth learning experience in ecology. Rose's self-chosen educational experiences were obviously much more expansive than anything available from her local high school. In these self-chosen experiences, her learning disabilities seemed almost nonexistent. In Brazil, her biggest challenge was learning Portuguese.

Rose also took advantage of local community resources. For example, she sampled classes in Tai Chi and liked them a lot. Her whole family had fun practicing this ancient martial art, and Rose benefited from its emphasis on self-discipline and the ability to focus. By now Rose had received her high school diploma by bypassing the system and taking the GED exam.

Rose's experiences illustrate the supportive roles parents, counselors and community experiences played in transforming a depressed and unmotivated youngster into a blossoming young adult. Rose's parents were her chief advocates—ensuring that Rose's difficulties were accurately identified and appropriately attended to. When the school fell short of meeting Rose's needs, her parents sought other options within the community that would offer more outlets for her abilities. They found a non-traditional setting that valued all students' gifts and talents. When she returned to public school, they supported her decision to continue in the arts magnet school and drop out of high school. They shared financial responsibilities with Rose to support outside educational offerings both at the magnet school and in her global wanderings. Finally, they sought out counseling to help her address her depression. Rose's counselor encouraged her to explore who she was and helped her identify strengths and talents, set meaningful goals, and trust her judgment. Rose herself sought out educational opportunities in the wider community that fit with her strengths and interests. By selecting and engaging in opportunities outside of school, she was able to find peer groups with whom she could identify. In these environments, Rose could see herself as a creative writer, artist, and social activist rather than a misfit in a culture that generally devalues the things that Rose values.

## Social and Emotional Issues

Gifted, learning-disabled students are often at risk for social and emotional difficulties because their exceptional talents and learning problems grate against each other. When such internal conflict spurs social and emotional problems, it inhibits talent development. The usual result, of course, is dramatic underachievement (Olenchak & Reis, 2002). Ongoing frustrations and challenges spawn negative patterns and reactions on the part of the students, families, and school personnel. Stereotyped perceptions and attitudes obstruct and often worsen attempts at dealing with academic issues (Mendaglio, 1993). Very few, if anyone, pay attention to the social and emotional outcomes of being gifted and learning disabled. Instead, the focus is on academic support and classroom management of inappropriate behaviors associated with learning disabilities or attention deficits.

To understand the kinds of support these students require, we need to recognize the possible stressors they face and how they affect social and emotional well being. It is also important to understand that the behavioral manifestations of coping with stress are often natural reactions to an unfriendly environment. Fortunately, Rose's parents were attuned to her needs. They saw her growing depression and unwillingness to conform to the school requirements as a cry for help. In response, they worked with Rose to construct an appropriate educational and psychological context that removed the school demands that exacerbated Rose's problems.

Unfortunately, Alphabet Children must often function and survive in an unfriendly world where they are judged and judge themselves according to what they cannot do. As a result, they may routinely experience extraordinary stress at school (Abeel, 2003; Baum & Olenchak, 2002; Mooney & Cole, 2000; Reis & Neu, 1994). Such stress stimulates a fight or flight response. For example, Blaine (see Chapter 4) physically lashed out at his peers and teachers when he felt jammed into a psychological corner. He expressed his frustration and high stress level in a single question to his mother, "Why did god give me ADHD? I wish I would die so other kids would feel sorry for me."

On the other hand, Samantha (introduced in Chapter 9) opted to flee rather than fight. She withdrew from situations that were sources of stress. In her latest book, *My Thirteenth Winter* (2003), Samantha described the ongoing insecurity about creating and sustaining social relationships she felt during her first year at college:

> Once in a while, my friends would decide they wanted to go out—to a dance on another campus or to a club in North Hampton or to a concert. Whenever I was invited, I always felt that familiar wave of insecurity and discomfort, and I would decline, making up an excuse for why I couldn't go. . . . Second semester

my involvement in the social scene continued to deteriorate. . . . I was invited to parties and dances more frequently but my reactions were always the same—anxiety and insecurity—my excuses continued. I had a paper to write or I would go to the library at the last minute so my friends couldn't find me and make me come with them. I spent Friday and Saturday nights alone among the library stacks. Sometimes, when friends came by my room, I would pretend I wasn't there, ignoring their knocks. (p. 166)

Such issues rarely resolve themselves and often deteriorate over time. Anthony Gregorc (personal communication, February, 2001) termed this downward spiral a *Burn Out Cycle*. First, students find themselves in a situation that they do not enjoy, that feels overwhelming, or that is not consonant with their values and interests. They begin to act out: they may complain, cause trouble in class, play hooky, take extra time off, or turn in papers late. If the stress continues, students may begin to demonstrate the second phase of the Burn Out Cycle—the physical manifestations. Here, the body responds to stressors by actually crying out physically. People report neck or back pain, stomach upset, diarrhea, headaches, eyestrain—a laundry list of physical ailments that are not imagined and are indicative of their emotional state. If no one addresses the causes of these symptoms, the sufferer heads for the final three phases of the cycle: "burning up, burning out, breaking down." In these phases, we see anxiety, severe depression, obsessive and compulsive behavior, or extreme inattentiveness and hyperactivity. When gifted students with attention or learning difficulties hit these last three phases, the social and emotional consequences are far more debilitating than the original academic problems (Meisgeier, Meisgeier, & Werble, 1978; Reis & Neu, 1994). According to Olenchak (1994), year after year of living through school-related frustration may require in-depth individual support in which students explore the issues they face.

What interventions can interrupt the Burn Out Cycle? How can we enlist the support of parents, counselors, and community resources to contribute to the healthy emotional development of these bright but challenged youngsters? Before jumping right to an intervention, we must identify the stressors these students face at different stages of development, the possible emotional and social consequences, and how these social and emotional issues could manifest themselves behaviorally.

Table 13.1 outlines the stressors, outcomes, and behavioral manifestations at each phase in the Burn Out Cycle.

| Table 13.1 Stressors, Emotional and Social Outcomes, and Behavioral Manifestations* | | | |
|---|---|---|---|
| **Stage** | **Stressors** | **Emotional and Social Outcomes** | **Behavioral Manifestations** |
| Elementary | Curriculum not aligned to child's strengths, styles, or interests<br><br>Inability to learn academics<br><br>Inability to make friends<br><br>Inability to attend to tasks<br><br>Unreasonable expectations of teachers and parents<br><br>Fear of embarrassment and looking stupid in front of peers | Lowered sense of academic self-efficacy<br><br>Negative perception of self worth<br><br>Frustration<br><br>Anxiety and depression | Complaints about school<br><br>Physical ailments<br><br>Avoidance behaviors<br><br>Aggressive responses<br><br>Inattention and hyperactivity<br><br>Withdrawal |
| Middle School | Increased demand for self-regulation (time management, organization, and self-discipline)<br><br>Increased demands for reading and writing proficiency<br><br>Fitting with social milieu of the classroom<br><br>Increased expectations of parents, teachers, and self | Perfectionism<br><br>Sense of being overwhelmed<br><br>Fear of failure and exposure of area of disability<br><br>Fear of success<br><br>Feelings of isolation and marginality<br><br>Feelings of despair and learned helplessness<br><br>Anxiety and depression | Underachievement<br><br>Total commitment to achieving excellence to the exclusion of outside social activities<br><br>Procrastination, avoidance of academic engagement<br><br>Boredom with usual classroom fare<br><br>Acting-out behaviors, immaturity |
| High School | High stakes tests<br><br>Written assignments and research papers<br><br>Academic requirements for graduation<br><br>Expectations for post-secondary opportunities<br><br>Pressures to fit in and not appear different<br><br>Expectations of self and others, especially in terms of future planning<br><br>Relationships | Feeling overwhelmed<br><br>Fear of failure<br><br>Fear of success<br><br>Anger<br><br>Feelings of isolation, disconnectedness, and alienation<br><br>Feelings of despair and learned helplessness<br><br>Anxiety and depression | Absenteeism<br><br>Underachievement<br><br>Seeking out inappropriate peer groups<br><br>Total commitment to achieving excellence to the exclusion of outside social activities<br><br>Procrastination, avoidance of academic engagement<br><br>Boredom and belief that school fare is irrelevant<br><br>Self-medicate with drugs or alcohol |

* by Susan Baum and Terry Neu

## How to Help

Parents and counselors play key roles in helping the Alphabet Child manage or alleviate obvious stressors. While both parents and counselors can seek out supportive resources from the community, each party offers has something unique to offer . The next sections of this chapter will elaborate on the vital roles these support systems play.

### Parents

Parents play two major support roles for their gifted child with learning or attention difficulties. The first is advocacy. It is the parents' job to ensure that the school recognizes and attends to the child's needs. The second role is home support of the child's academics, talent development, and social and emotional needs. In this role, parents may provide a shoulder to cry on, act as confidant (as much as a parent can be), collaborate on homework, assume the role of resident problem-solver, and seek resources for any situation that presents itself. Without such support, many GLD youngsters would fall apart. But there is a fine line, sometimes hard to discern, between protecting a child and overprotecting him or her. We have interviewed many parents about their role in helping their bright youngsters with special needs be socially, emotionally, and academically successful. The results of these inquiries show that parental roles need to change as students reach different stages or ages. Helping a student complete an assignment may work when seven-year-old needs to read a story for homework, but it probably won't work with a depressed 17 year old resisting parental assistance. Below, we explore in detail how parental roles shift.

### <u>Elementary School Stage</u>

**Advocacy Role.** Many times, parents are the first to recognize a problem as they see their once happy youngster become depressed, angry, or grow to dislike school. Some children become behavior problems and choose underachievement, developing perceptions of inadequacy and poor self-efficacy. Parents' primary role is to have the child's problem identified and ensure that a suitable academic program is put into place (see Chapter 8). The process begins with developing a positive relationship with the classroom teachers and other school personnel involved with the child. Discussing strategies that work at home and describing how the child excels at home can be help develop successful strategies for the classroom. If initial attempts to correct the situation are not successful, parents should ask for a complete psycho-educational evaluation. It is important to understand the legal rights afforded parents under IDEA (Individuals with Disabilities Education Act) legislation. If necessary, parents should retain a child advocate familiar with the complexity of Alphabet students. A good source for information is the state Learning Disability Association. (The web site for the Learning Disabilities Association of American (www.ldanatl.org) contains current information about IDEA and provides a roster of all states' Learning Disability Associations.) Once the learning difficulty is identified, parents should help educators develop an Individual Educational Plan (see Chapter 9).

**Home Support.** Parents should be partners with their children on homework assignments. Being a partner does not mean doing every other problem, but rather supervising and managing homework in a gentle and supportive fashion. For example, parents may need to create a calm, low stress, game-like environment where homework will take place and/or designate specific times—and time *limits*—for homework. The best time is usually directly after dinner rather than after school. Students need some down time after school to play and relax. When they arrive home, a positive "meet and greet" routine is more healthy than a "let's get back to work" reminder. For the moment, parents should avoid talking about schoolwork. Rather asking questions such as "What was fun today?" "Did you get to play at recess?" or, "What do you feel like doing before dinner?" sets a positive climate for communication. If the child arrives home upset, listening and providing hugs and snacks may soothe the situation. Parents need to use active listening and acknowledge that school is difficult.

When helping with homework, parents need to consider the child's preferred learning style. Some children need quiet places for study, and others need to be at the kitchen table with support nearby. Parents should allow their child to take regular and frequent short breaks. In addition, modeling time management techniques and teaching management skills shows the child how to carve tasks into small, manageable parts. At times when school is too stressful, many parents provide a mental health day and keep the child at home for a fun event, as described in Rose's story earlier in the chapter. Jonathan Mooney (Mooney & Coles, 2000) explained how his mother implemented "mental health days" for him:

> Once a week I waited outside my second grade classroom and listened to my mom argue with Mrs. C. "You are destroying this kid. Look at him. He doesn't shower. He doesn't talk. He has been diagnosed with depression. He's only seven. Every time you terrorize him with those . . . spelling words, he wants to kill himself." (I worked for three hours a night on my spelling that year only to fail every test.) Mrs. C replies, "Kids have to learn how to spell. Those are the rules. There are no exceptions, Mrs. Mooney." So my mother created the exceptions: "mental health days." Anytime I had a spelling test, we went to the zoo (p. 32).

Most important, parents must be enthusiastic about the child's gifts and talents. Showing excitement, pride, and love sets the stage for Alphabet Children to feel good about themselves, to make friends, and to have pro-social adult role models. Providing enrichment activities over the summer that enhance and develop the students' strengths, talents, and interests, may contribute to the child's well being, far more than remedial classes in reading.

### Middle School Years

All sorts of problems may surface for the first time during the middle school years. In addition, difficulties that seemed to have been solved at the elementary level may recur. Middle school classes require more reading, writing, organization, and time management. Students are vitally interested in fitting in socially and struggle to find a peer group with whom to identify. Gifted, learning-disabled students often try to hide their disability because they are afraid they won't fit in. To be perceived as a disabled youngster is, for some, unthinkable. During this stage, these students often struggle between dependence on their parents and an increasing need for autonomy. Parents may see their child begin to underachieve or their behavior worsen. As we saw in the case of Bryan (Chapter 11), he became the class clown and took on bullying behaviors in the playground. Students whose expectations to excel in school magnify may give up their social life and extra-curricular activities. On the other hand, students who perceive academic demands as too challenging may choose to stop trying. For these students, attribution theory (Chapter 7) kicks into gear. Failing for lack of trying is far preferable to putting forth effort and receiving a poor grade for it. Blaming failure on lack of effort may help protect self-esteem in the short term, but if the child gets caught in a cycle of failure/not trying/failure, feelings of helplessness may begin to surface.

**School Advocacy.** Because of hormonal changes, rapid physical and psychological changes, and shifting social group patterns, early adolescence can be a time of social and emotional turmoil. As a result, the parents have a more complex role to play. They must begin to relinquish to their child some of the responsibility for advocacy and expect and assist the child to do more self-advocacy. At the beginning of each year, parents should arrange a meeting with teachers, specialists, the counselor, and their child to review accommodations and negotiate a system in which the student can be proactive in taking advantage of accommodations. Strategies that deliver an accommodation without drawing undue attention can greatly diminish the stress an Alphabet Child feels. For example, if a students takes exams in the resource room, they should be able to report directly to the resource room without first checking in with the classroom teacher. Another strategy for delivering an accommodation might be to let all students use laptops for writing assignments if they want to.

**Home support.** At this stage, parents would be wise to avoid acting as a member of the homework police. If a child needs remedial support, hiring a tutor will enable parents to focus on the strengths of their child. Arranging a homework study session at home with a group of friends is one way to make sure that time is set aside for homework and projects. If the child asks for help with reading or editing written work, parents should pitch in. But at the same time, it is important not to allow the child to become overly dependent on assistance. Try to discriminate between what the child should be able to accomplish on her own and where she might appreciate or require help. These children need a flexible structure that offers plenty of authentic success opportunities and builds self-efficacy. Setting appropriate expectations and holding the student accountable will help him develop self-regulation and confidence. Parents might encourage their child to try out stress reduction activities such as yoga, karate, or Tai Chi, activities that may also help youngsters develop self-discipline.

As much as their time and energy permit, parents should search out opportunities for enrichment and talent development in the wider community (e.g., clubs, sports, talent classes, etc.). It is very important that GLD children engage in activities with other talented peers who have similar strengths or interests. Friends with whom these students can feel comfortable are essential for social development. There are many outstanding summer residential programs for gifted students that will enrich and develop the talents of the youngsters as well as provide them with a social peer group. (The National Association for Gifted Children (www.nagc.org) maintains a list of summer programs.)

## Secondary Level

In high school, gifted students with learning or attention difficulties are bombarded with new challenges. Classes for bright youngsters usually demand proficiency in—and expect lots of—reading, listening, and note taking. Students must complete long written assignments that involve synthesis and organization. High school is also filled with high-stakes exams, such as standardized tests, graduation exams, and entrance exams, that add to a GLD student's stress level, since scores steer students' academic and career futures. Many GLD students are also worried about selecting an accommodating college or university and meeting real or perceived expectations for continuing their education. Finally, concerns about fitting in and developing social relationships can continue to cause stress.

Stress that finds no release can result in students feeling depressed and overwhelmed. Some GLD students are still afraid to admit to their disability and struggle to maintain high levels of achievement. Others choose the path of least resistance and take low-level courses to avoid failure. With unidentified disability or inappropriate accommodations, these bright youngsters can become confused and depressed—some severely—over their academic stumbling. A favorite ploy for these students is to argue with their parents and teachers rather than assume responsibility for their poor achievement. Some have become accustomed to failure, and success becomes so strange and uncomfortable that they sabotage their own progress. In these cases, counseling and psychological support is vital.

**School Advocacy.** Parents and their children must continue to advocate for appropriate programs, including counseling. Meeting the needs of GLD students requires flexible thinking and creative problem solving, and families should consider both in-school and out-of-school educational opportunities. Internships, independent study, and on-line courses can be motivating possibilities. Once shameful, families may consider letting these students drop out of high school with integrity. Students who do not finish high school, receive a diploma, or score well on the college entrance exams, can still continue their education at institutes of higher education. (We discuss these possibilities later in the chapter.)

**Home support.** It is vital that parents hold their child accountable for his behavior, even if it means letting him fail. Well-meaning parents who overprotect children by rescuing them from natural consequences are probably doing them a disservice. These bright youngsters must learn to take responsibility for their decisions and behavior. If they continuously refuse to do their homework or refuse academic support, they will fail. Repeating classes or attending summer school may help these students comprehend the consequences of their behavior. If they cannot acquire minimal self-discipline before entering post secondary education, the odds are very strong that they will fail during their first year.

The most important support a parent can provide is a positive, healthy relationship with these complex youngsters. Expressing an interest in their goals, aspirations, and talents provides many openings for communication. Parents need to carefully listen to what their teen is saying; real communication requires active listening and allowing various points of view. Parents must seek professional help if their gifted but learning-disabled teenager is experiencing severe levels of depression, debilitating confusion about the future, or generalized anxiety.

## Counselors

The support of a capable school counselor is essential to meeting the social and emotional needs of Alphabet Children. Having an objective but empathetic professional, knowledgeable about the co-existence of gifts and talents with learning or attention difficulties, can ease the tension and frustration these students, their families, and teachers face. As Mendaglio (1993) put it, "Although the problem may be resident within the child, the intervention requires the designation of parents and teachers as clients of the counselor as well as they may inadvertently exacerbate the problem" (p. 37). Olenchak (1994) extended this idea to include any adults who may be outside the school and family, but who are involved with the student (e.g., scout leaders, little league coaches). The counselor can suggest mitigating strategies to all adults who interact with these special students. The role of counselor-as-child-advocate includes providing a safe haven for the child, communicating the child's needs to teachers and others who work with the student, working with families, providing group counseling sessions for the students, locating community resources, and helping with post-secondary planning.

**Providing a Safe Haven.** We believe that GLD students need someone within the school to provide a safe haven for them, a place where they can retreat when they are feeling overwhelmed. When stress consumes them and emotions are fragile, having an empathetic adult to talk to is crucial. Through active listening, the counselor can identify the problem and provide space, time, and strategies to reduce stress. The counselor's office can also be a place to drop by to share news, both positive and negative. Knowing that there is someone nearby who cares about the student as an individual can contribute greatly to the Alphabet Child's adjustment.

**Communicating Students' Needs.** Advocacy also involves communicating the GLD student's needs and problems with anyone who interacts with the child. Consider what one counselor wrote to help with a GLD student's transition to the next grade level:

> As Jordan's counselor, I wanted to take a few minutes to let you know a little about him. Jordan is a "twice exceptional" student: he is very gifted intellectually (IQ between 140-180), [but has been diagnosed] with ADHD . . . [and] depression. . . . [He] is being served on an IEP with Linda B. in a resource room setting once a day. Jordan is a visual spatial learner. During lecture, he may appear off task, but he is usually multiprocessing. He does not need to . . . [give] you his undivided attention to . . . [pick] up concepts. In fact, looking around or doodling allows him to remain relatively calm. Jordan has difficulty with processing speed. He needs more think time than most students to respond to questions. If he raises his hand to answer a question, please .

. . call on him. However, please avoid calling on him spontane-
ously in class unless you are prepared to wait or offer clues to
save him from discomfort. Jordan would benefit from frequent
reminders about due dates and test dates. Please remind him to
write them in his agenda. He has some difficulty with organization, so notebook checks might be useful. Jordan may take tests
in Ms. B.'s room if needed, and the tests can be sent to her if he
does not complete them in the classroom . . . He reads at well
above the collegiate level in terms of vocabulary. However, his
processing speed may interfere with his achievement unless accommodations are made. Jordan's previous experience in school
has been difficult. Please provide as much encouragement as you
can. His parents are very involved and you can email them any-
time with concerns. You can also work through me or Ms. B. I
hope we can make school a place this young man looks forward
to coming to! Thanks.

Sincerely,

Jan D.

**Working with Families.** The counselor can support the family by
helping them find positive ways to advocate for their child in school and
provide appropriate support at home. Parents need to understand the
unique characteristics of Alphabet Children, the stressors their children
are facing, as well as the social and emotional outcomes that result from
these challenges. They also need to recognize that a child's maladaptive
behaviors may spring from unresolved issues and stress. Counselors can
involve parents in small group meetings, parent workshops, or family
counseling sessions with the student. It might be necessary to provide
the family with names of family counselors if longer-term therapy is
indicated.

**Providing Group Counseling Sessions.** In group sessions, counselors can help Alphabet Children understand and cope with the unique
challenges they face. Group sessions send a clear message that these
youngsters are not alone, that others share the same challenges and frustrations as they do: "When one finds that he or she is 'not the only one,'
there is an immediate sense of relief particularly for gifted children with
learning disabilities, a group with relatively low incidence within a school
jurisdiction" (Mendaglio, 1993, p. 137). Members of the group can form

a positive, prosocial group, especially for those youngsters who have felt marginalized. In addition, students may be more attentive to suggestions and observations their peers make than those adults make. It is the role of the counselor, however, to teach students how to use constructive feedback techniques.

Regularly scheduled "rap" sessions give GLD students an excellent opportunity to confront their problems and together develop strategies for facing them. Such sessions might employ bibliotherapy, cinema therapy, role-playing, and discussion (Hébert & Spiers Neumeister, 2001: Hébert & Speirs Neumeister, 2002; Nicols & Baum, 2003). Engaging students in the arts is an effective approach for these students, especially because their communication strengths are often in nonverbal areas. Music, photography, and art therapies offer ideas to help students explore difficulties and then develop strategies for confronting them. (R. Wolf, personal communication May 1, 2003).

Susan Katz, a counselor who was concerned about the bright and learning disabled students in her school, developed the following rap session program. These rap sessions offer small groups of GLD students a non-threatening environment where they can fulfill their need for involvement, relevance, and thinking. In addition, conducting rap sessions on a regular basis helps teachers stay in touch with what is going on in these students' internal world and helps them structure the environment these students require for learning.

Rap sessions should satisfy some specific goals. They should

1. improve students' perceptions of self by providing opportunities to be listened to and accepted by others.
2. build trusting and caring relationships between adults and student and between the students themselves.
3. build communication skills (listening, verbal fluency, and language development—often areas of disability for GLD students).
4. help students identify areas of giftedness.
5. alert GLD students to their potential worth in society.
6. help students discover ways to compensate for a problematic weakness.
7. teach students to become their own advocates.
8. foster self-efficacy—the expectation that a particular task can be mastered (see Chapter 7).

There are specific guidelines to follow when conducting a rap session:

1.  Sit in a circle or around a table.
2.  Conduct an informal conversation in which students wait for the last person to finish speaking.
3.  Put downs, criticism, or gossip are outlawed.
4.  Confidentiality is assured.
5.  Everyone is entitled to give an opinion.

The adult's role in a rap session is to serve as the facilitator of interaction among the students. It is a time for the counselor to listen and learn about the students—not a time to moralize or to correct them. It requires sensitivity in areas where the students feel especially vulnerable and demands that the counselor anticipate the possible avenues that the discussion might take and create ground rules depending on the topic and how the discussion evolves. The counselor must assume the role of a good group discussion leader prepared to direct and redirect the rap. (There may be occasions in which student statements regarding physical abuse or emotional neglect require that the counselor report the incident.) The key to the success of this session is the facilitator's ability to formulate good questions. Some suggestions for possible discussion topics for GLD students in grades four and up include the following:

- What is a learning disability? What is a smart kid? What does smart mean? If someone says you are smart, what do they mean? Can you be smart and have a learning problem? What special problems do GLD students have?

- What is hard about being learning disabled and smart? What is hard about being very good at some things but not others? If you were a teacher and had a gifted student with a learning problem, what are some of the things you would do? Would not do? Suppose a kid had difficulty reading; how would you handle it?

- In what different ways do people communicate? How can people communicate without talking? Without writing? Which ones are you best at doing? Which do you enjoy most when others do them? What are the advantages of communicating in different ways?

- Why do people not do their work? Do you ever make up excuses for not doing your work? Why is it hard for you to do a big project? How can you make sure you finish something you start? Is not being able to read a good excuse? Is thinking that you cannot do it a good excuse? Are excuses acceptable?

- Do adults have to do everything well? Who are some people you learned about who had a learning problem and succeeded in spite of it? How did they compensate for their disability? If you were a friend to that person, how could you help? How can we help one another in this group? In our class?

- What happens when teachers do not understand what it means to be smart and have a learning disability? How can you communicate your difficulty to your teachers? When should you try to talk to your teachers about your problems? What can you tell your teachers about how you learn and communicate best? Can you offer some suggestions to your teacher that would help you be more successful in school?

Stress management should be another focus for group counseling sessions. *A Toolkit For Teens: Helping Adolescents Manage Their Stress* (Nicols & Baum, 2003) provides group session activities on time management, communication skills, stress management, conflict resolution, anger management, and strategies for dealing with difficult transitions and expectations. Figure 13.1 includes an excerpt from one group session. The objective for the session is to use creative thinking for time management.

**Seeker of Community Resources.** The counselor can serve as an advocate for a GLD student by finding opportunities for her to develop her talent or by providing an environment for at least part of the school day in which she can operate from a position of strength. Some of these opportunities may not be available through the school and parents may need to step in to ensure their child can take advantage of special classes, clubs, and organizations. Table 13.2 outlines some possibilities.

**Helping Students Plan for Post-Secondary Education.** Counselors play a key role in helping students plan for the future. It is vital that GLD students set career goals that complement their talents and interests. Once a student has some idea of the areas he or she might like to pursue, the next step is finding the right opportunities. Those pursuing post-secondary education must consider requirements for admission, the

### Making Time

**Group Size:**      Class

**Physical Set up:**      Normal Classroom setting – Teams of four students.

**Materials:**      Activity sheets for each student (2 per student), Blackboard, whiteboard or flip chart or overhead w/ time Scamper Table drawn or copied.

**Procedure:**      Meet & Greet: ask students to complete statement: If there could be one more hour in a day I would….

For most students, the response would include something desired such as sleep or more time to be with friends. Remind them to have time to do those kinds of activities, it is important to take things off their plate or find ways to consolidate tasks. Inform them that is the purpose of the day's session.

Teach Scamper Problem Solving Technique on next page. Do one sample problem   Have class brainstorm problem to solve and select their favorites for group discussion. Choose the same number of top problems as you have groups of four students. This way each team can work on a different problem.

Assign or allow groups to select preferred problem.

Distribute Activity Sheet and ask groups to SCAMPER the problem for 15 to 20 minutes.

Ask each group to report best three SCAMPER solutions.

**Follow up:**      Remind group that SCAMPER is intended to generate many more possible solutions to problems by considering different strategies. Ask how they think SCAMPER might be effectively used for other problems.

**In Depth Learning:**      Have students apply a SCAMPER solution to one personal but real problem in their lives and record their observations in their journals. Students should also record what SCAMPER stands for in their journal.

**Figure 13.1**. Sample group session activity.  (Nicols & Baum, 2003).

kinds of programs the school offers, and the availability of support for students with learning disabilities. For some students, mentorships or internships in areas of interest or talent may precede college entry. In fact, pursuing an internship directly after high school is often advantageous for students who are not quite ready for the college environment.

Many schools make accommodations in their entrance requirements for students with learning disabilities. Although some institutions still require entrance exams such as the SAT I and SAT II (formerly the Scholastic Aptitude Test), students with disabilities may use calculators, have more time on the test, and take the tests at home, on-line or in small groups. These adjustments have helped some GLD students score well. Fortunately, many universities forgo this requirement and use other criteria such as essays, interviews, portfolios, or simple scores on an intelligence test. In fact, some students who fail to finish high school or earn a high school diploma can still attend college. Samantha (introduced in Chapter 9) finished high school but did not pass the exit exam in math. However, Mount Holyoke College focused on her poetry and her essay

| Table 13.2 Community Resources (compiled by Terry Neu) | | |
|---|---|---|
| Resource | Description | Example |
| Local Talent Development | **Community Arts Centers** may have local theater groups, periodic musical performances, or art shows. Many of these centers offer individual or small group instruction. | Singing the Clues (an individual instruction to help students master singing two pieces of their favorite Blues music)<br><br>Introduction to Photography course |
| | **Local Museums** are wonderful resources that may also offer specialized courses of instruction in a related area. | A museum in New Haven, CT, highlights the engineering skills of Eli Whitney and offers after-school programs to encourage young inventors to build their own inventions |
| | **Society and Organizations** may offer training and opportunities to volunteer | Audobon Society bird-watching tours |
| | **Universities and Colleges** often have special exhibits or programs open to the public. | Student projects for an Engineering Department Fair are placed on public display.<br><br>An Anthropology Department demonstrates skills needed for archaeology digs. |

| | | Table 13.2 *continued.* | |
|---|---|---|---|
| **National Competitions** | | Each year the number of nationally organized individual or small group competitive programs increases. These programs encourage creative solutions and have benefited a number of the students we have worked with. | Odyssey of the Mind<br><br>Future Problem Solving<br><br>Destination Imagination<br><br>Model U.N.<br><br>International Science Fair<br><br>Math Olympiad<br><br>Young Writers projects<br><br>America First (cooperation between students and industry to build robots for specific tasks)<br><br>Battle Bots (student teams build robot that must accomplish a list of tasks) |
| **Clubs & Organizations** | | Part of the counseling process should include discovering student interests and strengths and matching students to organizations that provide talent development opportunities outside of school. | 4-H of America<br><br>Girl Scouts<br><br>Boy Scouts<br><br>Youth Orchestras and Choirs |
| **Special Schools** | | There are situations in which the regular education setting is not working for a specific student. Such a situation is not the fault of an individual school district, but results from a mismatch between system resources and the needs of a specific GLD student. The Counselor must be aware of alternative placements to recommend to parents. | Within District Special Programs: As mentioned in Chapter 11, several school districts have specialized programs to meet the needs of GLD students.<br><br>Magnet Schools: In Rose's case, the area arts magnet school proved to be a haven for her talents. Most states have a magnet school system that provides specialized curriculum for secondary students that varies from aircraft mechanics to the culinary arts.<br><br>Alternative Schools: A wide variety of private schools across the nation (as discussed in Chapter 11) provide the specialized environments GLD students need. |
| **Mentorships & Internships** | | Some corporations and businesses encourage their employees to give back to the community, which may include providing mentoring opportunities and internships for local youth. | |

as admission criteria. Once admitted, Samantha and other GLD students had the option of being excused from required courses such as foreign language and math, depending on their disability. Other students quit high school and attend a community college as preparation for eventual university entrance.*

To guide Alphabet Children through the process of finding an appropriate institution of higher learning, Coleman (1994) has articulated five questions students should ask themselves:

1. What areas of the curriculum are offered as majors, and do they meet with my interests?
2. What size campus will I feel comfortable with?
3. What are the students like? Will I fit in?
4. What extracurricular activities are available that I would be likely to participate in (sports, music, drama, fraternity/sorority, religious groups, etc.)?
5. What support services are available to help me with my learning disability? (p. 54)

We suggest two additional questions to help with decision-making:

6. What is the typical class size? (Most students with learning disabilities fare much better the smaller the class size.)
7. What are the entrance requirements?

Coleman also generated a list of questions students should ask regarding what kinds of support a particular institution offers (see Table 13.3). Decisions based on answers to these questions will increase the probability that Alphabet Children will choose institutions where they can be successful and comfortable.

Finally, Table 13.4 summarizes the kinds of social and emotional support parents and counselors can offer the Alphabet Child. Although the items in the table are associated with certain periods of development, they may be may be appropriate at any stage.

---

* For more information on nontraditional entrance requirements and support programs available at many colleges and universities., we recommend resources such as *Peterson's Colleges With Programs for Students With Learning Disabilities or Attention Deficit Disorders* (5th ed., 2000, but updated regularly). This guide presents the same information that marks other Peterson guides, but emphasizes institutions providing support for LD students. Other resources focus on particular disabilities. For example, Direct Learning lists on their web site (www.dyslexia-test.com/university.html) all universities in the world that have special accommodations for dyslexic students.

**Table 13.3. Questions to Ask Colleges About Support Services Available for LD Students (adapted from Coleman, 1994, p.55)**

*Who is eligible for support services?*
- What disability identification information is required? (including dates of testing)
- Are further diagnostic tests required or available? (IQ achievement, learning styles, study habits, career inventory)
- What are the costs, if any, of referral to, or placement in, the programs offered?
- Are qualified personnel available to interpret and explain results of testing?

*What academic supports are available specifically for LD students?*
- `Does the school provide
  - individual Education Plans?
  - note takers?
  - modified test taking options?
  - learning strategies seminars? (test taking, note taking, time management, highlighting text, outlining/webbing, study skills)
- What counseling supports are available?  Does the school provide support for
  - personal adjustment issues?
  - self-advocacy skills?
  - career guidance?

*What general academic support services are available? Does the school provide*
- math labs for extra help?
- writing centers for assistance?
- tutorial services?
- study session for classes?
- computer centers?

*What are the college's policies regarding*
- number of credit hours required for full-time students?
- extended drop period for LD students?
- taping lectures and classes?
- transferring credits from other institutions, especially community colleges?
- auditing classes prior to taking for credit?
- substitutions for some classes (e.g., American Sign Language for a foreign language requirement. See http://www.unm.edu/~wilcox/ASLFL/asl_fl.html)?
- grade point average for required for graduation?
- priority scheduling for LD students?
- selection of advisors?
- academic probation and failure?
- office hours for professors and instructors?
- teaching loads of professors?

**Table 13.3** *continued.*

*What compensation strategies are available to allow students to bypass their learning disabilities?*
- Books on tape?
- Voice compression tape recorders?
- Computers?
- Note takers?

*What lifestyle modifications can be made?*
- Private rooms?
- Dorm noise?
- Access to quiet study rooms?
- Library study carrel?
- Health services (especially if medication is used)?

**Table 13.4. Support Services***

| | **Role of Parent** | **Role of Counselor** | **Role of Community** |
|---|---|---|---|
| Elementary & Middle School Years | **Advocacy**<br>Develop a positive relationship with the teacher to explore issues and options.<br>Refer child for an evaluation.<br>Know rights.<br>Seek out an advocate who is familiar with bright students with academic difficulties.<br><br>**Home Support**<br>Become a homework partner.<br>Celebrate gifts.<br>Provide "mental health days."<br>Find appropriate peer group for play and fun activities.<br>Seek out talent development activities. | Offer family counseling.<br>Advocate in school for talent development.<br>Be an active listener for child, family, and teacher.<br>Coordinate communication. | Provide recreational opportunities such as scouting, arts involvement, science enrichment opportunities, karate |

\* by Susan Baum and Terry Neu

*Table continued on next page.*

| | **Table 13.4** *continued.* | | |
|---|---|---|---|
| **Secondary Years** | **Advocacy**<br>Ensure appropriate accommodations are in place.<br><br>**Home Support**<br>Hire a tutor to help with homework if necessary, arrange homework sessions at your house with friends.<br><br>Ensure there is an appropriate balance between school work and social activities. | Hold group counseling sessions with similar students.<br><br>Teach stress management strategies.<br><br>Arrange talent development opportunities such as mentorships. | Offer creative outlets such as sports programs, arts experiences, 4-H clubs, church organizations.<br><br>Offer stress reduction activities such as karate and, yoga,<br><br>Provide Outward Bound or other challenge programs |
| **Secondary Years** | **Advocacy**<br>Ensure student has appropriate program and accommodations.<br><br>**Home Support**<br>Focus on students goals, aspirations, talents and interests,<br><br>Within limits, allow natural consequences for irresponsible behavior. Let child fail if necessary.<br><br>Get professional help for depression or anxiety. | Ensure high school program is appropriate.<br><br>Advocate for student's participation in extra-curricular activities regardless of grades.<br><br>Offer career guidance.<br><br>Focus on post secondary opportunities that align with the student's strengths and interests.<br><br>Seek out community opportunities for talent development. | Provide mentorships, independent study and internships<br><br>Offer community service opportunities<br><br>Offer courses online or at community colleges. |

## Conclusion

This book reports what we have learned in the past twenty years studying and working with gifted students with learning and attention difficulties—Alphabet Children. We hope that you feel convinced that these students need and deserve appropriate attention. We believe that much more can be gained by emphasizing these students' strengths and interests. Students will develop skills for success as creative, productive adults more easily when learning is relevant and put into contexts that are personally meaningful.

We know that for these students to become successful adults, they will need to believe in themselves and their abilities. They must be made aware of their strengths and weaknesses so that they can set challenging but attainable goals. You will need to help them understand the role of effort and assist them in selecting environments that will nurture and validate them. Most importantly, they will need to accept their disability. Gifted learning-disabled adults who are successful in their lives talk about how overcoming hurdles has made them confident and committed. In fact, many report that their challenges have enriched their lives. Samantha Abeel (2003), the young poet mentioned earlier, commented:

> Over the years I have also come to view my learning disability as a rather strange and unusual gift. I believe it has allowed me to develop strengths I might not have otherwise developed.... We all come in unique packages with strengths and weaknesses, and somewhere there is a precious gift in all of us. I was blessed to have parents, mentors, and teachers who nurtured mine. No matter how difficult or complex the person in front of us may be, I have learned never to stop looking for his or her gift, as those around me never stopped looking for mine. (pp. 205-206)

## Epilogue

What happens when a student finally learns to become his or her own advocate and begins to make choices in his life that accentuate gifts and talents? As we described in Chapter 1, Neil was a bright, creative youngster who was failing dreadfully in high school. His special talent was photography. He enjoyed using his camera to study people: their joys, sorrows, and thoughts. With help from a tutor, Neil did graduate from high school. Both his tutor and his psychologist helped Neil understand his disability and his strengths. They taught him compensation strategies and made him aware of the possibilities in his life. The psychologist was particularly helpful in pointing out colleges and universities that had programs in photography and support services for LD students.

However, Neil was not ready to accept the fact that he had a disability or, for that matter, that school was for him. He decided that photography would remain his personal creative outlet, not to be compromised or exploited by the "outside world." His negative attitude toward school and his unwillingness to consider his options were all factors that contributed to Neil's decision not to go to college immediately. The summer after graduation found Neil painting houses and reading. That summer he read three books: an autobiography of Richard Nixon, a biography of Abba Eban, and one about the Holocaust. He remarked that now that school was over, he finally had time to learn.

But the next year found Neil unsuccessful at finding a job that he considered worthwhile. He began to see the need for further education as a means of accomplishing his goals. Neil enrolled in a local college and began to take the traditional required courses. Although he was able to pass the courses on his own, he gradually became convinced that he did have a disability. He explained, "I am not stupid. As a matter of fact, I am probably smarter than most of the kids here. Because I have a learning disability, things are more difficult for me. I have to put forth more effort and allocate more time for getting assignments done."

Still, after attending the local college for a couple of years, Neil felt that he was getting nowhere. The curriculum left him emotionally flat. His peers and professors were uninspiring, and he felt like he was attending a "diploma factory." He stopped attending classes and completing assignments. Rather than ruin his record by failing, he decided to withdraw from school altogether.

Over the next year, Neil worked for his father while he contemplated what he wanted to do with his life. He examined what kind of learning environment would nurture his values, learning strengths, and intellect. He questioned people he respected, other students with similar interests, and other knowledgeable sources. He finally made up his mind to attend Sara Lawrence University. He was initially admitted as a nonmatriculated student because the school was unconvinced that Neil's interest and productivity could be sustained. He made up his mind that he would show his professors—and himself as well—that he could excel. And excel he did! For his second semester, he was formally admitted to the program. At this writing, Neil has one semester remaining to complete his degree.

To what does Neil attribute his new determination, task commitment, and academic achievement? He thinks several factors contributed to his success. First and foremost was that he finally set a goal for himself that was personally meaningful. Second, he came to understand what kind of learning environment he needed. Specifically, Neil wanted an environment that respected his intellectual ability and where courses would be challenging and relevant. He desired a learning environment where his peers were his intellectual equals who, like himself, valued individual differences. Third, he wanted a school that cared about the individual and did not impose a boilerplate structure on students. Last, he wanted a school that encouraged independent studies, projects, and ongoing personal evaluation over exams and letter grades.

Sara Lawrence provided such an environment. Students attend small seminars where students lose their anonymity. As Neil puts it, "You become very involved in your learning because there is no choice." In addition to seminars, the school requires independent studies in which students meet individually and frequently with the professor. Students also interview prospective professors as part of their decision-making process in choosing courses.

Asked what his plans were upon completing school, Neil admitted that he was not certain. He felt that he would like to work for an organization whose major goals were to reduce prejudice and inequities in the world. He sees himself as someone who can make a difference. When asked about his future, Neil remarked, "I'm not concerned about my ability to do well in my life. Sara Lawrence really puts you in touch with what you can and cannot do. The professors build your confidence about your ability to succeed. I really feel that this unique experience has brought me to realize my fullest potential as a student. Most important, it has provided me with the courage to reach my potential as a productive adult."

Through Neil we can see some of the abstractions conveyed in this book come alive. Neil's self-awareness, his commitment to become a self-actualized adult, and his courage to shape an environment that validated him as a worthwhile person, were crucial to his success. To Neil and others like him, we offer hope and wish lifelong success.

# References

Abeel, S. (2003). *My thirteenth winter: A memoir.* NY: Orchard Books

Abeel, S., & Murphy, C. (2001). *Reach for the moon.* New York: Scholastic.

Abeel, S. & Murphy, C. (1993). *What once was white.* Travers City, MI: Hidden Bay Publishing.

American Psychiatric Association (1980). *Diagnostic and statistical manual of mental disorders* (3rd ed., text revision). Washington, DC: Author.

American Psychiatric Association (2000). *Diagnostic and statistical manual of mental disorders* (4th ed., text revision). Washington, DC: Author.

Ames, C. (1992). Achievement goals and the classroom climate. In D.H. Schunk and J.L. Meece (Eds.). *Student perceptions in the classroom* (pp. 327-248). Hillsdale, NH: Erlbaum.

Andermann, E.M., Eccles, J.S., Yoon, K.S., Roeser, R., Wigfield, A., & Blumenfeld, P. (2001). Learning to value mathematics and reading: Relations to mastery and performance-oriented instructional practices. *Contemporary Educational Psychology, 26,* 76-95.

Anderson, J.R. (1995). *Learning and Memory.* New York: Wiley.

Association for Children and Adults with Learning Disabilities. (1985). ACLD-proposed definition and rationale. LD Forum. Winter.

Asher, J. (1987). Born to be shy? *Psychology Today,* April, 56-64.

Baldwin L (1995). Portraits of Gifted Learning Disabled Students: A longitudinal study. Unpublished dissertation, Teachers College, Colombia University, NY.

Baldwin, J.D. & Baldwin, J.I. (2001). *Behavior principles in everyday life (4th ed.)* Englewood Cliffs, NJ: Prentice-Hall.

Bandura, A. (1986). *Social foundations of thought and action.* Englewood Cliffs, NJ: Prentice-Hall

Bandura, A. (1989). Human agency in social cognitive theory. *American*

*Psychologist, 44*,1175-1184.

Bandura, A. (1997). *Self-efficacy: The exercise of control.* New York: W.H. Freeman.

Bandura, A. (2002). Social cognitive theory in cultural context. *Applied Psychology: An International Review, 51,* 269-290.

Bandura, A., & Cervone, D. (1986). Differential engagement of self-reactive influences in cognitive motivation. *Organizational Behavior and Human Decision Processes, 38,* 92-113.

Bannatyne, A. (1974). Diagnosis: A note on recategorizing of the WISC-R Scaled Scores. *Journal of Learning Disabilities, 7,* 272-274

Barkley, R.A. (1992). A comparison of three family therapy programs for treating family conflicts in adolescents with ADHD. *Journal of Consulting and Clinical Psychology, 60*(3), 450—462

Barkley, R.A. (1995, May). A new theory of ADHD. Paper presented at the International Conference on Research and {practice in Attention Deficit Disorder, Jerusalem, Israel.

Barkley, R.A., & Murphy, K.R. (1998). *ADHD: A handbook for diagnosis and treatment* (2nd ed.). New York: Guilford Press.

Baum, S. (1985). *Learning disabled students with superior cognitive abilities: A validation study of description behaviors.* Unpublished doctoral dissertation, University of Connecticut, Storrs.

Baum, S, (2001, Spring). Wings mentor program. *Smart Kids with learning disabilities. 2 (8).* 2.

Baum, S., Cooper, C., & Neu, T. (2001). Dual Differentiation: An approach for meeting the curricular needs of gifted students with learning disabilities. *Psychology in the Schools, 38* (5), 477-490.

Baum, S., Cooper, C., Neu, T., & Owen, S. (1997). Evaluation of Project High Hopes. (Project R206A30159-95). Washington, DC: US Department of Education (OERI).

Baum, S., & Olenchak, F. (2002). The Alphabet Children: GT, ADHD and more. *Exceptionality 10*(2), 77-91.

Baum, S.M., Olenchak, F.R., and Owen, S.V. (1998). Gifted students with attention deficits: Fact and/or fiction? Or, can we see the forest for the trees? *Gifted Child Quarterly, 42* (2), 96-104.

Baum, S. & Owen, S. (1988). "High ability learning disabled students: How are they different?" *Gifted Child Quarterly, 32,* 321-326.

Baum, S., Owen, S., & Oreck, B. (1996). Talent beyond words: Identification of potential talent in dance and music in elementary students. *Gifted Child Quarterly, 40,* 93-102.

Baum, S., Owen, S., Oreck, B. (1997). Transferring individual self-regulation processes from Arts to Academics. *Arts Education Policy Review*, 98, 32-39.

Baum, S., Renzulli, J.S. & Hébert, T. (1995). *The prism metaphor: A new paradigm for reversing underachievement.* Storrs, CT: The National Research Center on the Gifted and Talented. (CRS 95310).

Baum, S., Viens, J., Slatin, B. with Gardner, H. (in press). *Multiple intelligences in the elementary classroom: Pathways to thoughtful practice.* Teachers College Press.

Berg, C. (2003). *How to aim a bouncing brain.* Boston: Sandberg Publishing.

Blanchard, K., & Johnson, S. (1985). The one-minute manager. New York: Berkley Books.

Blank, C., & Roberts, J. (1997). *Live on Stage.* White Plains, New York: Dale Seymour Publications.

Bloom, B.S. (1985). *Developing Talent in Young People.* New York: Ballantine Books.

Borchering, B., Thompson, K., Kruesi, M.J.P., Bartko, J., Rappaport, J.L., & Weingartner, H. (1988). Automatic and effortful processing isn't attention deficit/hyperactivity disorder. *Journal of Abnormal Child Psychology,* 16, 333-345.

Borkowski, J.G., Johnson, M.B., & Reid, M.K. (1987). Metacognition, motivation and controlled performance. In S.J. Ceci (Ed.), *Handbook of cognitive, social, and neuropsychological aspects of learning disabilities,* Volume II. Hillsdale, NJ: Erlbaum.

Brody, L. & Mills, C. (1997). Gifted children with learning disabilities: A review of the issues. *Journal of Learning Disabilities 30*(3), 282-

296.

Brophy, J.E. (1981). Teacher praise: A functional analysis. *Review of Educational Research, 51,* 5-32.

Buehler, R., Griffin, D., & Ross, M. (1994). Exploring the "planning fallacy": Why people underestimate their task completion times. *Journal of Personality and Social Psychology, 67,* 366-381.

Butler, D. (1998). A strategic content learning approach to promoting self-regulated learning by students with learning disabilities. In D.H. Schrunk and B.J. Zimmerman, (Eds.) *Self-regulated learning: From teaching to self-reflective practice* (pp. 160-183). New York: Guilford Press.

Carlson, C. (1986). Attention deficit disorder with hyperactivity: A review of preliminary experimental evidence. In B. Lahey and A. Kazdin (eds.) *Advances in child psychology clinical* ( pp. 3-48).

Chalfant, J. & Schefflin, M. (1969). *Central processing dysfunction in children: A review of research.* (NINDS Monograph No.9). Bethesda, MD: U.S. Department of Health Education and Welfare.

Chance, P. (1987) Master of mastery. *Psychology Today, 21*(4), 42-46.

Checkley, K. (1997). The first seven . . . and the eighth: A conversation with Howard Gardner. *Educational Leadership, 55*(1), 8-13

Clarizio, H.F., & McCoy, G.F. (1984). *Behavior disorders in children (3*rd ed.). New York: Harper & Row.

Clements, S. (1966). *Minimal brain dysfunction in children* (NINDB Monograph No. 3, Public Health Service, Bulletin No. 1415). Washington DC: U.S. Department of Health Education and Welfare.

Clinkenbeard, P. (1994, Fall). Motivation and the gifted student. AEGUS Newsletter.

Connecticut State Department of Education (1999). *Guidelines for identifying children with learning disabilities* (2nd ed.). Hartford, CT.

Conners, C. K. (1997). *Conners rating scales-Revised.* Toronto: Multi-Health Systems.

Coleman, M. R.(1994). Post-Secondary Education Decisions for

Gifted/Learning Disabled Students. The Journal of Secondary Gifted Education, V.3, 53-59.

Cowles, S. (2000). School experiences of artists. Paper presented at the meeting of the Social and Emotional Needs of Gifted Students Symposium. University of Connecticut, Storrs, CT.

Covington, M.V., & Omelich, C.L. (1977). "Effort: The double-edged sword in school achievement." *Journal of Educational Psychology, 71,* 169-182.

Cramond, B. (1994). Attention deficit-hyperactivity disorder and creativity: What is the connection? *Journal of Creative Behavior, 28*(3), 193-209.

Cruickshank, W. (1966). *The teacher of brain-injured children: A discussion of the bases for competency.* Syracuse: Syracuse University Press.

Cruikshank, W. (1967). *The brain injured child at home and in school.* Syracuse, NY: Syracuse University Press.

Cruikshank, W. (1977). Myths and realities of learning disabilities. *Journal of Learning Disabilities, 10,* 51-58.

Cruickshank, W., Bentzen, F., Ratzeburg, F., & Tanhauser, M. (1961). *A teaching method for brain-injured and hyperactive students.* Syracuse NY: Syracuse University Press.

Csikszentmihalyi, M. (1990). *Flow.* NY: HarperCollins Publishers

Csikszentmihalyi, M. (1996). *Finding Flow: The psychology of engagement with everyday life.* NY: Basic Books

Dabrowski, K., & Piechowski, M.M. (1977). *Theory of levels of emotional development* (Vols. 1 & 2). Oceanside, NY: Dabor Science.

Delcourt, M. (1998). What parents need to know about recognizing interest, strengths and talents of gifted elementary school children. Practitioners' Guide. National Research Center on the Gifted and Talented, Storrs, CT.

Denckla, M.B. (1989). Executive function, the overlap zone between attention deficit hyperactivity disorder and learning disability. *International Pediatrics, 4(2),* 155-160.

Dixon, J. (1983). *The spatial child.* Springfield, IL: Charles C. Thomas.

Dixon, J. (1986a). *Myself and others.* New Haven CT: Yale University, unpublished manuscript.

Dixon, J. (1986b). Ways of learning. New Haven, CT: Yale University, unpublished manuscript.

Dixon, J. (1989). "Integrative intelligence: What is it and how is it measured?" Paper presented at 2nd Annual Conference for the Education of Gifted Underachieving Students. New Haven, CT: Yale University, May 5, 1989.

Dixon, J. & Baum, S. (1986). *Focus on talent: An enrichment program for gifted/LD students.* State funded grant, Project Rescue, Litchfield, CT: Connecticut Department of Education.

Douglas, L.C. (1981). Metamemory in learning disabled children: A clue to memory deficiencies. A paper presented at the annual meeting of the Society for Research in Child Development, Boston, MA.

Douglas, V.I., & Parry, P.A. (1994). Effects of reward and nonreward on frustration and attention deficit disorder. *Journal of Abnormal Child Psychology, 22,* 281-302.

Dweck, C.S. (1986). Motivational processes affecting learning. *American Psychologist, 41,* 1040-1048.

Emerick, L.(1992). Academic underachievement among the gifted: Students' perceptions of factors that reverse the pattern. *Gifted Child Quarterly. 36(3)* 140-146.

Ertmer, P.A. & Newby, T.J. (1996). The expert learner: Strategic, self-regulated, and reflective. *Instructional Science, 24,* 1-24.

Farnham-Diggory, S. (1990). *Schooling.* Cambridge, MA: Harvard University Press.

Farley, F. (1986). The big T in personality. *Psychology Today,* March 43ff.

Feltz, D.L., & Landers, D.M. (1983). The effects of mental practice on motor skill learning: A meta-analysis. *Journal of Sports Psychology, 5,* 25-57.

Final Regulations, US Department of Education. (1999). Assistance to states for the education of children with disabilities and the early intervention program for infants and toddlers with disabilities. *Federal Register* 64, no. 48.

Fox, L., Brody, L. & Tobin, D. (Eds.). (1983). *Learning disabled/gifted children: Identification and programming.* Baltimore: University Park Press.

Gallagher, J. (1983). The Carolina Institute for Research: Early education for the handicapped. *Journal of the Division for Early Education,.* 7, 18-24.

Gallagher, J. (1990). *Teaching the gifted child, 3rd ed.* Boston: Allyn & Bacon.

Gardner, H. (1983). *Frames of mind: The theory of multiple intelligences.* New York: Basic Books, Inc.

Gardner, H. (1993) *Multiple Intelligences: The theory in practice.* New York: Basic Books.

Gardner, H. (1997). Multiple Intelligences as a partner in school improvement. *Educational Leadership 55(1)* 20-21.

Gardner, H. (1999). *Intelligence reframed: Multiple intelligence for the 21st century.* New York: Basic Books.

Gardner, H. (2000). Extraordinary deviations. In K. Kay (Ed.), Uniquely gifted: Identifying and meeting the needs of the twice exceptional student (pp. 195-196). Gilsum, NH: Avocus Publishing

Gelzheiser, L.M. (1984). Generalizations from categorical memory tasks to prose by learning-disabled adolescents. *Journal of Educational Psychology, 76,* 1128-1138.

Getzels, J. & Jackson, P. (1962). *Creativity and intelligence: Explorations with gifted students.* New York: John Wiley.

Goleman, D. (1995). *Emotional Intelligence.* New York: Bantam.

Good, T.L., & Brophy, J.E. (2003). *Looking in classrooms* (9th ed.). Boston: Allyn & Bacon.

Grolnick, W.S., & Ryan, R.M. (1987). Autonomy support in the classroom: Creating the facilitating environment. In N. Hasting and J. Schwieso (Eds.), *New directions in educational psychology: Behavior and motivation* (pp. 213-232). London: Falmer.

Guilford, J.P. (1959). Three faces of intellect. *American Psychologist, 14,* 469-479.

Guilford, J.P. (1962). *Intelligence, creativity and their educational implications.* San Diego, CA: Knapp.

Guilford, J.P. (1967). *The nature of human intelligence.* New York: McGraw Hill.

Hammill, D., Leigh, J., McNutt, S., & Larson, S. (1981). A new definition of learning disabilities. *Learning Disabilities Quarterly, 4,* 336-342.

Hammill, D., & Bartel, N., (1996). *Teaching students with learning and behavior problems: Managing mild to moderate difficulties in resource and inclusive settings. (6th edition.)* PRO-ED, Incorporated.

Harbar, J. (1981) Learning disability research: How far have we progressed? *Learning Disabilities Quarterly, 4,* 372-381.

Hendley, E.D. (1998). Development of WKHA inbred rat strain with genetic hyperactivity and hyperreactivity to stress. An invited symposium at the 5th Internet World Congress for Biomedical Sciences. Accessed January 15, 2003 at http://www.mcmaster.ca/inabis98/sadile/hendley0403/.

Hébert, T. P. & Speirs Neumeister, K. L. (2001). Guided viewing of film: A strategy for counseling gifted teenagers. *Journal of Secondary Gifted Education, 14*(4), 224 - 235.

Hébert, T. P. & Speirs Neumeister, K. L. (2002). Fostering social and emotional development of gifted children through guided viewing of film. *Roeper Review, 25,* 17- 21.

Hildreth, G. (1966). *Introduction to the Gifted.* New York: McGraw-Hill.

Hofstadter, D. (1985). *Metamagical themes.* New York: Basic Books.

Jellinek, M.S. (2003). Mirror, mirror, on the wall (editorial). *Archives of Pediatric and Adolescent Medicine, 157,* 14-16.

Kaufman, F. (1991, April) The courage to succeed: A new look at underachievement. Keynote address annual conference of the Association for the Education of Gifted Underachieving Students, University of Alabama, Tuscaloosa, AL.

Kaufman, F., Kalbfleisch, M.L., & Castellanos, F.X. (2001). Attention deficit disorders and gifted students: What do we really know? (RBDM 0105) Storrs, CT: University of Connecticut. The national research center on the gifted and talented.

Kavale, K., & Nye, C. (1981). Identification criteria for learning disabilities: A survey of the research literature. *Learning Disabilities Quarterly, 4,* 383-389.

Kirk, S. (1963). Behavioral diagnosis and remediation of learning disabilities. In Conference on Exploration into the Problems of Perceptually Handicapped Children (pp. 1-7). Evanston, IL: Fund for Perceptually Handicapped Children.

Kruger, J., & Dunning, D. (1999). Unskilled and unaware of it: How difficulties in recognizing one's own incompetence lead to inflated self-assessments. *Journal of Personality and Social Psychology, 77,* 1121-1134.

Levine, M. (2002). *A mind at a time.* New York: Simon & Schuster.

Lewis, R. & Doorlag, D. (1983). *Teaching special children in the mainstream.* Columbus, Ohio: Charles E. Merrill.

Ley, K., & Young, D.B. (2001). Instructional principles for self-regulation. *Educational Technology Research and Development, 49,* 93-103.

Licht, B.G. (1984). Cognitive-motivational factors that contribute to the achievement of learning-disabled children. In J.K. Torgenson and G.M. Senf (eds.) *Annual review of learning disabilities (Vol 2).* New York: Professional Press, 119-126.

Locke, E.L., & Latham, G.P. (2002). Building a practically useful theory of goal setting and task motivation: A 35-year odyssey. *American Psychologist, 57,* 705-717.

Loftus, E. (1996). *Eyewitness Testimony.* Cambridge, MA: Harvard University Press.

Loftus, E. & Palmer, J. (1974). Reconstruction of automobile destruction: An example of the interaction between language and memory. *Journal of Verbal Learning and Verbal Behavior, 13,* 585-589.

Luria, A. (1968). *The Mind of a Mnemonist.* New York: Basic Books.

MacKinnon, D. (1965). Personality and realization of creative potential. *American Psychologist, 27,* 717-727.

MacLeod, C. (1965) A comparison of WISC subtest scores of preadolescent successful and unsuccessful reader. *Australian Journal of Psychology.* 17, 220-228.

Maker, C.J., & Whitmore, J.R. (1986). *Intellectual giftedness in disabled persons.* Aspen, CO: Aspen Publishers, Inc.

Maslow, A.H. (1962). *Toward a psychology of being.* Princeton, NJ: Van Nostrand.

Maslow, A. (1968). *Toward a psychology of being* (3$^{rd}$ ed.). Princeton, NJ: Van Nostrand.

Meece, J.L. (1994). The role of motivation in self-regulated learning. In D.H. Schunk & B.J. Zimmerman (Eds.), *Self-regulation of learning and performance* (pp.25-44). Hillsdale, NJ: Erlbaum.

Mendaglio, S. (1993). Sensitivity: Bridging effective characteristics and emotions. *Journal of Secondary Gifted Education, 5*(1), 10-13.

Meisgeier, C., Meisgeier, C.,& Werble, D. (1978). Factors compounding the handicapping of some gifted children. *Gifted Child Quarterly, 22,* 325-331.

Mercer, C.D., Jordan, L., & Alsop, D.H. (1996). Learning disabilities definitions and criteria used by state education departments. *Learning Disabilities Quarterly 19,* 217-231.

Miller, G.A. (1956). The magical number seven, plus or minus two: Some limits on our capacity for processing information. *Psychological Review, 63,* 81-96.

Mooney, J., & Cole, D. (2000). *Learning outside the lines.* NY: Simon and Schuster.

National Joint Committee on Learning Disabilities. (1988). Letter to NJCLD member organizations. Towson, MD: Author.

National Institutes of Health (1998, November). Diagnosis and treatment of ADHD. *NIH Consensus Statement, 16*(2), 1-37.

Neihart, M. (2000). Gifted children with Asperger's syndrome. *Gifted*

*Child Quarterly, 44*(4), 222-230.

Neilson, M. E. (2002). Gifted students with learning disabilities: Recommendations for identification and programming. *Exceptionality, 10*(2), 93-111.

Nelson, C.M. (2000). Educating students with emotional and behavioral disabilities in the 21st century: Looking through windows, opening doors. *Education and Treatment of Children 23*(3), 204-222.

Nelson, K.C. (1989). Dabrowski's theory of positive disintegration. *Advanced Development, 1,* 1-14.

Nicols, & Baum, S. (2003). *A toolkit for teens: Helping adolescents manage their stress.* Washington, DC: Office of Overseas Schools.

Oettingen, G. (1995). Positive fantasy and motivation. In P.M. Gollwitzer & J.A. Bargh (Eds.), *The psychology of action: Linking cognition and motivation to behavior* (pp.219-235). New York: Guilford Press.

Olenchak, F.R. (1994). Talent development: Accommodating the social and emotional needs of secondary gifted/learning disabled students. *Journal of Secondary Gifted Education, 5*(3), 40-52.

Olenchak, F.R. (1999). Affective development and emotional giftedness. In N. Colangelo and G. Davis (eds.), *Handbook of gifted education.* Needham Heights, MA: Allyn & Bacon.

Olenchak, F.R. (2003). Affective development of gifted/LD students: A three-year study. *Understanding Our Gifted, 16*(2), 47-50.

Olenchak, F.R., & Reis, S.M. (2002) Gifted students with learning disabilities. In (M. Neihart, S. Reis, N. Robinson, & S. Moon, Eds.). The social and emotional needs of gifted children: What do we know?. Washington DC: National Association for Gifted Children.

Olson, J., & Mealor, D. (1981). Learning disabilities identification: Do researchers have the answer? *Learning Disabilities Quarterly, 4,* 389-392.

Orlick, T., & Partington, J.T. (1986). *Psyched: Inner views of winning.* Ottawa, Ontario: Coaching Association of Canada.

Oreck. B., Baum, S., & McCartney (2000) *Artistic talent development for urban youth: The promise and the challenge.* University of Connecticut. Storrs, CT: The National Research Center on the Gifted and Talented.

Perugini, E.M., Harvey, E.A., Lovejoy, D.W., Sandstrom, K., & Webb, A.H.(2000). The predictive power of combined neuropsychological measures for attention-deficit/hyperactivity disorder in children. *Child Neuropsychology, 6*(2), 101-114.

Pham, L.B., & Taylor, S.E. (1999). From thought to action: Effects of process-versus outcome-based mental simulations on performance. *Personality and Social Psychology Bulletin, 25,* 250-260.

Piechowski, M.M. (1991). Emotional development and emotional giftedness. In N. Colangelo & G. Davis (eds.) *Handbook of gifted education* (2nd ed.) Needham Heights, MA: Allyn & Bacon.

Piechowski, M.M., & Colangelo, N. (1984). Development potential of the gifted. *Gifted Child Quarterly, 28,* 80-88.

PL 95-561, Title IX, Part A. (1978). The gifted and talented children's education act of 1978, Section 902.

PL 100-297 (1988). Jacob K. Javits Gifted and Talented Students Education Act of 1988.

Polivy, J., & Herman, C.P. (2002). If at first you don't succeed: False hopes of self-change. *American Psychologist, 57,* 677-689.

Poplin, M. (1981). The severely learning disabled: Neglected or forgotten? *Learning Disabilities Quarterly, 4,* 330-335.

Reis, S.M. and others (1993). Why not let high ability students start school in January? The Curriculum Compacting Study. Research Monograph 93106.

Reis, S.M., & Neu, T.W. (1994). Factors involved in the academic success of high ability university students with learning disabilities. *The Journal of Secondary Gifted Education, 5* (3), 60-74.

Reis, S.M., Neu, T.W. & McGuire, J. (1995). Talent in two places: Case studies of high-ability students with learning disabilities who have achieved. Research Monograph No. 95114. Storrs, CT: The University of Connecticut.

Renzulli, J.S. (1977). *The enrichment triad model: A guide for developing defensible programs for the gifted and talented.* Mansfield Center, CT: Creative Learning Press.

Renzulli, J.S. (1978). What makes giftedness: Re-examining a definition. *Phi Delta Kappan, 60,* 180-184, 261.

Renzulli, J.S. (1997). The total talent portfolio: Looking at the best in every student. *Gifted Education International 12(2),* 58-63.

Renzulli, J.S., Smith, L.H., Callahan, C.M., White, A.J., & Hartman, R.K. (1976). *Scales for rating the behavioral characteristics of superior students.* Mansfield Center, CT: Creative Learning Press.

Renzulli, J.S., Reis, S.M., & Smith, L.H. (1981). *The revolving door identification model.* Mansfield Center, CT: Creative Learning Press.

Renzulli, J.S., & Reis, S.M. (1985). *The schoolwide enrichment model: A comprehensive plan for educational excellence.* Mansfield Center, CT: Creative Learning Press.

Renzulli, J.S. (1986). The three-ring conception of giftedness: A developmental model for creative productivity. In R.J. Sternberg, & J.E, Davidson (Eds.), *Conceptions of giftedness.* (pp. 53-92). Cambridge MA: Cambridge University Press.

Renzulli, J.S. & Reis, S.M. (1997). *Schoolwide Enrichment Model.* Mansfield Center, CT: Creative Learning Press.

Rimm, S.B. (1994). *Keys to parenting the gifted child.* Hauppauge, NY: Barron's.

Roe, A. (1953). *The making of a scientist.* New York: Dodd Mead.

Ross, D., & Ross, S. (1982). *Hyperactivity: Current issues, research and theory.* New York: Wiley.

Schiff, M., Kaufman, N., & Kaufman, A. (1981). Scatter analysis of WISC-R profiles for LD children with superior intelligence. *Journal of Learning Disabilities.*

Schunk, D.H. (1985). Participation in goal setting: Effects on self-efficacy and skills in learning disabled students. *The Journal of Special Education, 19,* 307-317.

Schunk, D.H., & Cox, P.D. (1986). Strategy training and attributional feedback with learning disabled students. *Journal of Educational*

*Psychology, 78,* 201-209.

Schunk, D.H., & Zimmerman, B.J. (Eds.). (1998). *Self-regulated learning: From teaching to self-reflective practice.* New York: Guilford Press.

Schwab Learning. (2002). *Assistive technology guide* (3rd ed.). Charles and Helen Schwab Foundation. http://www.schwablearning.org.

Schwarzer, R., Schmitz, G.S. & Daytner, G.T. (1999). *Teacher self-efficacy and collective teacher self-efficacy.* Department of Health Psychology, Freie University at Berlin.

Shaw, S.F., Cullen, J.P., McGuire, J.M. & Brinckerhoff, L.C. (1995). Operationalizing a definition of learning disabilities. *Journal of Learning Disabilities, 28*(4), 586-597.

Silverman, L. K.(1989). Invisible gifts, invisible handicaps. *Roeper Review, 12,* 37-41.

Silverman, L.K. (1993). The gifted individual. In L.K. Silverman (ed.), *Counseling the gifted and talented.* Denver, CO: Love.

Silverman, L.K. (1997). The construct of asynchronous development. *Peabody Journal of Education, 72*(3-4), 36-58.

Slavin, R.E. (2003). *Educational psychology: Theory into practice* (7th ed.). Boston: Allyn & Bacon.

Sternberg, R. (1988). The triarchic mind: A new theory of human intelligence. New York: Pergamon.

Sternberg, R. (1995). *A triarchic approach to giftedness.* Storrs, CT: National Research Center on the Gifted and Talented.

Sternberg, R. (1996). *Successful intelligence: How practical and creative intelligences determine success in life.* NY: Penguin Group.

Sternberg. R. (1997). What does it mean to be smart? *Educational Leadership, 54*(6), 20-24.

Stevens, G. & Birch, J. (1957). A proposal for clarification of the terminology used to describe brain-injured children. *Exceptional Children, 2,* 346-349.

Stock, J., & Cervone, D. (1990). Proximal goal setting and self-regulatory processes. *Cognitive Therapy and Research, 14,* 483-498.

Tannenbaum, A. (1983). *Gifted children: Psychological and educational perspectives.* New York: Macmillan.

Taylor, C. (1986). Cultivating simultaneous student growth in both multiple creative talents and knowledge. In Renzulli, J. S. (ed.) *Systems and models for developing programs for gifted and talented.* Mansfield Center, CT: Creative Learning Press, Inc.

Taylor, H.G. (1989). Learning disabilities. In E.J. Marsh & R. Barkley (Eds.). *Treatment of childhood disorders* (pp. 347-380). NY: Guildford Press.

Terman, L. (1959). *Genetic Studies of genius: The gifted group at mid-life.* Stanford, CA: Stanford University Press.

Terman, L., & Oden, M. (1947). *Genetic studies of genius: The gifted child grows up: Twenty-five years' follow-up of a superior group, Vol. 4.* Stanford, CA.: Stanford University Press.

Triesman, A.M. (1964). Monitoring and storage of irrelevant messages in selective attention. *Journal of Verbal Learning and Verbal Behavior, 3,* 449-459.

U.S. Department of Education. (1993). *National Excellence: A case for developing America's talent.* Washington, DC: Office of Educational Research and Improvement.

U.S. Office of Education. (1997). Education of handicapped children. *Federal Register* 42, 65082-85.

Van Tassel-Baska, J. (1992). *Planning Effective Curriculum for Gifted Learners.* Denver, CO: Love Publications.

Vohs, K.D., & Heatherton, T.F. (2000). Self-regulation failure: A resource depletion approach. *Psychological Science, 11,* 249-254.

Wallach, M.A. (1976). Tests tell us little about talent. *American Scientist. 64,* 57-63.

Wechsler, D. (1974). *Wechsler intelligence scale for children-revised (WISC-R).* New York: The Psychological Corporation.

Wechsler, D. (1991). *Wechsler intelligence scale for children-revised (WISC-III).* New York: The Psychological Corporation

Weiner, B. (1972). Attribution theory, achievement motivation, and the educational process. *Review of Educational Research, 42,* 203-215.

Weiner, B. (1992). *Human motivation.* Newbury Park, CA: Sage.

Weiner, B., Granham, S., Taylor, S.E., & Meyer, W. (1983). Social cognition in the classroom. *Educational Psychologist, 18,* 109-124.

Weinfeld, R., Barnes-Robinson, L., Jeweler, S., Shevitz, B. (2002). Academic programs for gifted and talented/ learning disabled students. *Roeper Review 24(4)* 226-233.

West, T. (1997). *In the Mind's Eye: Visual thinkers, gifted people with dyslexia and other learning difficulties, computer images and the ironies of creativity.* Updated Edition. NY: Prometheus Books.

Whitmore, J. (1980). *Giftedness conflict and underachievement.* Boston: Allyn & Bacon.

Whitmore, J. (1981). Gifted Children with handicapping conditions: A New Frontier. *Exceptional Children 48(2),* 106-114.

Winne, P.H. (1995). Inherent details in self-regulated learning. *Educational Psychologist, 30,* 173-187.

Winne, P.H. 92001). Self-regulated learning viewed from models of information processing. In B.J. Zimmerman and D.H. Schunk (Eds.), *Self-regulated learning and academic achievement: theory, research, and practice* (pp.153-189). New York: Longman.

Winner, E. (1996). *Gifted children, myths and realities.* New York: Basic Books.

Witty, P.A. (1958). Who are the gifted? In N.B. Henry (ed.), *Fifty-seventh yearbook of the National Honor Society of Education, Part II.* Chicago: The University of Chicago Press.

Young, J.D. (1996). The effect of self-regulated learning strategies on performance in learner-controlled computer based instruction. *Educational technology Research and Development 44,* 17-28.

Zentall, S.S. (1997, March). Learning characteristics of boys with attention deficit/hyperactivity disorder and/or giftedness. Paper presented at the annual meeting of the American Educational Research Association, Chicago.

Zimmerman, B. (1989). A social cognitive view of self-regulated academic learning. *Journal of Educational Psychology, 81,* 329-339.

Zimmerman, B.J. (2000). Attaining self-regulation: A social cognitive perspective. In M. Boekaerts, P.R. Pintrich and M. Zeidner (Eds.), *Handbook of Self Regulation* (pp.13-39). New York: Academic Press.

Zimmerman, B.J. (2002). Becoming a self-regulated learner: An overview. *Theory Into Practice, 41,* 64-70.

Zito, J.M., Safer, D.J., dosReis, S., Gardner, J.F., Magder, L., Soeken, K., Boles, M., Lynch, F., & Riddle, M.A. (2003). Psychotropic practice patterns for youth. *Archives of Pediatric and Adolescent Medicine, 157,* 17-25.

# Appendix A

# Sample Identification Activities

## Three-Dimensional Arts
compiled and developed by Anders Bachman
Freelance artist and Consultant

### Introduction:

This activity is designed to identify young artists with three-dimensional skills. Two lessons are described which tap students' spatial skills and give the observer opportunities to record behaviors in this domain.

### Behaviors to be observed:

Balance.
Form (dimensionality).
Clear communication of intent.
Unified design (parts to whole, inclusion/exclusion).
Experiments with ideas, materials, or techniques.
Combines disparate parts to create unique solution.
Uses detail to show complexity of ideas.
Uses tools and materials effectively.
Accepts and incorporates other's feedback.
Is able to talk about work.

### Organization for Learning:

The environment should have desk top space for each student, preferable arranged in a circle with an inlet to the center, or as a second choice, in small clusters. Each desk top should be covered with a piece of cardboard to protect it from the wire and to facilitate cleaning up.

### Activity Title: Creating Structures with Wire
### Time Frame: 45 minutes

### Materials:

2', 3', or 4' piece of wire (pliable)
one pair of needle-nose pliers
one pair of regular pliers per student

### Procedures:

The objective of this activity is to elicit three-dimensional thinking using a medium gauge wire to create your favorite food. We are going to

**294**    *Project* HIGH HOPES is Javits Act Program #R206R00001.

explore a little piece of our imagination and practice catching our images. What's fun about his for me is that both the images which you will each create today will be different from everyone else's. None of them will be right or wrong. We can all have some fun.

Imagine your favorite food sitting on the table in front of you. My favorite food is an apple. It's easy for me to create an example using it.

Example: Imagine a firm green apple. On the surface of this apple we are using a thin black magic marker to draw a continuous line which explores the surface of our apple, up and down the sides, over the bumps on the bottom, and up and around the stem. Maybe there is still a leaf attached to the stem, we'll explore it also. Imagine what the apple looks like now with a thin black line meandering around on its surfaces. Magically our thin black line turns into a stiff wire, and just as magically our apple disappears, leaving the stiff wire behind, describing its surfaces. Try to use this idea as a starting point or springboard when creating your wire object. Remember, you can pick any food. It doesn't have to be an apple.

One more thing, be careful of the tools. Make sure that the pliers do not get anything in their working parts, and make sure that the end of your wire is not bothering someone else. At the end of our session, after we clean up, we can have a short show and tell. We will begin cleaning up at _____.

*Project* HIGH HOPES is Javits Act Program #R206R00001.

## Drama Activities
compiled and developed by Jason LaRosa
Eastern Connecticut State University

### Introduction:
The exercises are designed to produce many different behaviors, and there seems to be enough overlapping of intended behaviors to ensure each student a fair chance at exhibiting the greatest range of behaviors over the entire session.

Please realize although the two Performing Arts sessions are designed to identify gifts in movement and the dramatic arts, the two disciplines share much common ground in their beginning stages. The exercises outlined below are designed to provide the students with the widest possible range of verbal and physical stimuli in order to produce the desired behaviors.

### Behaviors to be Observed:
Uses facial expressions.
Uses expressive voice.
Uses body language.
Shows clear communication of intent.
Creates elaborate movements, characters, or skits.
Accepts and incorporates others' feedback.

### Organizing for Learning
You will need a large, open room or an average classroom with desks, tables, etc. cleared. All corners, piles of desks, etc. should be cushioned (ideally with gym mats, foam rubber, etc.) in smaller rooms. The students should wear clothes suitable for sitting on the floor and comfortable footwear (students may be asked to remove shoes for easier movement and to prevent injury). Finally, ice-packs and a first aid kit should be in the room for minor injuries.

*Project* HIGH HOPES is Javits Act Program #R206R00001.

**Activity Title: Explosions**
**Time Frame: 5 minutes**

**Materials:**
   Ice pack or alternative medical care in case of emergency.

**Procedures:**
   Students will walk around the room, leaving plenty of space between themselves and others. At a signal (handclap or flick of the lights) they will "explode out of the walk and into a freeze. After two rounds, the students will be instructed to mime performing a task from their freeze position (example: arms akimbo, fists on top of each other, and legs parallel in an open stance could become swinging a baseball bat). The task should be sustainable long enough for the instructor and observers to see it.

**Activity Title: Machines**
**Time Frame: 10 minutes**

**Materials:**
   Ice pack or alternative medical care in case of emergency.

**Procedures:**
   One student starts a motion, another student joins in with a complementary motion, other students fill in with motions complementing the positive and negative space created by the first two students. The result of this exercise should be a creation of automated motion created by bodies working in harmony.

**Activity Title: Hello!**
**Time Frame: 5 minutes**

**Materials:**
   Ice pack or alternative medical care in case of emergency.

**Procedures:**
   The leader will provide a brief introduction of himself, identify a space where he and the students will be performing the activities, and

---

outline the activities.

The group and leader stand in a circle. The leader addresses each student with "Hello" punctuated with a wave and certain attitude. Once the leader addresses each student, he will change the wave and the attitude and repeat. The activity will end after four rounds or after each student who desires to lead a round has done so.

**Activity Title: First Thing In the Morning**
**Time Frame: 15 minutes**

**Materials**

Ice pack or alternative medical care in case of emergency.

**Procedures:**

This is a mime exercise. The leader will explain that we will demonstrate what we do first thing in the morning and will encourage the students to try the exercise and guess each other's activities. If possible, the instructor should find out what each student will be demonstrating so he can help revise each student's work for clarity and detail.

*Project* HIGH HOPES is Javits Act Program #R206R00001.

## Engineering and Design
compiled and developed by Bill Brown
Director, Eli Whitney Museum and Workshop

### Introduction:
Engineering has been considered a strength area of the spatial child. Students with strong spatial skills seldom have instruction modified to elicit this strength area. This activity has been designed to capitalize on spatial strengths by presenting a problem faced by Leonardo da Vinci. As Leonardo approached this problem through the use of testing models, students will follow his example as they explore basic concepts in engineering and design. Little or no verbal directions are needed, as students use visual cues to actually construct the original model, then test and modify to increase the distance achieved by their car. There area multiple possible solutions generated by students to this problem.

### Behaviors to be observed:
Actively manipulates materials.
Tries to predict outcomes.
Understands the main concepts of today's topic.
Product shows clarity of thought and focused plan of action.
Puts materials together in a unique way.
Explains the logic of alternative solutions.
Shows problems solving by pursuing and unprompted investigation.

### Organization for Learning:
Set up a materials table. Arrange work tables in a manner which allows the students to move to different locations with ease. Make sure there is easy access to a hallway or other area in which the completed vehicles have plenty of room to run.

### Activity Title: Building Rubber Band Powered Vehicles, da Vinci Style
### Time Frame: 70 minutes

### Materials (list per student):
2 axles
2 front wheels
2 rear wheels

*Project* HIGH HOPES is Javits Act Program #R206R00001.

4 eye screws
small nails
1 12x3/4x4 soft would board
hammer
large rubber bands

**Procedures:**

Students will be introduced to the work of Leonardo da Vinci. da Vinci had conceived of a spring-powered vehicle using the mechanisms commonly found in wind-up clocks. Show students the drawing and ask students, "What do you think this is? How might it work?" Demonstrate the spring power used to run a clock and ask for student feedback. Show students a mock up of Leonardo's cart which has been altered to run on rubber bands. Wind up the cart and let it travel across a table or floor. Ask students for the noted differences they notice between the design of the cart and automobiles they are familiar with. Take out enough parts to assemble a demo four-wheeled car. Model the construction technique with a limited amount of teacher talk.

Key points for students to observe include:
using a nail to start the eye screw hole
placement of the wheels on the axles
anchoring a nail on the front to attach the rubber bands (without smashing an axle)
attaching a rubber band to the back axle
winding up the back wheel

Allow time for students to complete their model. Emphasize that they will need to make adjustments to increase their car's distance after they test their model each time. While students are constructing their model, mark off a testing track at five foot intervals. A tiles floor with 12" tiles is ideal, but if this is not available, use masking tape to mark off appropriate intervals. Typically, students finish their prototypes at different times. As students finish, have them test their vehicle on the track. Make sure to keep accurate records for each test they conduct. Also, be sure to debrief each student after each test and elicit students' alterations for extended runs.

*Project* HIGH HOPES is Javits Act Program #R206R00001.

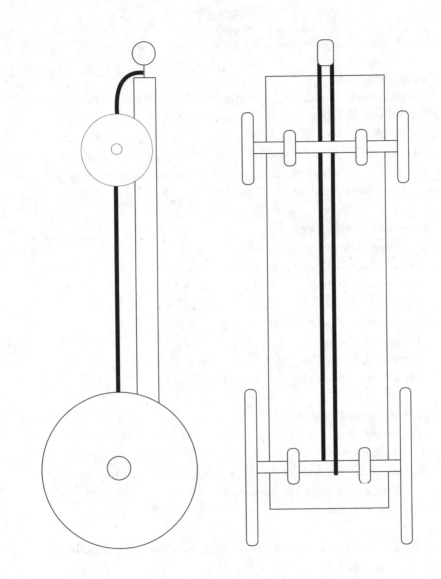

## Zoology
compiled and developed by Julie Henry
Dept. of Ecology and Evolutionary Biology, University of Connecticut

### Introduction:
Reptiles and amphibians have always held a certain fascination for some students. This lesson is designed to draw out the naturalist by sing common salamanders, frogs, lizards, and turtles. Through the careful use and examination of live specimens student behaviors that are highly valued in science such as observation, comparison, and contrasting skills can be identified in students.

### Behaviors to be Observed:
Displays curiosity by asking relevant questions.
Shows a lot of knowledge related to today's topic.
Actively manipulates materials.
Communicates clearly the results of the project.
Systematically tests hypothesis.
Tries to predict outcomes.
Represents ideas in the form of a model.
Finds means of overcoming obstacles in problem solving.

### Organization for Learning:
The room should have long tables for specimen display and for student work areas. Be sensitive to some students' fear of reptiles and amphibians. Caution: some specimens should not be held by students. The specimens should be arranged in individual tanks that can be manipulated for observation.

### Activity Title: Comparing and Contrasting Reptiles and Amphibians
### Time Frame: 55 Minutes

### Materials:
Terrarium (-ia)
Salamander(s)
Lizard(s)
Turtle
Frog

*Project* HIGH HOPES is Javits Act Program #R206R00001.

Drawing paper and pencils with erasers (paper can be divided up into sections and prelabled)

Photographs or slides of child, dog, bird, reptile, amphibian, fish

**Procedures:**
1. First, ask children what pets they have to see if they have an image in their experience to relate to. Children will probably have additional or different answers to the ones listed. Talk about these answers. Compare animals listed above, starting with the most complicated and progressing to least complicated. Ask students: What are the similarities? What are the differences?

2. Observation of two very different amphibian/reptiles . . . such as turtle and frog. Looking at the two will allow them to feel comfortable about making contrasts and will provide a warm-up for the next exercise. As we look at the animals we will talk about the same body parts and exercise 3.

3. Observation of salamander and lizard. Draw and talk about the following for each organism:
   Head: eyes, ears, mouth, nostrils
   Limbs: leg, feet, toes, claws, tail
   Body: movement, limb placement
   Skin: texture, color, etc.
   Behavior
   Habitat

4. Compare and contrast the salamander and the lizard. Some points probably will have been made earlier, but they can be repeated for emphasis. At this point, reptiles and amphibians can again be a topic to talk about (adaptations to land etc.). Children's experience with these organisms can be solicited at this time.

---

# Appendix B

# Reproducible Forms

# Reproducible Forms

| STRUCTURED INTERVIEW | | |
|---|---|---|
| 1. | Describe this child's interests. | |
| 2. | Have you observed situations in which this child | |
| | • becomes totally absorbed in a particular subject area? | Yes / No<br>If yes,<br>please explain. |
| | • has discussed adult topics such as politics, religion, or current events? | Yes / No<br>If yes,<br>please explain. |
| | • becomes self-assertive, stubborn or aggressive. | Yes / No<br>If yes,<br>please explain. |
| | • avoided tasks? | Yes / No<br>If yes,<br>please explain. |
| | • was particularly curious? | Yes / No<br>If yes,<br>please explain. |
| | • was highly imaginative? | Yes / No<br>If yes,<br>please explain. |
| | • was humorous or seemed to be aware of nuances of humor? | Yes / No<br>If yes,<br>please explain. |

**PERSONALIZED TALENT DEVELOPMENT PLAN**

F. Richard Olenchak, Ph.D.

Beginning _____ and Ending _____

Student _____ Date _____

Classroom Teacher(s) _____ Grade _____

Mentor _____ Updates _____

Current Interests _____

| TALENT DEVELOPMENT ACTIVITIES | FREQUENCY & LOCATION | GUIDING ADULT | PROPOSED OUTCOMES & DATES |
|---|---|---|---|
|  |  |  |  |
|  |  |  |  |
|  |  |  |  |
|  |  |  |  |
|  |  |  |  |
|  |  |  |  |

Student's Signature _____

Parent's Signature _____

Mentor's Signature _____

Signatures of School Faculty Involved

_____

_____

Signature of School Administrator _____

## SEAT: Self-Efficacy for Academic Tasks
by S.V. Owen and S.M. Baum

### Instructions for Administering the SEAT
The portions in *italics* should be read aloud to the students.

### Step 1
(The purpose of this step is to determine how each child rates his/her ability to perform the behaviors listed.)

*The paper lists some things kids do in school. I want you to tell me how good you are at these things. For example, if I ask about WRITING A REPORT, you decide whether you are good at writing a report, just okay at writing a report or bad at writing a report. Look at the faces on the paper. A smiling face means you are good at something, and a frowning face means you are bad at it. The face in the middle means that you are okay or average. For each behavior, circle the face that you think best describes how well you do that thing. I will read the first one aloud, and you circle the face that best describes how well you do the activity.*

Read the first item aloud, and wait for the children to circle the face chosen.

*Are there any questions?*

Read the rest of the behaviors, and ask them to choose one face that best describes how well they do that activity. Do all 34 items this way. Do not pay any attention to any of the other words under the faces for now.

Walk through the group and check to see if each child is proceeding correctly. Only after all the children have completed the first step, go on to Step 2.

(The purpose of the final two steps is to determine the child's perception, or attribution, for success at the things s/he does well.)

### Step 2
*Now look at your paper. You have circled different faces. Find the first happy face you circled. Please think about why you are good at that activity. Is it because you are smart, because you try very hard, because you are lucky, or because the activity is easy? After you decide, circle the most important reason that you are good at that task. Only choose one reason.*

*Now do the same for each activity where you circled with a happy face.*

STOP AND WAIT FOR ALL CHILDREN TO COMPLETE THIS SECTION. Walk through the group and check to see if each child is proceeding correctly. Only after all the children have completed the first step go onto Step 3.

## Step 3

*Look at the paper one last time, but this time find the first frowning face you circled. Now decide why you are not good at this task. Is it because you don't feel smart, because you do not try hard, because you are unlucky, because the task is too hard, or because you are shy? Decide which of these reasons is the best and circle the reason.*

*Do the same thing for the rest of the frowning faces you circled.*

Grade_____ Boy [ ] or Girl [ ] Name_____

## WHAT GRADES DO YOU USUALLY GET IN SCHOOL? (Check one)

[ ] A's
[ ] B's
[ ] C's
[ ] D's
[ ] F's

[ ] A's and B's
[ ] B's and C's
[ ] C's and D's
[ ] D's and F's

### How Good Are You at These Things?

**1. Writing a report**

| Smart | Try Hard | Lucky | Easy |
|-------|----------|-------|------|

| Not Smart | Don't Try | Un-lucky | Too Hard | Too Shy |
|-----------|-----------|----------|----------|---------|

**2. Teaching other kids**

| Smart | Try Hard | Lucky | Easy |
|-------|----------|-------|------|

| Not Smart | Don't Try | Un-lucky | Too Hard | Too Shy |
|-----------|-----------|----------|----------|---------|

**3. Answering when a teacher calls on you**

| Smart | Try Hard | Lucky | Easy |
|-------|----------|-------|------|

| Not Smart | Don't Try | Un-lucky | Too Hard | Too Shy |
|-----------|-----------|----------|----------|---------|

**4. Talking to other students about a school subject**

| Smart | Try Hard | Lucky | Easy |
|-------|----------|-------|------|

| Not Smart | Don't Try | Un-lucky | Too Hard | Too Shy |
|-----------|-----------|----------|----------|---------|

5.  **Talking to a teacher about a school subject**

☺

| Smart | Try Hard | Lucky | Easy |
|---|---|---|---|

😐

☹

| Not Smart | Don't Try | Un-lucky | Too Hard | Too Shy |
|---|---|---|---|---|

6.  **Doing social studies projects**

☺

| Smart | Try Hard | Lucky | Easy |
|---|---|---|---|

😐

☹

| Not Smart | Don't Try | Un-lucky | Too Hard | Too Shy |
|---|---|---|---|---|

7.  **Talking about a subject in front of the class**

☺

| Smart | Try Hard | Lucky | Easy |
|---|---|---|---|

😐

☹

| Not Smart | Don't Try | Un-lucky | Too Hard | Too Shy |
|---|---|---|---|---|

8.  **Doing homework**

☺

| Smart | Try Hard | Lucky | Easy |
|---|---|---|---|

😐

☹

| Not Smart | Don't Try | Un-lucky | Too Hard | Too Shy |
|---|---|---|---|---|

9.  **Taking important tests**

☺

| Smart | Try Hard | Lucky | Easy |
|---|---|---|---|

😐

☹

| Not Smart | Don't Try | Un-lucky | Too Hard | Too Shy |
|---|---|---|---|---|

10. **Obeying class rules**

☺

| Smart | Try Hard | Lucky | Easy |
|---|---|---|---|

😐

☹

| Not Smart | Don't Try | Un-lucky | Too Hard | Too Shy |
|---|---|---|---|---|

**11. Taking short tests the teacher gives**

| Smart | Try Hard | Lucky | Easy |
|-------|----------|-------|------|

| Not Smart | Don't Try | Un-lucky | Too Hard | Too Shy |
|-----------|-----------|----------|----------|---------|

**12. Using a dictionary**

| Smart | Try Hard | Lucky | Easy |
|-------|----------|-------|------|

| Not Smart | Don't Try | Un-lucky | Too Hard | Too Shy |
|-----------|-----------|----------|----------|---------|

**13. Writing a letter**

| Smart | Try Hard | Lucky | Easy |
|-------|----------|-------|------|

| Not Smart | Don't Try | Un-lucky | Too Hard | Too Shy |
|-----------|-----------|----------|----------|---------|

**14. Doing art projects**

| Smart | Try Hard | Lucky | Easy |
|-------|----------|-------|------|

| Not Smart | Don't Try | Un-lucky | Too Hard | Too Shy |
|-----------|-----------|----------|----------|---------|

**15. Taking part in music activities**

| Smart | Try Hard | Lucky | Easy |
|-------|----------|-------|------|

| Not Smart | Don't Try | Un-lucky | Too Hard | Too Shy |
|-----------|-----------|----------|----------|---------|

**16. Doing a science experiment**

| Smart | Try Hard | Lucky | Easy |
|-------|----------|-------|------|

| Not Smart | Don't Try | Un-lucky | Too Hard | Too Shy |
|-----------|-----------|----------|----------|---------|

**17. Paying attention when a teacher is talking about a subject**

| Smart | Try Hard | Lucky | Easy |
|-------|----------|-------|------|

| Not Smart | Don't Try | Un-lucky | Too Hard | Too Shy |
|-----------|-----------|----------|----------|---------|

**18. Following directions**

| Smart | Try Hard | Lucky | Easy |
|-------|----------|-------|------|

| Not Smart | Don't Try | Un-lucky | Too Hard | Too Shy |
|-----------|-----------|----------|----------|---------|

**19. Asking questions in front of the class**

| Smart | Try Hard | Lucky | Easy |
|-------|----------|-------|------|

| Not Smart | Don't Try | Un-lucky | Too Hard | Too Shy |
|-----------|-----------|----------|----------|---------|

**20. Writing a story or poem**

| Smart | Try Hard | Lucky | Easy |
|-------|----------|-------|------|

| Not Smart | Don't Try | Un-lucky | Too Hard | Too Shy |
|-----------|-----------|----------|----------|---------|

**21. Solving math word problems**

| Smart | Try Hard | Lucky | Easy |
|-------|----------|-------|------|

| Not Smart | Don't Try | Un-lucky | Too Hard | Too Shy |
|-----------|-----------|----------|----------|---------|

**22. Knowing math facts**

| Smart | Try Hard | Lucky | Easy |
|-------|----------|-------|------|

| Not Smart | Don't Try | Un-lucky | Too Hard | Too Shy |
|-----------|-----------|----------|----------|---------|

**23. Writing neatly**

☺                    😐                    ☹

| Smart | Try Hard | Lucky | Easy |
|-------|----------|-------|------|

| Not Smart | Don't Try | Un-lucky | Too Hard | Too Shy |
|-----------|-----------|----------|----------|---------|

**24. Reading aloud in front of other students**

☺                    😐                    ☹

| Smart | Try Hard | Lucky | Easy |
|-------|----------|-------|------|

| Not Smart | Don't Try | Un-lucky | Too Hard | Too Shy |
|-----------|-----------|----------|----------|---------|

**25. Reading silently**

| Smart | Try Hard | Lucky | Easy |
|-------|----------|-------|------|

| Not Smart | Don't Try | Un-lucky | Too Hard | Too Shy |
|-----------|-----------|----------|----------|---------|

**26. Reading library books**

☺                    😐                    ☹

| Smart | Try Hard | Lucky | Easy |
|-------|----------|-------|------|

| Not Smart | Don't Try | Un-lucky | Too Hard | Too Shy |
|-----------|-----------|----------|----------|---------|

**27. Doing workbook pages in reading**

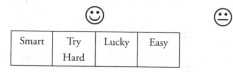

| Smart | Try Hard | Lucky | Easy |
|-------|----------|-------|------|

| Not Smart | Don't Try | Un-lucky | Too Hard | Too Shy |
|-----------|-----------|----------|----------|---------|

**28. Playing games in gym**

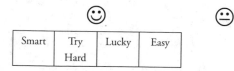

| Smart | Try Hard | Lucky | Easy |
|-------|----------|-------|------|

| Not Smart | Don't Try | Un-lucky | Too Hard | Too Shy |
|-----------|-----------|----------|----------|---------|

### 29. Working on a computer

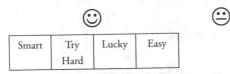

| 😊 | | | | | 😐 | | 😞 | | | | |
|---|---|---|---|---|---|---|---|---|---|---|---|

| Smart | Try Hard | Lucky | Easy | | Not Smart | Don't Try | Un-lucky | Too Hard | Too Shy |
|---|---|---|---|---|---|---|---|---|---|

### 30. Spelling

| 😊 | | | | | 😐 | | 😞 | | | | |
|---|---|---|---|---|---|---|---|---|---|---|---|

| Smart | Try Hard | Lucky | Easy | | Not Smart | Don't Try | Un-lucky | Too Hard | Too Shy |
|---|---|---|---|---|---|---|---|---|---|

### 31. Finishing seatwork

| 😊 | | | | | 😐 | | 😞 | | | | |
|---|---|---|---|---|---|---|---|---|---|---|---|

| Smart | Try Hard | Lucky | Easy | | Not Smart | Don't Try | Un-lucky | Too Hard | Too Shy |
|---|---|---|---|---|---|---|---|---|---|

### 32. Doing exercises in gym class

| 😊 | | | | | 😐 | | 😞 | | | | |
|---|---|---|---|---|---|---|---|---|---|---|---|

| Smart | Try Hard | Lucky | Easy | | Not Smart | Don't Try | Un-lucky | Too Hard | Too Shy |
|---|---|---|---|---|---|---|---|---|---|

### 33. Working with other kids in class

| 😊 | | | | | 😐 | | 😞 | | | | |
|---|---|---|---|---|---|---|---|---|---|---|---|

| Smart | Try Hard | Lucky | Easy | | Not Smart | Don't Try | Un-lucky | Too Hard | Too Shy |
|---|---|---|---|---|---|---|---|---|---|

### 34. Doing a report on a school subject

| 😊 | | | | | 😐 | | 😞 | | | | |
|---|---|---|---|---|---|---|---|---|---|---|---|

| Smart | Try Hard | Lucky | Easy | | Not Smart | Don't Try | Un-lucky | Too Hard | Too Shy |
|---|---|---|---|---|---|---|---|---|---|

## Scoring the SEAT

Eleven scores can be derived from the SEAT. The first two describe the student's perception of competence on school-related tasks. The other nine are percentages reflecting how often a student offers a particular reason for an academic success or failure.

Directions for Scoring the Self-Efficacy Ratings
1. **Overall sense of academic self-efficacy**
   - Count the number of times the happy face was chosen and multiply that sum by three.
   - Count the number of times the neutral face was chosen and multiply that sum by two.
   - Total the number of frowning faces chosen.
   - Total the weighted scores from each category above to determine the overall score.

2. **Sense of academic failure**
   - Total the number of frowning faces chosen.

### Directions for Deriving Attribution Scores
1. **Success explanations**
   - Count the number of Success perceptions (Happy faces chosen).
   - Total the number of each attribute selected to explain success.
   - Divide each attribution total by the number of successes (from first step) to determine percentage of times a particular attribution is given. Because there are four possible explanations for success, there will be four percentages possible. Of course, if the child does not choose a particular explanation, the child will have a percentage explanation of zero.

2. **Failure explanations**
   - Count the number of frowning faces chosen.
   - Count the number of times each failure attribution was selected. Note that there are five choices for failure.
   - Divide each attribution for failure total by the number of total

failures to determine the percentage that particular attribution was chosen to explain a failure experience.

| Average SEAT Scores for Various Groups (Grades 4-6) | | | |
|---|---|---|---|
| | Gifted Students | LD Students | GLD Students |
| Overall Self-efficacy | 91 | 79 | 78 |
| Academic Failure | 1 | 4 | 6 |

| Average Group Attribution Percentage Scores | | | |
|---|---|---|---|
| | Gifted Students | LD Students | GLD Students |
| Success—ability | 31% | 29% | 23% |
| Success— effort | 31% | 32% | 41% |
| Success—ease of effort | 37% | 28% | 37% |
| Success—luck | 2% | 7% | 3% |
| Failure—lack of ability | 5% | 5% | 2% |
| Failure—lack of effort | 17% | 29% | 33% |
| Failure—task difficulty | 15% | 21% | 33% |
| Failure—bad luck | 5% | 6% | 11% |
| Failure—shyness | 3% | 14% | 26% |

# Index